Gambling
without
Guilt
**The Legitimation of an
American Pastime**

Gambling without Guilt

The Legitimation of an American Pastime

John Rosecrance
University of Nevada at Reno

Brooks/Cole Publishing Company
Pacific Grove, California

Consulting Editor: *Roy Roberg*

Brooks/Cole Publishing Company
A Division of Wadsworth, Inc.

Printed in the United States of America

10 9 8 7 6 5 4 3 2 1

Library of Congress Cataloging-in-Publication Data

Rosecrance, John D.
    Gambling without guilt : the legitimation of an American pastime /
John Rosecrance.
      p.   cm.
    Bibliography: p.
    Includes index.
    ISBN 0-534-08954-2 : $10.00
    1. Gambling—United States—History.   2. Compulsive gambling.
3. Gambling. I. Title.
    HV6715.R67   1988
    363.4'2'0973—dc19   87-24419
                                          CIP

Sponsoring Editor: *Claire Verduin*
Editorial Assistant: *Linda Ruth Wright*
Production Editor: *Fiorella Ljunggren*
Manuscript Editor: *Lynne Y. Fletcher*
Permissions Editor: *Carline Haga*
Interior and Cover Design: *Roy R. Neuhaus*
Cover and Chapter Opening Illustration: *Roy R. Neuhaus*
Art Coordinator: *Sue C. Howard*
Interior Illustration: *Graphic Arts*
Typesetting: *TCSystems, Shippensburg, Pennsylvania*
Printing and Binding: *Malloy Lithographing, Inc., Ann Arbor, Michigan*

To my father,
who never placed a bet in his life

Foreword

The Contemporary Issues in Crime and Justice Series introduces important topics that until now have been neglected or inadequately covered to students and professionals in criminal justice, criminology, law, political science, psychology, and sociology.

The volumes cover philosophical and theoretical issues and analyze the most recent research findings and their implications for practice. Consequently, each volume will stimulate further thinking and debate on the issues it covers, in addition to providing direction for policy formulation and implementation.

In *Gambling without Guilt*, John Rosecrance has written an insightful, comprehensive, and entertaining treatise on the history and scope of gambling in America. While he has done an admirable job of surveying the available literature on the gaming industry, his greatest contributions may lie in his ethnographic accounts of gambling environments and his personal accounts of his own gambling experiences spanning over thirty years. As such, Rosecrance's work represents an effective blending of theory and practice that provides support for his major thesis—namely, that gambling has been legitimated in the United States, primarily through its acceptance by the middle class.

Additional poignant insights offered by Rosecrance, which further chide against traditional beliefs, include the reasons people gamble and the amount of influence organized crime has on gambling operations. Regarding the former, he argues persuasively that problem gambling cannot be adequately explained by the traditionally accepted medical model; that is, there is little empirical evidence to suggest that such behavior is either compulsive or pathological in nature. Accordingly, the single treatment of abstinence imposed by most medical programs has serious limitations and, in some cases, may be counterproductive to the effective treatment of problem gambling. With respect to the Mob's influence on gambling, Rosecrance notes that the available research on illegal gambling does not indicate that such activity is inevitably linked with organized crime. For example, he suggests that most bookmakers are just that—bookmakers. Usually they are not members of organized crime, nor are they violent; they are "businessmen" simply trying to get an edge.

In questioning the medical model, Rosecrance offers a new definition of problem (compulsive) gambling, as well as an alternative treatment model. This new approach adds to our knowledge of problem gambling and could lead to more effective treatment programs for individuals with such a problem. He also adds a new dimension to the study of gambling behavior: the idea that social rewards (most gambling is done in groups) play a large part in gambling activities. The chapter describing the social worlds of gambling is not to be missed.

Another interesting dimension is the coverage of international gambling. Gambling, we learn, enjoys worldwide participation and interest, and there are recurring parallels between the United States and Anglo European countries with respect to the spread of gambling and attempts at control. In the final chapter, which deals with the future of gambling and its further legitimation, important economic, social, and political impacts and policies are discussed. Overall, this book provides a comprehensive view of the gaming industry and raises some thought-provoking questions regarding the influence of gambling on our society.

Roy Roberg

Preface

Gambling in the United States has recently become institutionalized and socially accepted. *Gambling without Guilt: The Legitimation of an American Pastime* examines the development and significance of changing American attitudes toward gambling. The book is suitable for use as a text in courses on gambling or as a supplement to courses in social problems, deviance, political science, or criminal justice.

A unique feature of this book is the inclusion of the participants' point of view—a perspective often overlooked by traditional research on gambling and one that adds authenticity, accuracy, dimension, and color to the subject.

The first four chapters provide a comprehensive overview of gambling in the United States. Chapter 1 presents a basic framework for understanding this complex activity and its impact on American society. Chapters 2 and 3 explore the history of gambling from the perspective of American gambling policies and practices. Chapter 4 describes the methods used by various academic disciplines to explain gambling behavior.

The remaining chapters focus on specific aspects of gambling. Chapter 5 explores the distinct social worlds that surround the five main forms of gambling: horse race gambling, sports betting, poker playing, casino gaming, and the buying of lottery chances. Chapter 6 examines the reasons illegal wagering continues to thrive despite broad legalization and challenges the assumption that organized crime controls illegal bookmaking. Chapter 7 argues for redefinition of the term *compulsive gambling* and reexamination of the effectiveness of treatment programs based exclusively on the medical model, while also proposing an alternative model for problem gambling. Chapter 8 describes the coping mechanisms regular gamblers use to mitigate the effects of inevitable losses and delineates the pragmatic strategies that offer clues to the origins and treatment of problem gambling. Chapter 9 travels to England and other European countries, as well as Australia, to explore international gambling traditions and compare them with those in the United States. The final chapter looks toward the future, predicting trends and problems in gambling practices and regulation.

Acknowledgments

I am grateful to the following reviewers, who made very helpful comments and suggestions: Jay S. Albanese of Niagara University, James H. Frey and Terry Knapp of the University of Nevada at Las Vegas, and Stanley B. Yeldell of Glassboro State College. I greatly appreciate the valuable source material and encouragement provided by William Eadington of the University of Nevada, at Reno. I am also indebted to the staff at Brooks/Cole for their contributions to the book, especially Claire Verduin and Fiorella Ljunggren, and to Lynne Fletcher, who deserves special thanks for her skillful editing.

John Rosecrance

Contents

Gambling Today

The operators of all commercial gambling games have a guaranteed advantage, an edge. Upon this edge and the attraction of risk an enormous institution has been raised. Today gambling is a major American leisure industry.

Vicki Abt, James F. Smith, and Eugene M. Christiansen*

On a summer day in New York City, a businessman on his way to work places bets at an Off-Track Betting (OTB) office on races to run later that day at Saratoga Race Track.

In Washington, D.C., a retired school teacher boards a bus with his friends for a trip to Atlantic City, where he plans to play the slot machines.

In a Miami suburb, a widow buys a paper to check out the entries for the night's dog races at Hollywood Track.

In Chicago, the owner of a florist shop calls his bookie to bet on the Cubs, who are playing on TV that day.

In Minneapolis, a fire fighter getting off work buys the *Racing Form* for a trip to Canterbury Downs Race Track.

In Fargo, North Dakota, a farmer purchases a book on blackjack at a local pharmacy to improve his betting strategy at the low-stakes casino games offered in town.

In Las Vegas, several members of the Elks Club from Omaha are getting off a plane for their annual gambling junket.

In Gardena, California, a homemaker heads to a legal poker parlor for a few hours of cards.

In San Francisco, shoppers at the checkout stand of a supermarket stop to purchase lottery tickets in the Better Life Sweepstakes.

In Seattle, secretaries at an aircraft plant pool their money to purchase several tickets on the Progressive Pick Six at Longacres Race Track.

All of these people are participating in forms of gambling, activities that presently are viewed as socially acceptable behavior. While only a few years ago gambling was considered slightly deviant by conven-

* From *The Business of Risk*, by Vicki Abt, James F. Smith, and Eugene M. Christiansen (Lawrence: University of Kansas, 1985), p. x.

1

tional society, it is now an integral part of mainstream American life. Historically, Americans have alternated between fascination with and repulsion to gambling. They have passed stringent antigambling laws and then refused to support the prosecution of offenders. Even though time spent gambling was considered wasteful idleness, gamblers often found regular participation socially rewarding. On the one hand, gambling was socially unacceptable; on the other, it was permissible as long as part of the proceeds went to charity. In addition, gamblers who won consistently were admired as professionals, whereas persistent losers were branded as degenerates. Recent developments, however, have resolved much of this ambivalence.

The growing public acceptance of gaming and its increasing legalization have combined to effectively remove much of the moral stigma previously attached to gambling. There is an economic basis for the reduction of moral opposition to gambling, namely, that gambling has come to be widely viewed as a "painless" way for governments to raise revenue without increasing taxes. This viewpoint has been accepted by the American public to such an extent that the social stigma against participation has been lifted. Americans can now gamble without guilt or criticism from their peers. Social acceptability and legalization have fueled a dramatic increase in gambling participation, the magnitude of which has yet to be either fully acknowledged or adequately understood. For better or worse, gambling has become part and parcel of the American life-style. It is time that we begin to understand some of the societal ramifications of the legitimation of gambling.

Scope of Gambling

During 1986, wagering on gambling games in the United States totaled $198.7 billion, an amount that represented almost 6 percent of the nation's aggregate personal income. Between 1982 and 1986, wagering, both legal and illegal, increased $47.5 billion, or 31.4 percent.[1] These figures refer to gross wagering, or *handle,* the bulk of which is redistributed in transfer payments from losers to winners. The amount actually lost by gamblers—that is, retained by gambling operators—was pegged at $22.6 billion in 1986.[2] If these revenues were placed into a hypothetical holding company, such a company would be fifteenth on a list of the largest American corporations. There is no evidence that gambling by Americans has peaked; on the contrary, most indicators point to continuing legalization and increased participation.

Presently forty-six states sanction some form of gaming; only Mississippi, Hawaii, Indiana, and Utah have refused to jump on the gambling bandwagon. The states permitting various forms of gambling are presented in table 1-1 (pp. 4–5). Bills are pending in state legislatures, several ballot issues face voters, and considerable congressional debate continues—all directed toward increasing the scope of legal gambling. Moreover, citizens of those states that prohibit gambling or that lack large-scale operations by no means refrain from participation. In many cases they wager illegally through bookies or take frequent trips to nearby gambling states.

Illegal betting continues as a viable presence on the gambling scene, and there is little indication that its significance will decline in the foreseeable future. The operators of illegal games have successfully adapted to legalization and, bolstered by a virtual monopoly of sports betting, have maintained an impressive market share.[3] Enforcement of antigambling laws, with the exception of federal violations, is almost nonexistent;[4] thus illegal games continue to operate with relative impunity.

In attempting to explain increases in gambling, researchers have suggested that legalization, fueled by a desire for government revenue, and social acceptability have stimulated participation by giving potential gamblers opportunities close at hand as well as easy entry.[5] Others have said that economic factors such as the rise in discretionary income and differential tax regulations have encouraged gambling.[6] Although these explanations all have some merit, another generally overlooked dynamic should be considered: the acceptance of gambling by the middle class. The contention that middle-class acceptance has boosted gambling participation must be substantiated by further research; however, preliminary observations indicate that it may be a significant factor in the legitimation of gambling.

Middle-Class Participation

Differential access to gaming based on social strata is an American tradition. Gambling by the American upper classes, whether on horses, cards, casino games, oil, real estate, or stocks, has always been tacitly approved.[7] From the landed aristocracy of colonial times to the rich and famous of the 1980s, wagering by wealthy persons with discretionary income has been sanctioned by American society. In addition, the working class, despite the efforts of reformers, has long been familiar with various forms of gambling.[8] Conversely, the stolid middle class has not actively participated in gambling until recently. Middle-class Americans traditionally have disdained the fickleness of gambling for the certainty of gradual asset accumulation. Recent developments, however, have encouraged middle-class participation.

Although no scientific data concerning class participation in gambling exist, market surveys done by casinos have indicated a significant increase in wagering by middle-income bettors.[9] Several large casinos, such as Caesars, Holiday Inn, and Bally's, have recently geared their

Table 1-1   States with legalized gambling

State or district	Bingo	Horse racing	Lotteries	Dog racing	Jai alai	Sports betting	Off-track betting	Casinos
Alabama	x	x	⋯	x	⋯	⋯	⋯	⋯
Alaska	x	⋯	⋯	⋯	⋯	⋯	⋯	⋯
Arizona	x	x	x	x				
Arkansas	⋯	x	⋯	x	⋯	⋯	⋯	⋯
California	x	x	x	⋯	⋯	⋯	⋯	⋯
Colorado	x	x	x	x	⋯	⋯	⋯	⋯
Connecticut	x	x	x	x	x	⋯	x	⋯
Delaware	x	x	x	⋯	⋯	⋯	⋯	⋯
Florida	x	x	x	x	x	⋯	⋯	⋯
Georgia	x	⋯	⋯	⋯	⋯	⋯	⋯	⋯
Hawaii	⋯	⋯	⋯	⋯	⋯	⋯	⋯	⋯
Idaho	⋯	x	x	⋯	⋯	⋯	⋯	⋯
Illinois	x	x	x	⋯	⋯	⋯	⋯	⋯
Indiana	⋯	⋯	⋯	⋯	⋯	⋯	⋯	⋯
Iowa	x	x	x	x	⋯	⋯	⋯	⋯
Kansas	x	⋯	x	⋯	⋯	⋯	⋯	⋯
Kentucky	⋯	x	⋯	⋯	⋯	⋯	⋯	⋯
Louisiana	x	x	⋯	⋯	⋯	⋯	⋯	⋯
Maine	x	x	x	⋯	⋯	⋯	⋯	⋯
Maryland	x	x	x	⋯	⋯	⋯	⋯	⋯
Massachusetts	x	x	x	x	⋯	⋯	⋯	⋯
Michigan	x	x	x	⋯	⋯	⋯	⋯	⋯
Minnesota	x	x	⋯	⋯	⋯	⋯	⋯	⋯
Mississippi	⋯	⋯	⋯	⋯	⋯	⋯	⋯	⋯
Missouri	x	x	x	⋯	⋯	⋯	⋯	⋯
Montana	x	x	x	⋯	⋯	⋯	⋯	⋯
Nebraska	x	x	⋯	⋯	⋯	⋯	⋯	⋯
Nevada	x	x	⋯	x	x	x	x	x

operations toward attracting middle-class gamblers. Polls taken by racetrack officials, OTB operators, and lottery sponsors also point to significant wagering by middle-class patrons.[10] These surveys, coupled with the views of gambling operators such as casino officials, lottery personnel, and racetrack managers (as revealed during personal interviews), all indicate a notable increase in middle-class gambling.

A significant factor in middle-class approval of gambling has been wholesale legalization. The availability of legal gambling has stimulated interest in and acceptance of this activity. Although it has been commonly assumed that gamblers, regardless of the legality of games, would "always find a way to get a bet down,"[11] this was not the case

Table 1-1   (continued)

State or district	Bingo	Horse racing	Lotteries	Dog racing	Jai alai	Sports betting	Off-track betting	Casinos
New Hampshire	x	x	x	x	...	...	...	...
New Jersey	x	x	x	...	...	...	...	x
New Mexico	x	x	...	...	...	...	...	...
New York	x	x	x	...	...	...	x	...
North Carolina	x	...	...	...	...	...	...	...
North Dakota	x	...	...	...	...	...	...	x*
Ohio	x	x	x	...	...	...	...	...
Oklahoma	x	x	...	...	...	...	...	...
Oregon	x	x	x	x	...	...	...	...
Pennsylvania	x	x	x	...	...	...	...	...
Rhode Island	x	x	x	x	x	...	...	...
South Carolina	x	...	...	...	...	...	...	...
South Dakota	x	x	x	x	...	...	...	...
Tennessee	x	x	...	...	...	...	...	...
Texas	x	...	...	...	...	...	...	...
Utah	...	...	...	...	...	...	...	...
Vermont	x	x	x	x	...	...	...	...
Virginia	x	...	x	...	...	...	...	...
Washington	x	x	x	...	...	...	...	...
West Virginia	x	x	x	x	...	...	...	...
Wisconsin	x	x	x	...	...	...	...	...
Wyoming	x	x	...	...	...	...	...	...
Dist. of Columbia	x	...	x	...	...	...	...	...

* North Dakota allows low-stakes casino betting (maximum bets $2), with proceeds going to charity.

among middle-class bettors, who often didn't know the whereabouts of bookies, or felt uncomfortable in the sub rosa world of illegal gambling. The present availability of officially sanctioned gambling, however, now enables them to participate in an activity in which heretofore they were hesitant to join; for instance, middle-class patrons who would never venture into working-class bars to bet horses can now feel comfortable wagering at OTB shops or teletrack theaters. Those who might not consider betting with numbers runners gladly purchase lottery tickets of which a share of the profits is earmarked for schools. Many middle-class people who previously didn't patronize illegal casinos (often because they didn't know of their existence) now plan their leisure activities around casino gaming. Legalization and the social acceptability that accompanies it have allowed some middle-class gamblers to wager openly and to discuss their participation with peers.[12] "Closet gamblers" no longer feel they need to keep their wagering secret.

The transition of gambling from a private to a public activity has generally been accompanied by an increase in wagering. The comments of a college professor from Minnesota are representative of this shift:

> I always liked to play the horses, and I knew a local bookie who would take my bets. However, I always felt somewhat sleazy about phoning him and getting some action. I certainly didn't discuss wagering with my colleagues or in-laws. My wife knew I bet sometimes, but not how much I really liked to. When racing was approved—thank goodness—and Canterbury Downs opened, I was in hog heaven. I couldn't wait to begin betting with both hands. Now most of the college goes—even my father-in-law has gone—and I can talk horses with the other professors. Some of us have even worked up sort of a handicapping seminar, where we all get together and compare notes. I sure like it better these days; just wish I could get a few more winners. Did you say you knew something about the horses? Well, last Saturday . . .

Opposition to Gambling

Some observers question my contention that gambling has been legitimated, citing as countertrends continued opposition to its presence by various groups and regions, the defeat of new gambling proposals, and the negative publicity given to some existing operations. Nevertheless, evidence that gambling in the United States has been legitimated and that it will remain so for the forseeable future exists. Although there undoubtedly will be periodic swings in the public's acceptance of gambling, the pendulum is unlikely to move far enough to cast serious doubts on gambling's legitimacy. Gambling is firmly established as an American recreational activity, and its revenue contributions to government entities have been institutionalized. States now depend on these dollars to fund basic services such as hospitals, road construction, schools, and welfare agencies. The die has been cast; there is no returning to a time when gambling was relatively insignificant and its presence unobtrusive.

Although opposition to gambling still exists, it has been fragmented, persisting only as pockets of resistance. Opponents of gambling per se represent a minority and parochial view. Church groups no longer present a united front. On the contrary, many churches now support gambling and have themselves become dependent on revenues from bingo or from Las Vegas Nights. The opinion of Billy Graham is typical of the growing church tolerance toward gambling. After visiting Las Vegas in 1978, Graham said he found the resort "a nice place to visit" and indicated that although he himself did not gamble, the Bible says nothing definitive against the practice.[13] The Catholic church, always neutral toward gambling, recently acknowledged that playing bingo was the second most common parish activity.[14] Some legislators, like Florida's Senator Bob Graham, are opposed to gambling on the grounds that it weakens society's values, but many accept the viewpoint of Florida's commissioner of education, Ralph Turlington, who supports lotteries. After examining the Maryland lottery, Turlington argued, "Have the people there quit work? Are they less moral today? Are they less American?" He contends that the people in Maryland are, in fact, better off.[15] While the Mormon church continues to oppose lotteries on the grounds that they "add to the problems of the financially disadvantaged,"[16] such a perspective is not supported by the overwhelming majority of Americans, who have consistently approved lotteries.

Resistance to some types of gambling games continues. Casino gaming has been defeated in many jurisdictions. The failure of casinos to revive the overall economy and general vitality of Atlantic City has caused other communities to seriously question the benefits of casino gaming. These ballot defeats are not indictments of gambling in general but rather of casino gaming in particular; many of the same states that have turned down casinos have wholeheartedly embraced lotteries and pari-mutuel wagering. Sports betting, except for abortive efforts in Delaware and Western Canada, has not been considered appropriate for legalization. The unwillingness to consider legalizing sports betting stems in large part from the small profit margins and large risks inherent in this type of operation.[17] Millions of Americans show little compunction about illegally wagering on sports events with bookies or in office pools. The amount of money bet on the Super Bowl (most of it illegally) exceeds that for any other wagering event. In fact, much of the opposition to legalization of new games comes from operators of existing gaming ventures who are fearful of increased competition. Horse racing interest groups have been vocal opponents of lotteries and casinos, whereas operators of existing state lotteries adamantly oppose the institution of a national lottery.

Author's Perspective

Most authors emphasize a particular perspective, which in turn affects the material chosen for inclusion in their books. In this book I emphasize ethnographic, or firsthand, accounts of actual gambling environments. I believe that participant observation of gambling social worlds is essential to a full understanding of this phenomenon. In many instances, accounts of naturally occurring gambling groups differ considerably from those derived from experimental, clinical, or survey data.[18] Firsthand observers frequently demystify and debunk well-established gambling stereotypes. Although I have been careful to include diverse perspectives and information gleaned from varied sources and methodologies, I also demonstrate in this book a preference for ethnographic inquiry.

One of the problems in doing research as a participant observer is the difficulty of gaining entry to the group under study. Historically, academicians have not had much personal experience with gambling environments.[19] My inquiry into gambling, however, has been enhanced considerably by thirty-two years of gambling experience.

When I was 17 years old, several of my friends and I heard on the radio that harness racing was opening in our town. None of us knew anything about horse racing, but it sounded exciting, so we agreed to go. We dressed as we thought racetrackers would look: Jimmy wore a checkered sport coat, Dick put on a loud shirt, and I borrowed my father's wide-brimmed hat. On entering the track, we bought Clocker Dan's nightly picks for a dollar. Pooling our money, we bet five dollars on Dan's first selection. When the horse crossed the finish line three lengths in front of its competition, my friends and I looked at each other with unabashed awe: our horse had actually won! During the course of the evening, I "figured out" that horses with the name of Hanover were swift runners, and I convinced my friends that we should "chuck it all in" on Hanover Rex in the eighth race. We put twenty dollars on the horse, and it proved my theory by winning easily. After collecting the winnings, I knew that I was on to something.

So began a gambling odyssey that was to take me throughout the world, from palatial gaming clubs to back-room poker games and rundown, outlaw racetracks. During my gambling career, I have both experienced the dizzying heights of winning streaks and unbeatable rushes and suffered agonizing losses and confidence-shattering bad beats. I have come to know all manner of gamblers and their social worlds: those of poker players, horse racing devotees, sports bettors, casino gamesters, and lottery participants. Some could be considered occasional bettors; some, regular players; some, professionals; others, degenerates. It was to better understand an activity that had become both my bane and my sustenance that I turned to academic research, returning to college in mid-life to complete a long-delayed Ph.D.

Both in graduate school and since, I have attempted to analyze and describe gambling using the tools of science in order to render it comprehensible. When I explained this to one of my horse playing buddies, he said, "It never hurts to have a lot of information." I have worked diligently to give the reader the benefit of information garnered from the world of gambling as well as from the world of academia.

Two frequently asked questions are best answered immediately: "Are you a professional gambler?" and "Are you a compulsive gambler?" Several times in my life I have depended on gambling for my main income, and I have, in fact, considered myself a professional. Presently, though I remain a regular participant, I am not dependent on gambling winnings and therefore no longer consider myself a professional. I do not fit the traditional model of a compulsive gambler. Although I have on occasion lost more than my allotted "limit," I have never resorted to excessive borrowing, chasing, or mortgaging in an attempt to garner funds for gambling. I consider myself a controlled gambler; that is, I am able to keep my gambling losses within manageable parameters. Controlled gambling is not synonymous with worry-free gambling, however. In common with all serious gamblers, I have experienced the periodic losing streaks that are an integral part of this activity. Indeed, much of my empathic insight into gambling comes from having shared negative consequences with other gamblers.

Summary

Gambling today is an established, mainstream American leisure activity. Gambling is also big business! Revenues gained from patrons who lose appear prominently on the balance sheets of large corporations and state legislatures, as well as illegal operators. While recognizing that the American attitude toward gambling has historically been ambivalent, in this book I contend that much of that ambivalence has been resolved in favor of continuing acceptance and increasing participation. This resolution came about as moral opposition to gambling declined, in large part overcome by legislation, economic imperatives, and social acceptability. I also suggest that increasing middle-class participation may be an important factor in the acceptance accorded gambling. Further, I emphasize the importance of firsthand observations of naturally occurring gambling groups, as ethnographic accounts of real-life gambling situations often differ from those developed by traditional research methods.

Notes

1. Eugene M. Christiansen, "The 1986 Gross Annual Wager Part I: Handle," *Gaming and Wagering Business* 8 (July 1987): 7–14.
2. Eugene M. Christiansen, "The 1986 Gross Annual Wager Part II: Revenue," *Gaming and Wagering Business* 8 (August 1987): 6–20.
3. Although estimates of the scope of illegal gaming vary widely (see chapter 6), Christiansen's figures are considered highly credible. He estimates (August 1987, p. 6) that illegal operators retain 24.9 percent of gross gambling

revenues. For an understanding of the virtual monopoly that illegal bookies have on sports betting see Richard Sasuly, *Bookies and Bettors* (New
York: Holt, Rinehart & Winston, 1982).

4. Jane A. Morrison, "Illegal Bookmaking Helps Fill Coffers of Organized
   Crime," *Reno Gazette Journal*, 21 July 1986, p. 2c.
5. Robert L. Custer, "How Problem Gamblers Can Get Help," *U.S. News and
   World Report* 88 (January 1980): 75
6. I. Nelson Rose, *Gambling and the Law* (Hollywood: Gambling Times,
   1986).
7. T. H. Breen, "Horses and Gentlemen: The Cultural Significance of Gambling among the Gentry of Virginia," *William & Mary Quarterly* 34 (April
   1977): 239–257.
8. John Rosecrance, "The Next Best Thing: A Study of Problem Gambling,"
   International Journal of the Addictions 20 (December 1985): 1727–1739.
9. Jane A. Morrison, "Caesars Begins Catering to Middle-Income Crowd,"
   Reno Gazette Journal, 31 August 1986, p. 1F.
10. Oliver Quayle, *A Study of Betting on Sports in New York City: Study
    #1493* (New York: Oliver Quayle Co., 1972); Roxanne Arnold, "Scratching
    for Ticket to Big Spin," *Los Angeles Times*, 22 July 1986, p. 1 sec. 1.
11. U.S. Senate Committee of Commerce, "Hearing on Regulation of Interstate
    Parimutuel Wagering," *Serial No 95-39* (Washington, D.C.: U.S. Govern-
    ment Printing Office, 1977), p. 57.
12. James H. Frey and I. Nelson Rose, "The Role of Sports Information Services
    in the World of Sports Gambling," *Arena Review* 11 (May, 1987), p. 51.
13. John M. Findlay, *People of Chance* (New York: Oxford University Press,
    1986), p. 203.
14. "Bingo Popular Church Activity," *Tahoe Daily Tribune*, 8 September
    1986, p. 3A.
15. John Dillin, "State Lotteries—Lure of the 'Painless Tax,' " *Christian Sci-
    ence Monitor*, 9 July 1985, p. 1.
16. "Mormons: Lotteries Bad," *Reno Gazette Journal*, 1 October 1986, p. 1A.
17. See William R. Eadington, "Sports Betting and Pari-Mutuel Wagering," in
    The Gambling Studies, ed. William R. Eadington (Reno: Bureau of Busi-
    ness and Economic Research, University of Nevada, Reno, 1985), pp. 225–
    235, and Roger Larson, *No Winners* (St. Paul: Ipse Dixit Press, 1978), pp.
    88–89.
18. Robert D. Herman, *Gamblers and Gambling* (Lexington, Mass.: D.C. Heath,
    1976), p. 66.
19. David M. Hayano, *Poker Faces* (Berkeley: University of California Press,
    1982), p. 153.

Gambling through the Nineteenth Century

This day did go to Nu. Mark. for the race matches. Had news of a strong steed, Caesar, from Ned Wells the draper. Did place 3 pd. did see Caesar be out run. Drank pear cider with Ned. Swear to Goody [wife?] will wager no moor.

Diary excerpt from a New York merchant, 1666*

Two ideas have dominated the history of gambling in the United States: the working class should be protected from gambling, and gaming is permissible in some contexts but not in others. In practice, both of these ideas proved problematic. Workers invariably have refused to be protected from gambling, and allowing some gaming has made it difficult to restrict other games.

Throughout American history there have been ups and downs in gambling participation; boom times have been followed by reform movements to curtail or restrict gaming. During these periodic changes, efforts to shield the working class from the temptation of gambling remained constant. However, the task of protecting America's workers from the siren lure of gambling has always proved difficult. Reflecting on past efforts to control gambling, Julian Lapides, a state senator from Baltimore, succinctly described the problem: "The poor are willing suckers and it's hard to defend a group that doesn't want to be defended."[1] The next two chapters will analyze why efforts to restrict gambling proved so difficult, and explain how gambling eventually achieved social acceptability.

Americans have a long history of participating in various forms of gambling. In order to present the material effectively, I have divided the historical review into sections based on chronological time frames: (1) gambling before 1830, (2) pre–Civil War gambling, and (3) post–Civil War gambling.

* From *Win or Lose: A Social History of Gambling in America*, by Stephen Longstreet (Indianapolis: Bobbs-Merrill, 1977), p. 35.

11

Gambling before 1830

Reports of early Indian societies indicate that gambling played an important role in the lives of the first Native Americans. The Onondagas of New York were legendary gamblers who regularly wagered their possessions in dice sessions. The Iroquois people, which included the Onondaga tribe, played a variation of dice called Hubbub using peach pits with one side seared by fire. William Wood described this game in 1634: "Five stones were placed in the dish on the ground and as violently thumping the platter, the bones mount changing colors with the windy wisking of their hands to and fro, which action in that sport they much use, smiting themselves on the breast and thighs, crying Hub Hub Hub. They may be heard playing this game a quarter of a mile off."[2]

The Narragansett Indians of Rhode Island and the Chumash of the Northwest often gambled for days in sessions during which the worldly goods of entire tribes might change hands. Eastern Indian tribes played a form of football with goals approximately one mile apart. During these contests, vast amounts of wampum were gambled on the outcome, with a reckless abandon that amazed early explorers. Francois Xavier de Charlevoix, in the early eighteenth century, observed that losing Hurons gambled until they were stripped naked and, in a desperate effort to recoup, frequently upped the ante by offering themselves, their wives, and their children as slaves for specified periods.

Lotteries

While the Indians threw dice or wagered on the outcome of sporting events, the first efforts to colonize America were being financed by English lotteries. In 1611, the Virginia Company of London was in financial difficulty because of the unexpectedly high start-up costs of its plantation project in Virginia. Mounting debts, coupled with the colony's problems in developing marketable exports, led the directors to seek other funding schemes. Company officials, encouraged by the success of lotteries in Europe, lobbied and were granted a franchise from the Crown to conduct similar drawings in England. Profits from the lotteries were earmarked for the Virginia Colony.

Between 1612 and 1615, the Virginia Company held four raffles in London, marketing tickets by advertising that purchasers of a lottery ticket were honoring both God and country. The company promised that "So worthie an enterprise" would advance the cause of "Christian truth, the honor of our nation, & benefite of English people."[3] At the same time that company officials were attempting to hype lottery sales in England, they were trying to check gambling in Virginia. Responding to reports that gaming, idleness, and vice were rampant in the colony, the Virginia Company incorporated antigambling ordinances into

Jamestown's first legal code. Although these codes were generally ineffective in curbing the growth of gaming in Virginia, they represented a peculiar perspective. The curious logic that allowed and encouraged gambling in one context but disapproved and outlawed it in another was to characterize the American gambling experience and foster an ambivalence that has only recently begun to be resolved.

The Puritans of Massachusetts were opposed to gambling on the grounds that such activity was immoral. Cotton Mather's pronouncements were representative of this viewpoint. On several occasions he condemned gambling as "an appearance of evil and as such . . . forbidden in the word of God."[4] A series of blue laws were passed to inhibit and restrict gambling. Although gaming with dice and cards, especially among the lower classes, continued in Massachusetts,[5] legal prohibitions severely restricted the growth of gambling during the seventeenth century in the Northeastern colonies. However, in the early eighteenth century, when massive funds were needed for the construction of colleges, roads, and churches, these same colonies turned to a familiar vehicle—the lottery.

Lotteries seemed an ideal method to raise funds from colonists, who possessed little cash and who complained vociferously of overtaxation. In many instances the shortage of currency made it difficult for governments and entrepreneurs to fund capital investments. The selling of lottery tickets allowed the government to pool money from many purchasers, in quantities sufficient to fund costly projects. Colonists who balked at paying taxes to local governments were willing to purchase lottery tickets authorized by those same governments.

The first lotteries in America were private enterprises; merchants used them to dispose of inventories; developers, to sell real estate; and farmers, to improve their land. As these private ventures became more commonplace, they came under the scrutiny of colonial governments. Government efforts to restrict lotteries were motivated by a familiar combination of paternalism and self-interest. In 1719, the Massachusetts General Court lambasted lotteries for tempting the "Children and Servants of several Gentlemen, Merchants, and Traders . . . into a vain Expense of money."[6] In 1732, the Rhode Island legislature restricted lotteries on the grounds that they "lead unwary persons into a foolish expense of money which may tend to the great hurt of the government."[7] In 1747, the New York State Legislature criticized lotteries for causing "Pernicious Consequences to the public" because they encouraged "numbers of Labouring people to assemble together where such lotteries are usually drawn."[8]

Colonial governments, rather than banning private lotteries, undertook to regulate them, and by 1750, most states officially authorized their operation. Unauthorized lotteries were deemed illegal. Many of those authorized were operated by municipalities, churches, public utilities, and schools. Examples of authorized lotteries during this period are numerous. In 1744, Rhode Island funded a project to pave the streets of Newport City. In 1746, lottery proceeds went to the founding of Kings College, later to be known as Columbia University. In 1747, Benjamin Franklin conducted a lottery to finance a strengthening of Philadelphia's defenses. In 1765, the trustees of St. Paul's Church in Philadelphia used the lottery to retire their construction debt. The Massachusetts Faneuil Hall Lottery of 1762, drawn to repair one of Boston's municipal buildings, was typical of lotteries during this period. The following listing[9] shows how funds from this lottery were distributed.

1	prize of	1,000	is	1,000	dollars
1	" "	500	is	500	"
2	" "	200	are	400	"
12	" "	100	"	1,200	"
20	" "	50	"	1,000	"
20	" "	20	"	400	"
30	" "	10	"	300	"
200	" "	6	"	1,200	"
1200	" "	4	"	4,800	"

1486 Prizes   10,800
4514 Blanks

6000 Tickets at 2 dollars each is $12,000
        To be paid as prizes   10,800
Remains for the use of Faneuil
        Hall $ 1,200

During the eighteenth century, lotteries were ubiquitous. Lottery proceeds were used to endow many of America's best-known colleges, including Yale, Harvard, Dartmouth, Williams, Brown, Princeton, North Carolina, and Pennsylvania. Paving projects, bridge repairs, public granaries, jail constructions, and lighthouse placements were also funded by lottery proceeds. Lotteries ranged in size from one with a prize of thirty thousand pounds, created to build two bridges, a fence, and a jail in Rent County, Rhode Island, to another offering forty pounds, established to repair a Massachusetts township bridge. Encouraged by the success of lotteries, the fledgling Continental Congress authorized a United States Lottery to help pay for the war with England, exhorting purchasers to contribute to the "great and glorious cause."[10] After some initial success, ticket sales slumped badly, and the national lottery was disbanded before the war ended. In the years following the Revolutionary War, lotteries grew in popularity: once again, money for public works was scarce, and taxation systems were not well established. By 1795, about two thousand authorized lotteries were in operation. The list of drawings and prizes required half a column of small print in New York newspapers.[11]

As the nation's population grew, lotteries increased in size and scope. More ambitious plans for expansion and improvements required the large sums that could be obtained from lottery proceeds. Lotteries became more national and more complex in their operation. While the first drawings were often conducted by volunteer private citizens, by the early nineteenth century, a new breed of operators had emerged: ticket brokers and lottery contractors. Brokers bought up large blocks of tickets at a discount and then resold them at regional outlets. Contractors assumed control of running and advertising the larger lotteries for a fee or percentage.

Horse Racing

Lotteries were not the only gambling games available in colonial times. Horse racing was a popular activity from the start of colonialization. In 1610, Jamestown received its first shipment of racehorses, a total of seven. In 1620, the Virginia Company shipped twenty mares, "beautiful and full of courage,"[12] and racing began in earnest. The first horse races were informal affairs run over a short distance. The early colonists found that the cost of clearing large spaces of land precluded the building of traditional racecourses. Instead, they developed a type of contest peculiar to America—quarter horse racing. Early racing enthusiasts laid out a straight course about a quarter of a mile long over existing roads or on relatively level land (often hastily cleared of trees). Races were all-out sprints from one end of the track to the other. Typically a race matched two horses who were ridden by their owners. Spectators bet with one another on their favorites; often the wagers involved tobacco or livestock as well as cash. This type of racing flourished in seventeenth century Virginia and was also found in the Northeastern colonies. A Plymouth decree of 1674 stated that "whatever person shall run a race with a horse kind in any street or common road shall forfeit 5 shillings in money forthwith to be levied by the Constable."[13] In Philadelphia, the town council repeatedly warned that racing horses on Sassafrass Street was forbidden. Their warnings were not heeded and Philadelphians dubbed this thoroughfare Race Street, a name that later was made official.

In Virginia, the large planters or gentry controlled horse racing and considered it their exclusive sporting domain. Laws were passed forbidding members of the working class to wager on horse races.[14] An advertisement of an upcoming race meeting in the *Virginia Gazette* underscores the exclusiveness of racing; the purpose of the contests, it states, is to furnish the county's "considerable Number of Gentlemen, Merchants, and credible Planters an opportunity for collective Friendship."[15] The notice warned that spectators must behave with "Decency and Sobriety, the Subscribers being resolved to discountenance all Immorality with the utmost Rigour."[16]

The gentry often wagered heavily on the outcome of quarter horse races. In 1693, for example, two Virginia planters wagered four thousand pounds of tobacco (about one year's harvest) and forty sterling shillings on the speed of their horses.[17] The gentlemanly participants often found themselves in disagreement over the terms of their wager or the fairness of the race. Rather than resort to duels, the gentlemen sought redress in the courts. In the late seventeenth and early eighteenth centuries, Virginia courts were besieged by litigious planters seeking arbitration in disputes over horse races. To discourage court suits, it became an established practice for gentlemen to sign a wagering contract prior to the actual race contest. In 1690, a Henrico County, Virginia, court dismissed a gambling suit since "noe Money was stacked down nor Contract in writing made one of wch in such cases is by the law required."[18]

Charges of interference or "josselleing" during races were commonplace, and witnesses were often called to describe what had occurred during a questionable race. Reverend James Blair, a leading Virginia clergyman and founder of William and Mary, once testified in a suit stemming from a race between Captain William Scione and Robert Napier. In another case, a Rodhan Kenner testified that his horse had an insurmountable lead when his opponent's brother sprang from the bushes and "did holler and shout and wave his hand over his head in the horse's face." The horse shied and ran sideways, causing gentleman Kenner to lose the race. After a lengthy trial, a jury ruled against the plaintiff, holding that such conduct did not constitute "foule play."[19]

According to a Virginia historian, horse racing served as a solidifying social force for the colonial gentry. Participation in events that barred social inferiors fostered a sense of elitism:

> The exclusiveness of horse racing strengthened the gentry's cultural dominance. By promoting these public displays the great planters legitimized the cultural values which racing symbolized—materialism, individualism, and competitiveness. These colorful, exclusive contests helped persuade subordinate white groups that gentry culture was desirable, something worth emulating; and it is not surprising that people who conceded the superiority of this culture readily accepted the gentry's right to rule. The wild sprint down a dirt track served the interests of Virginia's gentlemen better than they imagined.[20]

As colonial America grew and prospered, quarter horse racing declined in popularity; at the same time, planters began constructing traditional circular racecourses, initiating formal racing seasons and buying and registering purebred horses. The particularly American hell-for-leather sprint remained popular in underdeveloped areas of the West, however. Quarter horse races continued to be run on the frontier and today remain popular in western states such as Oklahoma, New Mexico, and California.

The first recognized racecourse was built on Long Island in 1665. Governor Richard Nicolls presided at the inaugural race meeting held at Hempstead Plains. Racegoers from New York thronged to the track in such large numbers that, on occasion, the Brooklyn Ferry couldn't transport everyone during the daylight hours, so some were forced to stay overnight on Long Island. Subsequent racetracks were built in Maryland, New Hampshire, South Carolina, Pennsylvania, North Carolina, and Virginia. These new courses were usually large ovals that could accommodate races of between three and four miles. Several horses ridden by jockeys would race for purses put up by race organizers. The following announcement appeared in a Maryland newspaper on April 23, 1761.

> To be run for on Thursday, the 28th of May, on the usual race ground at Alexandria, a purse of fifty pounds, three times around the ground (being near three miles) the best in three heats, by any horse, mare or gelding, 14 hands to carry 10 stone, below that measure weight for inches. . . .
>
> The horses to be entered on the Monday before the race with the managers, Mr. George Washington, Mr. John Carlyle and Mr. Charles Digges.
>
> . . . Each horse to pay fifty shillings entrance on the first day and twenty-five shillings on the second day.
>
> All differences that may arise, will be decided by the managers.[21]

By the end of the eighteenth century, race meetings were an established part of American life. As horse racing became larger and more complex, professional trainers and jockeys were hired to prepare and ride the horses. Betting, which at first was between a few individuals, became more widespread. In order to facilitate increased wagering, a group of individuals known as stake holders or pool sellers emerged. For a percentage, these people would hold, or pool, the collective wagers of gamblers and pay the winners. This practice developed into a more sophisticated form of pool selling, in which one party would give odds on the chances of prospective horses. In this manner a market was created for betting, and a practice begun that became known as bookmaking. By 1830, pool sellers were conducting business at many racetracks in America.

Cards and Dice

In addition to lotteries and horse racing, colonists avidly gambled with cards and dice. In 1624, such gaming could even be found among the clergy, so that a Virginia assembly deemed it necessary to enact the following statute: "Mynisters shall not give themselves to excess in drinking or yette spend their tyme idelie by day or by night, playing at dice, cards or any unlawful game."[22]

The early Dutch settlers in New York gambled on a card game called lansquenet, using a deck of seventy-three cards. Games of cards and dice were popular at local taverns, as is evident in the remarks of a New Jersey grand jury: "Servants, and the sink of ye town and country assembled and congregated together for the more secure indulgence of the several fashionable, and without your Honors interposition, legal diversions of cards, dice, drinking, cursing, swearing and the whole train of debaucheries incident to such infamous places . . ."[23]

Harvard undergraduates played cards so assiduously that regents found it necessary to fine the players five shillings—the most expensive of the collegiate vices. In 1661, Plymouth Colony ruled that servants and minors caught gambling with cards would be "publicly whipt."[24]

Thomas Jefferson, while righteously proclaiming that "gaming corrupts our disposition and teaches us a habit of hostility against all mankind," often gambled at cards. While composing the Declaration of Independence in June 1776, he noted in his personal log: "Lost at Backgammon 7/6. Won at Backgammon 7d 1/3. Won at cross and pyle, 3 and 3/4 d [the match game?]. Mrs. Jefferson, lost at cards 1/3. Lost at lotto [a form of bingo], 18/d."[25] Benjamin Franklin used his printing company to manufacture playing cards that were sold at post offices throughout Pennsylvania. Henry Clay was a noted poker gambler and on one occasion won a $40,000 pot from a northern industrialist. Andrew Jackson was a notorious gambler who early in his career staked his horse on a dice roll and won.

The popularity of cards and dice in postrevolutionary America encouraged the commercialization of these games. Entrepreneurs opened halls, saloons, and parlors that offered gamblers a place to indulge in card playing and dice throwing. This development made it possible for skillful players to earn a living from their gambling activity, and a new occupation emerged—the professional gambler. New games like faro, craps, roulette, and three-card monte were introduced, games that could be easily manipulated to provide the operators with an unfair advantage. Crooked roulette wheels, rigged faro boxes, card marking, and dealing from the bottom of the deck increased the profits of unscrupulous gambling operators. The American frontier of the nineteenth century proved to be fertile ground for the spread of commercialized gaming. Gambling businesses flourished as steamboats and railroads forged westward. Gambling establishments, often called dens, dotted the waterfront and railyards of Louisville, St. Louis, Charleston, New Orleans, and Chicago, even as the practices of professional gamesters were becoming the subject of public scrutiny.

Pre–Civil War Gambling

By 1830, lotteries, horse racing, and card and dice games had achieved widespread acceptance and legality in America, and sizable profits could be gained from willing participants. Gambling had in large part become commercialized and was now being operated by lottery brokers, stake holders, and gamesters. The emergence of a profession of gamblers whose income came directly from gaming proceeds was to change the course of gambling in America. Gambling was no longer predominantly a private activity conducted in drawing rooms, down back country roads, in exclusive clubs, or in darkened taverns. It had been taken over by professionals who operated openly and profited by their skill and expertise. The vast potential for profit often encouraged the new breed of professional to engage in cheating, fixing, and rigging. Professional gamblers, because of their alleged penchant for cheating, became known as blacklegs. The disapproval directed against them can be seen in a traveler's guide to the frontier, which labeled "gaming adventurers, blacklegs as the lowest class of people on the frontier" and warned visitors to steer clear of such confidence men.[26]

Public reaction to reports of cheating and fraudulent schemes perpetrated by gambling professionals led to a round of reforms that altered the face of gambling in America. From 1830 to 1860, confidence that gambling could be properly regulated waned, and many jurisdictions opted for outright prohibition. Although gaming was not banned in all areas, the gambling profession developed an unsavory reputation that blocked gambling's legitimation.

Lotteries

Changing public opinion toward the operation of lotteries ushered in a reform movement that eventually swept through the United States. Between 1825 and 1833, several large lotteries were wracked by scandals of mismanagement and outright fraud. A bogus lottery, exposed in 1831, had collected over $400,000 and paid out no prizes. In 1833, an antilottery group revealed that the Union Canal Lottery of Pennsylvania had sold over $5 million in tickets though they had been authorized sales of only half a million. In New York, the lottery contracting firm of Yates and McIntyre was indicted by an 1830 grand jury that found its methods of distributing prizes "a much apparent mystery."[27] In Boston, lottery brokers were accused of selling fictitious tickets for a profit of $1 million. Maine legislatures were shocked when an 1835 audit discovered that lottery directors had received over $10 million in expenses out of a total of $16 million collected. Other states and municipalities uncovered similar irregularities, and lotteries generally fell out of favor.

Editorial opposition to lotteries reflected a paternalistic protection of the working classes. Ticket sellers were accused of "assailing the poor man at his labour, entering the abode of the needy, and by holding out false promises of wealth, induc[ing] him to hazzard his little all on the demoralizing system."[28] A New York grand jurist of this period summed up the public's new view of lotteries, describing games "as evil of the most alarming nature both in a pecuniary and moral point of view."[29] Between 1833 and 1840, twelve states had specifically banned lotteries; most other states followed suit, and by 1865 no authorized lotteries remained in the United States. Although there was a short-lived revival of lotteries after the Civil War, only the Louisiana lottery was to achieve prominence. When it was banned in 1894 after rumors of massive fraud, legal lotteries disappeared from the United States for the next seventy years.

Horse Racing

In the years preceding the Civil War, horse racing, especially in the Eastern states, fell into disfavor. Attempts to open new racetracks were thwarted by legislatures, and existing tracks suffered a decline in business. A turf historian noted that racing was "sinking lower and lower in the North until Fort Sumter was fired upon."[30] The decline of racing during this period can be attributed to the public's increasingly negative perception of track insiders and professional gamblers. The emerging entrepreneurs of the turf were no longer gentry or established society scions. Instead, according to a Yale University observer, they represented "the most objectionable classes of society, with no real interest in sport, who were constant patrons of the track and found devious ways of making a living from their racing connections."[31] A newspaper columnist described the opening of a Long Island race meeting in 1856:

> They had come out in strength, this racing world—this huge agglomeration of gambling and fraud, of weakness and wickedness. . . . This "fancy" profession is surrounded by an atmosphere of immorality almost as fatal as fascinating; and although undoubtedly many of our most honorable men interest themselves in "sporting events" what are their numbers compared with those we meet upon the road—men whose interest in them is the interest of "sharps" and "gamblers"?[32]

The professionalization of horse racing was intertwined with the emergence of bookmakers, who as odds makers were concerned with profit margins rather than improving the thoroughbred breed. In order to increase profits, bookmakers, with the help of track insiders (trainers, grooms, and jockeys), occasionally conspired to fix races. The order of finish was manipulated in such a way that the general public lost the vast majority of its wagers. When accounts of race fixing (termed in racing lore "doing business") first surfaced, antebellum reformers attacked bookmakers as a scurrilous lot that deprived honest laborers of their hard-earned money. Racetrack professionals were reviled for their chicanery, and gambling critics urged governments to uphold "industrious habits" and discourage wagering on horse races.[33] While racing opponents were mildly successful in persuading some state legislatures not to sanction proposed race meetings, their more lasting impact on the course of gambling came from convincing the public that horse racing was basically crooked. This perception, despite herculean efforts by race promoters to the contrary, has stigmatized horse racing to this very day. Although bettors returned to racetracks in droves after the Civil War, they found it difficult to dispel the notion that somehow they were being "taken."

Cards and Dice

The round of reforms directed against cards, dice, and other casino games can be directly traced to events that occurred in Vicksburg, Mississippi, July 5–7, 1835. At that time, Vicksburg was a typical frontier town in that casino gaming was tolerated, widespread, and openly conducted, Several gambling casinos catered to a bustling town of 2,500 that was becoming an important cotton center and railroad terminus. Compatibility with gaming had earned Vicksburg the title "the liveliest gambling place in the whole Southwest."[34] By 1835, a sizeable middle class existed—a group that believed the ubiquity of gambling blacklegs was severely damaging Vicksburg's reputation and inhibiting commercial growth.

In June 1835, Vicksburg officials uncovered an alleged plot to arm Negro slaves for the purpose of overthrowing white rule. The conspirators belonged to a shadowy group called the Clan of the Mystic Confederacy, which supposedly included some white gamblers who planned to profit from the disruptions that would follow an armed insurrection. The "plot" was foiled and five "confessed" slaves were hung on June 30. The gambler–conspirators were never located, but by July 4 strong public sentiment against anyone connected with gaming had risen. When a drunken gambling saloon owner disrupted a July 4th gathering, antigambling interests seized the initiative, forming a vigilance committee made up of the town's "better citizens" and passing a resolution ordering "all professional gamblers" to leave Vicksburg within twenty-four hours.

On July 6, the vigilantes marched through town tearing down the casinos and burning gambling paraphernalia such as cards, dice, faro boxes, and roulette wheels. Five professional gamblers who had refused to leave town were summarily hung, while several others were tarred and feathered. The wrath of the vigilance committee was de-

Notice.

AT a meeting of the citizens of Vicksburg on Saturday the 4th day of July, it was

Resolved, That a notice be given to all *professional* GAMBLERS, that the citizens of Vicksburg are resolved to exclude them from this place and its vicinity, and that *twenty-four hours* notice be given them to leave the place.

Resolved, That all persons permitting Faro dealing in their houses, be also notified, that they will be prosecuted therefor.

Resolved, That one hundred copies of the foregoing resolutions be printed and stuck up at the corners of the streets, and the publication be deemed notice.

Vicksburg, July 5, 1835.

Figure 2-1   This broadside evinced a change of attitude toward sharps in the old Southwest. Professional gamblers in Vicksburg, Mississippi, learned that citizens intent on erasing vestiges of the frontier would back their resolutions with popular vigilante force. (*Courtesy of the Mississippi Department of Archives and History, Jackson, Mississippi*)

scribed by a local resident: "At this time while I am writing they are whipping, tarring and feathering for stealing. They have driven the gambler from this town and all law is according to the will of the victors. All gamblers that can be found are hung, insurrectors hung, other offence, whipping. If a man says aught against the [militia] Company's proceedings he is either whipped or hung."[35]

The actions taken by the Vicksburg committee encouraged other antigambling groups, and a wave of reform swept frontier towns from Mobile to Chicago. Several jurisdictions banned gambling altogether, while others made it difficult for casinos to operate openly. The authorities of Natchez, a notorious gambling center, threatened casino owners with vigilante action. Most of the gambling operators heeded the warning and left on steamships heading westward. Signs in public squares ordered "sporting men" to leave town. The manufacture and distribution of cards and dice was prohibited in some towns.

The more established Eastern cities also participated in the antigambling fervor. In New York, Horace Greeley, editor of the *New York Tribune,* campaigned diligently for the abolition of gaming. He convinced businessmen to join him in forming the New York Association for the Suppression of Gambling. The goal of the organization, according to an association member, was "to pluck the victim from the gambler's clutches." Most of this protection was to be afforded the working classes, who, according to Greeley and his associates, were being regularly fleeced by gambling blacklegs. After considerable lobbying by antigambling forces, the 1851 New York legislature passed several antigambling ordinances, which, according to backers, "if faithfully enforced would close every gambling hell within the state."[36] Some of New York's gaming establishments did in fact close, while many moved underground and operated by bribing enforcement officials. The reforms directed against casino gaming during this period had two effects: many gambling casinos were forced to operate illegally, and open gaming moved westward to the gold fields of Colorado and California, the frontier towns of Kansas and Texas, and the riverboats of the Mississippi.

The reforms that began in the 1830s were directed mainly against gambling professionals. Stimulated by accounts of fraudulent schemes perpetrated by professionals, antigambling sentiments were sustained by reformers' distrust of the gamesters, who thwarted traditional values. The professionals' public gaming was anathema to upholders of the traditional values of thrift and hard work. Whereas the gentry had gambled with their peers, professionals were encouraging all classes to participate. To antigambling reformers, it was clear that the hard-working working classes needed protection from the gambling sharpers— even though workers enthusiastically declined such protection. Although antigambling laws were passed and gamblers were run out of town, workers and others continued to seek out gambling games. After the Civil War, participation increased significantly and gambling was soon to experience a renaissance.

Post–Civil War Gambling

The post–Civil War period was a time of industrial and territorial expansion. Gambling was to play a significant role in that era. From 1870 to 1900, gambling flourished in the United States in a manner reminiscent of postrevolutionary activity. From New York to San Francisco, gambling casinos dominated local economies, horse racing groups built lavish new racetracks, and policy games proliferated in urban neighborhoods.

Policy Games

Most states (with the notable exception of Louisiana) had banned lotteries. Policy games were developed to fill that void. Policy was based on the drawing of numbers from one to seventy-eight by spinning a wheel. Typically, twelve to fifteen numbers would be drawn, with players betting that among them would be numbers of their choice.

Bettors could select from one to four numbers in various orders and sequences. The following list depicts typical policy payouts.

> *Day Number*—Any number from one to seventy-eight played as one of the eleven to fifteen drawn and appearing anywhere on the winning list. On this the policy shops paid 5 to 1.
>
> *Station Number*—A number played to appear in a specified position on the list. The odds were 60 to 1.
>
> *Saddle*—Two numbers to appear anywhere on the list. Odds, 32 to 1.
>
> *Station Saddle*—Two numbers to appear at specified positions on the list. Odds, 800 to 1.
>
> *Capital Saddle*—Two of the first three numbers drawn. Odds, 500 to 1.
>
> *Gig*—Three numbers to appear anywhere on the list. Odds, 200 to 1.
>
> *Horse*—Four numbers to appear anywhere on the list. Odds, 680 to 1.

The actual odds of choosing any winning combination were obviously much higher than indicated. For instance, more than 30,000 saddles, about 75,000 gigs, and almost 1.5 million horses are possible.[37]

Policy gaming, a forerunner of numbers and keno, appealed to low-income players since bets as small as five cents were taken. Outlets for selling policy numbers and posting winning combinations were called policy shops. Dream books (used to select numbers) such as the *Wheel of Fortune* and *Old Aunt Dinah's Policy Dream Book* were popular best-sellers. Policy tickets were sold by agents or runners who roamed the urban ghettos collecting bets. The runners typically received 15 percent of whatever they collected. Although bets were often small, the volume of business proved extremely lucrative. During the 1880s, New York City had over seven hundred policy shops, and a cartel called the Central Organization operated policy games in twenty cities, including Chicago, Baltimore, Philadelphia, Richmond, and Washington.[38] The following passage describes policy shops in New Orleans during that period.

> Visitors to New Orleans in the 80's remember well the open policy booths in the main business streets of the city, and the lines and crowds of negroes and whites that thronged the "book," seeking to bet their nickels and dimes on the innumerable combinations of figures which superstition or fancy dictated. There were policy booths in front of laundries, barrooms, groceries and markets. There were instances where as much as $5,000 was paid for a stand if the location were favorable enough, which might not be more than four feet square of space, with a small chair and table. More than a hundred policy shops existed in New Orleans.[39]

Policy, except in Louisiana, was never legalized, and operators continued in business by paying for protection from official harassment.

When policy operators failed to pay the required protection, they were subject to being arrested or closed down. When, in 1870, many policy operators refused to pay for protection, police raided many policy shops in New York City. This action convinced the operators to pay up, and the next day they were all allowed to reopen their shops. Those who ran the policy rackets often manipulated the numbers drawn to ensure that only a few bettors held winning combinations. Regardless of illegality or chicanery, by the end of the nineteenth century, playing the policy was an established part of urban America. In New York City, for example, over one million persons are estimated to have purchased tickets regularly.

Horse Racing

After the Civil War, horse racing attracted an increasing number of participants and spectators, entering what some were to call the "golden age of the turf." New racetracks were built throughout the United States, horse breeding became a major industry, the training and maintenance of thoroughbreds became a recognized occupation, owning racehorses was considered prestigious, and "doping out" a winner became a national pastime. Heightened interest in racing was fueled by the ability of racing patrons to easily and quickly wager on their selections. Rapid wagering and accurate payouts were facilitated by the proliferation of bookmaking. Bookies were an integral part of racing and were accorded places of importance at every racetrack. Each track set aside a betting ring near the finish line with a group of stalls in which bookmakers and their writers quoted odds, accepted bets, and paid off winners. The open-sided ring was roofed, and blackboards listing the horses' names, jockeys, post positions, weights, and odds were hung over each stall. Odds were changed according to each bookmaker's calculations and general betting patterns. Bookies and their assistants stood on platforms so they could keep apprised of the odds being offered by their competitors.

Bookmakers paid the tracks a fee for their place in the betting ring. Choice positions in the ring required a special membership fee; in 1888, the cost of joining the Metropolitan Turf Association (a leading bookmaking syndicate) was seven thousand dollars—more than the cost of a seat on the stock exchange.[40] In 1894, the *New York Herald* estimated that at Brighton Beach, a New York racetrack, about sixty bookmakers were in operation, with a gross handle in excess of one million dollars per day. The same newspaper described the bookmaking process:

> The whole art of bookmaking lies first in judgment, and second in the mental ability to quickly calculate the percentages. . . . When you can do all that without difficulty you can gather your capital in a valise . . . and begin business with the utmost certainty that every man's hand will

be against you and your hand will be against all men. It is surprising the way bookmakers watch each other. A cat and a mouse are no comparison. Every one of them carries big glasses with which he is constantly sweeping the bookmaking horizon. In this way they catch the fluctuation of odds just as a Wall Street broker reads the tape. A very important feature of modern bookmaking is the "outside man" whose duties are multifarious. In the first place, he must know everybody, particularly the big bettors. The little plungers always take care of themselves. He must notify his book of what is going on in different parts of the ring, out of range of the bookies' keen vision. For instance, if the bookmaker is laying even money against Armitage on one side of the ring, and his "outside man" rushes up with the information that "Mike" Dwyer's commissioners have knocked the price to four to five on the opposite side, the bookie would be obviously foolish to lay anything higher. A good "outside man" can save his book a great many dollars through the medium of keen eyes and prompt action.[41]

The post–Civil War popularity of racing is reflected in the fact that on October 24, 1877, the United States Congress adjourned to attend a horse race at Pimlico Track in Baltimore. This was the only time that Congress has adjourned to attend a sporting event. Horse racing was truly a national endeavor: the West boasted of tracks in Sacramento, San Francisco, Boise, and Denver; in the Midwest, Cincinnati, Chicago, St. Louis, and Detroit offered race meetings; the South had tracks operating in Louisville, Lexington, Nashville, Memphis, Mobile, and New Orleans; and on the East Coast, all states except Maine offered some racing, with the largest tracks being in New York, Boston, and Washington, D.C.

The types of races offered at these tracks were no longer the four-mile marathons of the eighteenth century but typically were scheduled at distances between one mile and one and one-quarter miles. Sprint racing with distances of six to seven furlongs was introduced during this period and became popular with patrons. Large breeding farms were established in Kentucky and Tennessee to produce large numbers of racing horses. Race bettors known for their expertise or courage became popular figures. Bet-A-Million Gates, famous for his six-figure wagers, was a colorful character at racetracks during this era. He told one of his betting companions, "For me there's no fun in betting just a few thousand. I want to lay down enough to hurt the other fellow if he loses and enough to hurt me if I lose."[42] One of the most renowned horse players of this or any other period was George Smith, better known as Pittsburgh Phil. His prescription for success was an elaborate record-keeping system, an objective approach, and an unstinting dedication to the task of picking a winner. His philosophy is clearly stated in his own statement of purpose:

The racing man should arise in the morning, cool and clear-headed and with the first opening of his eyes he should again take up the problems of the day. The horses come before him at once, and they never leave until after the contest is decided. I think about them the very first thing when I awaken, weighing them in one light and from one standpoint and another. As I dress and eat my breakfast I am placing them here and there, giving each a chance until at last from all standpoints I decide which one in a truly and perfectly run race, devoid of the hundred or more unlooked for incidents that can happen, should be the winner.[43]

Pittsburgh Phil's system of keeping charts of races and records of horses' past performances was soon copied by others, who subsequently published a form sheet detailing important data related to racing events. Racing fans eagerly purchased such sheets, encouraging the compilation of even more complex data. This trend culminated in the printing of the *Daily Racing Form,* later known as the bible of horse players. The availability of pertinent information significantly increased interest in horse race wagering. No longer were bettors dependent on personal knowledge of a horse's capabilities or on the opinions of stable workers. Track devotees could wager on races based on data readily available for their consideration, and they didn't have to be at the track to feel confident of their selection. Thus, the development of a form sheet was an important catalyst in the emergence of offtrack betting. This form of wagering was further enhanced by improvements in telephone and telegraph communications. Accurate information concerning entries and results could now be relayed from the track to farflung locations.

Gamblers wanting to bet on horse races, even when not actually present, found their needs satisfied by bookmakers who opened betting parlors known as poolrooms. Chafetz, in his classic study of gambling, *Play the Devil,* describes a poolroom at the end of the nineteenth century:

> Poolroom was a misnomer. Its chief furnishings were a blackboard, telephone, telegraph, and ticker tape, folding chairs, slips of paper, and the day's issue of the Chicago *Racing Form* or the New York *Telegraph.* Few of its customers played pool. An information bureau sent the names of horses scratched and where the odds stood over the wires a half hour before each race. The patrons bet accordingly, in person or via phone or runners. Ten to fifteen minutes before starting time the bureau submitted a final summary of the odds as the betting at the track had affected them, and a second wave of betting went on till an employee called "post" and "time." The official report of the race was read out in staccato snatches as the ticker transmitted it. Winners were announced, bets paid off, and betting began at once on the next race, with clients given a half hour to get their money down.[44]

A magazine interview with a bookie of the 1890s described the financial aspects of operating a poolroom: "I had a poolroom on 3rd Avenue near 37th Street. It was about a fifth rate room. My rent was $100 and I gave about $1200 each month to square the game with the police and certain anti-vice societies. Then there was my help, my telegraph and my telephone bills. After all were paid I had for the season of seven months over $54,000."[45]

Handbooks provided another form of offtrack betting. Operators of this type of book did business at small neighborhood stores, on city corners, or in the customer's home or workplace. Bets as low as five cents were taken, and operators depended on volume business. Pari-mutuel wagering—in which bettors were paid off in proportion to the amount of money bet on each horse, and therefore established their own odds—was tried at several racetracks in the 1870s and 1880s. At the time, however, the system was not well received and after a brief trial was discontinued. The bookies were unalterably opposed to this form of wagering and actively lobbied against its use. In addition, the first pari-mutuel machines were sometimes cumbersome. Pari-mutuel wagering was an idea whose time had not yet come, and bookmakers remained in full control of wagering.

Cards and Dice

Cards and dice, the staples of casino gaming, also flourished in post–Civil War America. The Western frontier remained a legendary gambling territory, while the more-established cities of the East, South, and Midwest witnessed a rebirth of enthusiasm for gambling casinos called "dens," "saloons," "houses," "palaces," "hells," "pits," "halls," and "parlors." Poker became the most popular betting card game in America, and the ability to bluff and keep a cool demeanor during a poker hand was deemed a sterling quality. Grover Cleveland so admired the poker-playing ability of John Carlisle that he appointed him secretary of the treasury.

Legendary gamblers appeared on the American scene. George Devol plied his trade playing three-card monte and faro on Mississippi steamboats, Wild Bill Hickock dealt poker in Cheyenne, Doc Holiday and Wyatt Earp ran a card club in Tombstone, Soapy Smith operated plush gambling halls in the Yukon Territory, Cornelius Vanderbilt played for hundreds of thousands in no-limit poker games with American industrialists, and Colonel Bradley opened a sumptuous betting club that catered to Palm Beach society.

While players flocked to gambling establishments to indulge their fascination with cards and dice, society withheld approval of these activities. The experiences of George Canfield illustrate the ambivalence toward casino gambling that dominated this period. Canfield got his start dealing cards in a resort owned by a New Hampshire society leader. Arrested during a police raid (the owner had neglected to pay his police protection), he served six months in jail after being vigorously prosecuted by Samuel P. Colt, who later became president of U.S. Rubber. After being released, Canfield opened a faro game in New York

City, where he regularly paid police protection. As his game prospered, the cost of protection escalated. Canfield then purchased a fashionable gambling casino at Saratoga Springs. He refurbished the casino in a style reminiscent of Monte Carlo, importing ornate furniture, hiring the finest European chefs, and requiring participants to dress in formal attire. In New York City, Canfield bought a palatial gambling hall near Delmonico's restaurant and catered to the city's wealthy. Both of these casinos were allowed to operate because Canfield paid 10 percent of the profits to police officials. When he refused to pay more, his casinos were raided and he was arrested and charged with illegal gambling. After lengthy legal proceedings, Canfield pled guilty and paid a one-thousand-dollar fine. He resumed operating his casinos but once again refused to pay exhorbitant police protection fees. After being involved in several incidents with the police and grand juries, and after being the subject of negative editorial comments, Canfield closed his casinos and retired to live out his life in a New York brownstone. Although he had been fantastically successful and was considered the "prince of gamblers" for his honestly run games,[46] Canfield lamented that, in the end, the hypocrisy of police officials and city fathers had pushed him out of the gaming business.

The invention of a mechanical device helped to revitalize gambling establishments. At the end of the nineteenth century, technologists developed a gambling device that was a forerunner of the slot machine. The Little Gem was designed to produce poker hands on spinning reels. For as little as a nickel, gamblers could pull the lever and attempt to line up a royal flush and win five dollars. These machines were later equipped with fruit figures, and the search for three lemons began. By the beginning of the twentieth century, although firmly established as part of American life, gambling was once again to experience a period of reform and subsequent retrenchment.

Summary

Gambling has always been an integral part of American life. Native Americans were avid gamblers, and Jamestown, the first permanent white settlement, was funded in large part from English lottery sales. Horse racing, cards, and dice were popular diversions of the early colonists. Municipal improvements, industrial expansion, and educational institutions were funded from the proceeds of colonial lotteries. Even though gambling was popular in early America, however, it was also roundly condemned on moral and legal grounds. Religious, civic, and military leaders called for prohibitions against gambling. Opponents of gambling, often citing its dangerous effects upon the working classes, led reform movements that inhibited to some degree gambling's growth and acceptance.

The most effective of these reform movements developed between 1830 and 1860. During this period, reformers denounced gambling professionals, whose unethical practices had outraged the American public. Gambling was never completely eradicated, however, and after the Civil War, patrons once again flocked to racetracks, casinos, and policy games. In spite of this increased participation, Americans still held ambivalent views toward gambling, and it remained a vulnerable target of reformers. Gambling had not yet achieved legitimacy.

Notes

1. Ronald Alsop, "State Lottery Craze Is Spreading, But Some Fear It Hurts the Poor," *Wall Street Journal,* 24 February 1983, p. 31.
2. Henry Chafetz, *Play the Devil* (New York: Potter Publishing, 1960), p. 8.
3. John M. Findlay, *People of Chance* (New York: Oxford University Press, 1986), p. 13.
4. Gilbert Geis, *Not the Law's Business* (New York: Schocken, 1979), p. 223.
5. Chafetz, *Play the Devil,* p. 17.
6. John S. Ezell, *Fortune's Merry Wheel* (Cambridge, Mass.: Harvard University Press, 1960), p. 20.
7. Ibid., p. 21.
8. Chafetz, *Play the Devil,* p. 21.
9. Ezell, *Fortune's Merry Wheel,* p. 32.
10. Findlay, *People of Chance,* p. 33.
11. Herbert Asbury, *Sucker's Progress* (New York: Dodd, Mead, 1938), p. 76.
12. William H. P. Robertson, *The History of Thoroughbred Racing in America* (Englewood Cliffs, N.J.: Prentice-Hall, 1964), p. 7.
13. Ibid., p. 8.
14. Chafetz, *Play the Devil,* p. 16.
15. T. H. Breen, "Horses and Gentlemen: The Cultural Significance of Gambling Among the Gentry of Virginia," *William & Mary Quarterly* 34 (April 1977), p. 251.
16. Ibid., p. 250.
17. Ibid., p. 252.
18. Ibid., p. 254.
19. Ibid., p. 255.
20. Ibid., p. 257.
21. Robertson, *The History of Thoroughbred Racing in America,* p. 25.
22. Chafetz, *Play the Devil,* p. 13.
23. Ibid., p. 17.
24. Stephen Longstreet, *Win or Lose: A Social History of Gambling* (Indianapolis: Bobbs-Merrill, 1977), p. 30.
25. Ibid., p. 37.
26. Findlay, *People of Chance,* p. 47.
27. Ezell, *Fortune's Merry Wheel,* p. 207.
28. Ibid., p. 203.
29. Ibid., p. 206.
30. Charles B. Parmer, *For Gold and Glory* (New York: Carrick & Evans, 1939), p. 93.
31. Ibid., pp. 92–93.
32. Ibid., p. 93.

33. Findlay, *People of Chance*, p. 42.
34. Ibid., p. 65.
35. Ibid., p. 68.
36. Chafetz, *Play the Devil*, p. 94.
37. For a graphic illustration of how difficult it was to "hit" a policy number see Asbury, *Sucker's Progress*, pp. 90–105.
38. Asbury, *Sucker's Progress*, p. 101.
39. Ibid., pp. 96–97.
40. Chafetz, *Play the Devil*, p. 267.
41. Robertson, *The History of Thoroughbred Racing in America*, pp. 95–96.
42. Chafetz, *Play the Devil*, p. 363.
43. Edward Cole, *Racing Maxims and Methods of Pittsburgh Phil* (New York: American Bank Note, 1908), pp. 24–25.
44. Chafetz, *Play the Devil*, p. 375.
45. Ibid., p. 376.
46. Both Chafetz, *Play the Devil*, pp. 318–339, and Asbury, *Sucker's Progress*, pp. 421–467, devote entire chapters to the exploits of Richard Canfield.

Gambling in the Twentieth Century

It is evident from our survey that gambling is a very wide-spread phenomenon in the United States. In 1974, according to estimates projected from our sample, 61 percent of all adult Americans placed some kind of bet for money.

Survey Research Center Report, National Probability Sample of
U.S. Population*

This chapter continues the historical review of gambling in America. It is divided into the following categories, which reflect significant chronological developments:

1. Turn-of-the-century reforms
2. Prewar gambling
3. Postwar crime hearings
4. Contemporary legitimation

Although the twentieth century began with another round of reforms, gambling as usual proved resilient. Continued efforts to protect working classes from the evils of gambling and to restrict gaming to approved areas proved unsuccessful. Ultimately the forces of legitimation were to prevail.

Turn-of-the-Century Reforms

The antigambling reform movements of the early twentieth century, unlike those before the Civil War, were not motivated primarily by outrage over the chicanery of professional gamblers. The professionalism of gambling operators was assumed, and reports of gambling trickery no longer aroused massive indignation. Antigambling campaigns were initiated and sustained by the merging of evangelical reformers and pragmatic politicians. This was the age of populist reform, rural stirrings of righteousness, and antidrinking sentiments that were to culminate in passage of the Volstead Act, which prohibited the sale of

* From "The Micro and Macro Dimensions of Gambling in the United States," by Maureen Kallick-Kaufmann, *Journal of Social Issues* 35, No. 3 (1979), p. 10.

liquor. Opposition to gambling was a by-product of these sociohistorical trends. Although reformers failed to stamp out gambling, they did succeed in driving the games underground, denying them respectability and thus delaying significant middle-class participation.

Policy Games

The confluence of moral reform and political expediency was evident in New York City's campaign against policy games. Dr. Charles Parkhurst, pastor of the Madison Square Presbyterian Church, had long railed against the evils of gambling from the pulpit and from his position as president of the Society for the Prevention of Crime:

> Policy houses flourish in New York as thick as roses in Sharon. They are open to the initiated at any hour of day or night. They are eating into the character of some of what we are accustomed to think of as our best and most promising young men. They are a sly and constant menace to all that is choicest and most vigorous in a moral way in the generation that is now moving onto the field of action. But if you convict a man for keeping a gambling hell in this town you have to do it in spite of authorities and not by their aid.[1]

The good doctor was generally considered a crackpot whose reputation had been sullied because of his presence at a "dance of nature" where nude parlor girls played leapfrog. However, Dr. Parkhurst's society found an ally in William Travis Jerome, a minor justice who enthusiastically joined the gambling crusade not only by issuing warrants against policy houses but by accompanying the raiding parties. Judge Jerome became an instant celebrity and explained his actions to the *New York Independent:*

> The gamblers in almost every instance received warning, and were enabled to save themselves and their paraphernalia. . . . I took measures to prevent this "tipping off," as it is called, and going with a raiding party held court immediately in the evil resort itself, and got positive evidence of the character of the place, and names and addresses of the patrons who were caught, etc. The usefulness of this lies in the fact that juries are loathe to believe the evidence of spies who get into the gambling houses under false pretenses. The raids have been so successful that a great deal of evidence has been secured and many indictments found. We seem to be on the track of the great men who are or were responsible for the recent disgraceful condition of affairs.[2]

With the wholehearted support of Dr. Parkhurst and his society members, Judge Jerome, pledging to close policy games, was elected district attorney of New York in 1901. A month after the election, with the support of the new district attorney, agents of the antigambling society raided the offices of Al Adams, the acknowledged king of policy games and head of the multicity policy syndicate called the Central Organization. Adams was arrested and released. Like most charged with gambling, he expected to plead guilty and pay a small fine. District Attorney Jerome, however, was determined to make an example of Adams and informed the press that a sentence of prison for the policy king would be the first salvo in a vigorous antigambling campaign. After protracted legal proceedings in 1903, Adams was sentenced to eighteen months in Sing Sing Prison. This sentence effectively discouraged policy game operators in New York and elsewhere. After his release from prison, Adams did not return to policy writing. No other individual was able to gain control of policy gambling; other cities cracked down on policy games, and many operators left the business for other gambling ventures. According to Asbury, noted historian and author of *Sucker's Progress,* "by 1905 policy playing was definitely declining, and within another ten years it was no longer an important phase of American gambling."[3]

Horse Racing

Horse racing also was adversely affected by antigambling reforms of the early 1900s. A combination of morality and political savvy was successful in prohibiting racing in state after state. In Pennsylvania, Reverend Wilbur F. Crafts, president of the International Reform Bureau, convinced a key legislator, M. A. Cassatt, to reverse his position on a pending bill that would allow racing in the state. The legislator's defection was crucial, and the bill was defeated. Sam Jones, a popular evangelical preacher, stumped the South exhorting his followers to rid the land of two evils—the saloon and the racetrack. A turf historian described the ensuing political fallout: "More than one office seeker, looking for sensational planks for his platform, found them now in the slogans: Down with the Saloon! Down with Racing! Long before 1912 the southern states started going dry—legally. But in 1906 the last horse race was run in Andrew Jackson's stronghold, Tennessee. And Georgia, Alabama, most of the neighboring states, thrust racing from their borders."[4]

Congressional figures, sensing the tenor of the times, banned racing from the District of Columbia. In Missouri, Joseph Folk, a gubernatorial candidate, made gambling reform a key plank in his campaign. Despite the efforts of gambling operators who contributed heavily to his opponent, Folk was elected and made good on his campaign promises by promptly closing the racetracks. In Texas and Louisiana, church groups supported antigambling legislators who subsequently banned horse racing in their respective states. During the 1908 campaign, candidates for the California State Legislature had to declare whether or not they would support an antiracing bill. The president of the YMCA, noted church leaders, and leading newspapers actively supported the bill. Intimidated by these interest groups, in 1909 California legislators outlawed racetracks, despite racing's popularity. This led a social commentator to say that "Puritanism [was] the inflexible doctrine of Los Angeles."[5] By 1911, only six states allowed horse racing, and ninety-five tracks on the national circuit had closed.[6]

The antigambling reforms also affected offtrack betting. By 1900, betting parlors and poolrooms depended on Western Union to supply them with up-to-date racing information. Entries, scratches, jockeys, results, and payoffs were transmitted by telegraph to poolrooms throughout the United States. Western Union officials defended the transmission of racing news on the grounds that they were obliged to carry all messages unless they were clearly obscene. Church leaders led by Dr. Parkhurst, censured Western Union for distributing racing information. They convinced U.S. Senator Chauncey M. Depew, a Western Union board member, to pressure company directors. When Depew threatened to resign and hinted that he might entertain criminal action against the company for aiding and encouraging a felony, officials decided to discontinue their race wires and racing information services. Many poolrooms closed, and offtrack betting was severely limited. Henry Stedeker, a veteran New York bookmaker, mused, "I think that the demand of 50,000 or more people who cannot go to the racetracks but who still wish to bet will not be unsupplied long."[7] The bookmaker's observation proved accurate when a few months later the Payne News Agency provided accurate racing information to all who subscribed to its service. In 1910, Mont Tennes, a Chicago gambling operator, reorganized the news agency and in so doing established a virtual monopoly over the transmission of racing data. The monopoly allowed Tennes to control his customers and led to the formation of powerful bookmaking syndicates with national connections. By charging standard fees, Western Union had allowed customers equal access to offtrack bookmaking. In contrast, an illegal wire controlled by powerful underworld figures provided the leverage for the development of bookmaking cartels.

Events surrounding horse racing reform in New York typify the ambiguous status of gambling during this period. Since 1887, the state had passed legislation, such as the Ives Bill and the Percy Gray Law, that appeared to prohibit gambling at racetracks but in fact served to approve track bookmakers, as long as they were licensed by the track. In 1906, Charles Hughes, running on a reform platform, soundly defeated William Randolph Hearst for governor. To satisfy his backers, on whom he counted for backing in a presidential bid, Hughes pressed for legislation outlawing wagering at racetracks. After lengthy maneuvering, the 1909 state legislature made it illegal "for anyone to state the current price odds on horses, seek bets on horses and locate himself in a more or less permanent position, and to set down in writing or the like any bets on horses."[8]

The bill took effect in 1911, and the racing season was dark in New York State for the first time since 1665. In 1913, the New York Court of Appeals, under much pressure from racing interests, sanctioned a form of oral betting at racetracks, and the horses ran again in the empire state. Betting at the track was now legal as long as it was conducted by word of mouth, with no money being transferred when the bet was placed and no receipt given. The new gimmick satisfied the legal niceties, and officials accepted the charade that horse players and bookies were only engaged in verbal betting. In actual practice, players were betting much as they had before, since the bookmaker had never recorded a wager unless the bettor proffered a cash payment. The duplicity of oral betting continued until 1934, when a more liberal law approved open bookmaking.[9]

Casinos

At the turn of the century, reform-minded politicians took direct aim at casino gaming throughout the United States. The years between 1900 and 1912 saw numerous state and local initiatives directed against gambling operations. These initiatives were generated by district attorneys, judges, assemblymen, mayors, and police officials eager to satisfy the public mood for reform. Public opinion was molded by religious leaders who put together traveling revival shows that toured the country preaching against the evils of gambling and drinking. These religious meetings, held under large tents, featured reformed gamblers who gave vivid testimonials as to the chicanery and crookedness of the "sporting life." Chafetz describes the relationship between the appearance of traveling evangelists and gambling reform: "Even after the evangelists delivered their last exhortations and the gamblers gave their last demonstrations, folded their tents, and headed for sinners in the next town, anti-gambling fervor ran high. Ministers and local civic leaders would pressure the authorities to raid local dens of chance and smash slot machines and paraphernalia they seized."[10]

In cities from New York to San Francisco, reform administrations spurred by religious leaders closed down gaming casinos. Cleveland, Detroit, Pittsburgh, Buffalo, Chicago, Denver, San Francisco, and New Orleans all raided gaming operations. Hot Springs, Arkansas, known as the "Monte Carlo of the Midwest," had several gambling clubs that offered faro, roulette, poker, dice, and slot machines. In 1910, Judge Woods, elected on a pledge to rid Hot Springs of the "gambling hells," closed down all the casinos. French Lick, Indiana, long known as an open gambling town, severely restricted the operation of its many casinos. The course of gambling reform in Canton, Ohio, is typical of what occurred in many locales. In 1911, two traveling preachers, Quinn and Ashby, convinced Canton officials that gambling was rampant in their town. The officials prevailed upon the sheriff, who responded by raiding two of the largest gambling halls. According to police reports, several wagons of gambling paraphernalia were taken to the dump and burned. After a few months, the raided casinos reopened to business as usual. Reverend Recard, pastor of the United Brethren Church, described local conditions: "Gambling is the bottomless pit among the slime holds and its mouth is open in Canton. The city is known among the good and wise to the ends of the earth as the home of McKinley. It is also known in great circles of shysters whose fingers are always pointing to the purses of others. To these it is known as a safe retreat and a fat pasture."[11] Quinn and Ashby returned to Canton and secured evidence of continued gambling. They once again convinced Canton council members to take action, and the sheriff was ordered to "clean up the town." Subsequently, ninety gambling arrests were made; operators, convinced of the council's resolve, closed their casinos and left town.

Local reform efforts often prompted state legislatures to prohibit or restrict gambling. In 1907, New Mexico and Arizona passed statewide antigambling laws that banned even card playing at home. Nevada followed suit, prohibiting all gambling in 1910. New York, California, Missouri, Illinois, and Alabama legislatures passed bills to facilitate action against illegal gaming operators. Bet-A-Million Gates (who had once wagered thousands on the number of flies lighting on a sugar cube) echoed a commonly held view of gambling participation during a speech before the Methodist church in Port Arthur, Texas, on December 5, 1909: "Don't gamble. Don't play cards. Don't bet on horse races. Don't speculate in wheat. Don't speculate on the stock exchange. Don't throw dice. Don't shirk honest labor. Don't be a gambler." Gates's last statement to the religious conclave, however, proved prophetic for the American public: "Once a gambler, always a gambler."[12]

Prewar Gambling

In the 1920s and 1930s, gambling made an impressive comeback, and by 1940, an American Institute of Public Opinion poll revealed that 54 percent of American adults had gambled at least once in the prior year.[13] Although gambling was back in favor, its structure and format had changed considerably since the halcyon days of the 1890s. Policy had largely been supplanted by numbers games; bingo and church lotteries were accepted and established gambling ventures; horse race gambling was conducted through a pari-mutuel system regulated by individual states; offtrack wagering was dominated by large syndicates who had gained a monopoly over information dissemination; and the first legal casinos had appeared.

Numbers

With policy writers in disarray from reform efforts of the early twentieth century, a new numbers game was introduced, and by the 1920s it had captured the fancy and bets of former policy players. Numbers players chose a number between 1 and 999, and if their number appeared, they were paid off at odds of approximately 600 to 1. The winning numbers, published daily, were based on the results of three races at a designated racetrack. Numbers gambling was introduced to Harlem in the 1920s by West Indian immigrants. Blacks helped organize and run these fledgling enterprises, whose popularity soon spread to white neighborhoods. Numbers games were started in other large cities, including Chicago, Philadelphia, and Detroit, and then spread to urban areas throughout the United States. Blacks continued to play an important part in numbers gaming, and this influence was often converted into political and economic power bases. By the start of World War II, approximately 10 percent of the U.S. population regularly played the numbers.[14]

Although lotteries were strictly forbidden, during the Depression church groups turned to bingo and other lottery games as a way to raise funds. This trend continued to such an extent that by 1940 almost 25 percent of Americans reported that they gambled on church lotteries. This level of participation coincided with the adoption by the 1940 Federal Council of Churches of a statement condemning gambling on the grounds that "great masses of people are indulging in this vice."[15] In 1942, the New York police commissioner expressed an opinion shared by many when he said, "Bingo and similar games would be viewed as unlawful except under the auspices of the church." Mayor Fiorello LaGuardia expressed the opposite view, maintaining that "if bingo is unlawful in one place, it cannot be lawful in another."[16] LaGuardia's comment, which could also be applied to gambling in general, pinpointed a dilemma that only recently has begun to be resolved.

Horse Racing

Horse racing was revived in the 1920s and 1930s as track operators convinced legislators that an officially sanctioned pari-mutuel system would profit states significantly. Colonel Matt J. Winn, president of Churchill Downs, was an important figure during this period because he was able to convince Kentuckians to resist the antigambling fervor that had caused neighboring states to ban horse racing. Winn literally dusted off pari-mutuel machines that were in the back of the track's storehouse and put them into use. In an attempt to improve racing's image, the colonel banished bookmakers from the track and promised state officials to keep them away permanently. Through the pari-mutuel system advocated by Winn, which deducted the state's share from each wager, the state was assured a constant source of revenue. The combined promise of state revenues and an improved image was enough to convince legislators (some of whom represented constituencies where horse breeding farms were an important part of the local economy) that horse racing should be tolerated, and in 1906, Kentucky legalized a pari-mutuel system for horse race wagering.

During the reform era, Kentucky remained an example of a state in which horse racing could exist and prosper. In 1920, Maryland also passed a law authorizing track pari-mutuels, and a gradual movement toward this form of betting was underway. As the Depression exacerbated states' problems with revenue collection, the licensing of pari-mutuel horse racing increased. By 1935, Illinois, Louisiana, Florida, New Hampshire, West Virginia, Ohio, Michigan, Massachusetts, Rhode Island, Maine, and Delaware had passed enabling legislation to cash in on the pari-mutuel bonanza. In 1938, when California received over $3 million in revenue from its participation in legalized horse race gambling, several other states fell in line. In 1940, New York, the last bastion of bookmakers, expelled its bookies and installed state-sanctioned betting machines.

Although rising attendance and wagering figures in prewar America clearly demonstrated that horse racing was back in a big way, it was a decidedly new game. Bookmakers, who had been the lifeblood of racing, were now banished to the poolrooms; they didn't fit the new image of horse racing as a state-regulated activity. Racetrack operators were no longer independent entrepreneurs who could run their businesses as they saw fit. They were now partners with the state and therefore had to confer with administrative bodies such as racing boards or state commissions to make significant changes in racing practices. State stewards, charged with protecting the public interest, were appointed to oversee daily track operations. Racetracks within the same state were not allowed to openly compete with one another and instead had to petition a racing commission for allotted racing dates.

State control lent an aura of respectability to horse racing and significantly increased its acceptability. States now actively participated in activities that previously had been tolerated at best and often prohibited. From the public's perspective, gambling on horse races had been accorded a clear stamp of legitimacy. Track officials advertised that racing had been purged of its criminal elements and was now a wholesome enterprise backed by the good offices of the commonwealth. Not surprisingly, many people were wondering whether or not other forms of wagering could continue to be condemned as illegal and immoral now that horse race betting was sanctioned and supported by the states.

Heightened interest in horse racing also stimulated offtrack wagering in poolrooms and betting parlors. Increased demand for racing information encouraged publishing magnate Mo Annenberg to move into the business of disseminating racing information. In the 1920s, Annenberg bought off and muscled out other purveyors of track data and gained control over all racing information. He owned the *Daily Racing Form* and the *Morning Telegraph* (indispensable racing guides) and controlled the racing wire (over which race entries and results were carried), in addition to printing scratch and wall sheets that listed horses running at racetracks throughout the United States. Annenberg used his monopoly to extract maximum profits from the legions of bookmakers who needed the information. In 1937, Annenberg described his control of racing services: "We in the racing field own three-quarters of the globe and manage the balance. In other words, the few little nations that are left have to pay us tribute to continue. Now why isn't that the most beautiful and most satisfactory position to be in which ought to satisfy even me."[17] In 1939, Annenberg was indicted for income tax evasion and, as part of a plea bargain, sold off the illegal race wire, paid an $8-million fine, and served a short prison sentence. According to police informants, those who succeeded Annenberg as controllers of the race information wire were connected to organized crime. Their control of racing information would be the subject of the Kefauver committee investigations of the 1950s.

During the 1920s and 1930s, the layoff system became an integral part of bookmaking. Under this system, bookies who took large wagers and wanted to ensure against possible loss placed, or *laid off*, some of the bet with a more financially established bookmaker. The practice of layoff betting, usually conducted over the telephone, facilitated the development of national syndicates with large sums of ready cash to back up their wagering position. Arnold Rothstein, a notorious gambler, started a layoff system in New York in about 1914, taking bets from bookmakers throughout the East and Midwest until his murder in 1928. Frank Ericson and Frank Costello, both reputed to have mob connections, operated large layoff businesses that catered to bookmakers wanting to hedge their bets throughout the United States and Canada.

Casinos

The fire-and-brimstone evangelists who toured the country at the beginning of the twentieth century invariably linked gambling and drinking as interrelated evils. Their warnings were to prove prophetic during the 1920s, when bootleggers and casino operators merged their interests. Partnerships between rum runners and gambling club owners were advantageous to both parties, and the ensuing business realignments changed the structure of illegal gaming in the United States. These mergers fostered the development of regional gambling centers controlled by organized-crime figures. The experience of bootleggers in coordinating the distribution and marketing of liquor were transferred to the management of gambling complexes. Large-scale bootlegging operations were predicated on cooperation among regional entrepreneurs. These same informal networks were employed to run gambling halls in such places as Hot Springs, Arkansas, Newport, Kentucky, New York, Philadelphia, Boston, and Atlantic City.

After bootleggers and gamblers joined forces, casino owners found it difficult to operate independently of syndicate influence. The leading casinos of the 1920s and 1930s were run by such infamous crime figures as Lucky Luciano, Bugsy Siegel, Al Capone, Jack Geizik, and Sam Giancana. Although to infer that bootleggers suddenly took over all gambling halls would be simplistic, their influence was hard to deny. The progressive infiltration of criminal bootleggers into casino gaming has been described by historian Mark Haller:

> In cities like New York, Cleveland, and Chicago, for instance, bootleggers began to invest in gambling enterprises early in their careers. At first they co-existed with traditional gambling entrepreneurs, but because of the relative youthfulness of bootleggers and the willingness of some to employ violence, their influence spread gradually until they and their partners became predominant influences. Often, indeed, their coordination of gambling was only part of their investment in and coordination of the nightlife and commercialized entertainment of a city—nightclubs, bars, juke boxes, legal liquor distribution, and other related enterprises. As bootleggers, many had begun to move into these other areas of entertainment at the same time that they invested in gambling, so that gambling must be seen as part of a larger set of investments.[18]

In the depths of the Depression, Florida legalized slot machines (most of which were placed in casinos) in an effort to increase state revenues and spur local economies. Legalization seemed to achieve both purposes, since in a two-year period 12,500 slot machine handles were pulled to the tune of $65 million, with the state's share of the take exceeding $2 million.[19] Church groups vociferously complained that slot machines were taking the nickels and dimes of common laborers— nickels and dimes that more appropriately should have gone into savings accounts. The complaints of church leaders were heeded, and in 1937, Florida abandoned its experiment with legalized slot machines. While slot machines were being righteously destroyed, Colonel Bradley's sumptuous Palm Beach Casino Club, catering to wealthy socialites, remained untouched by either police raiding parties or the ire of church members.

As Florida was beginning its slot machine venture, El Monte and Gardena, California, were licensing gambling in poker rooms even though playing cards for money in one's home was illegal. In addition, in 1931, the sleepy mining state of Nevada sanctioned easy divorce and casino gaming in an effort to find desperately needed new sources of revenue. By 1940, six gaming casinos, or clubs, were operating in Las Vegas. On the eve of World War II, though the importance of gaming to the Las Vegas economy was growing steadily, tourists still regarded Hoover Dam as the area's major attraction. Still a local phenomenon, Nevada's gaming industry had yet to take on national significance. Findlay described the informal atmosphere, slow pace, and innocence that characterized early Nevada casinos:

> Early operations were known as "clubs" rather than casinos, suggesting an atmosphere of intimacy and exclusiveness. These clubs, more akin to corner groceries than to the supermarkets of gambling that appeared afterwards, functioned with none of the sensation that later casinos created. Bettors generally risked only little sums, and observers mostly agreed that the business was small, even harmless. Instead of the shady and corrupt gambling dens that they had anticipated, visitors found insubstantial and seemingly innocent clubs. Local residents prided themselves not on the economic success of gaming but rather on its upright character.[20]

Crime Hearings

The next major development on the American gambling scene was the 1950–1952 Kefauver committee investigation into the links between gambling and organized crime. Like the traveling evangelists at the turn of the century, Senator Estes Kefauver took his hearings to cities (fourteen in all) throughout the United States. Publicity for the hearings was generated through the fledgling medium of television. Kefauver investigators took for granted (often without independent corroboration) that organized crime controlled gambling. Witness after witness (drawn from enforcement agencies) testified that gambling was controlled by the mob and that gaming proceeds were used to finance a multitude of nefarious syndicate activities, including loan sharking, prostitution, drug dealing, and bribery. In addition, the Kefauver committee presented evidence of massive police corruption and concluded that large-scale illegal gambling was possible only with the cooperation of paid-off policemen. According to Kefauver informants, the mob controlled its profitable bookmaking empire through monopoly of the race wire. They further alleged that the mob controlled casino gaming (including slot machines) and numbers rackets.

The committee recommended far-ranging federal legislation to restrict and prohibit gambling. At the same time, it called on state and local agencies to step up their enforcement of antigambling laws already on the books. Although the Kefauver committee hearings were widely publicized, the recommendations did not spur immediate action. On the federal level, the only significant legislative action taken was the 1952 Wagering Tax Act, which required gamblers to pay a 10 percent excise tax on any wagers they accepted and to purchase a fifty-dollar gambling stamp. The act did not provide funding for enforcement, however, and its provisions were rarely enforced. On the state and local level, some superficial investigations were initiated; a 1967 report by the President's Commission on Law Enforcement and Administration of Justice summed up these efforts:

> There was a brief series of investigations in cities where the Senate Committee had exposed organized crime operations and public corruption, but law enforcement generally failed to develop the investigative and prosecutive units to root out the activities of criminal cartels. . . . Not even the horrified national reaction caused by the Kefauver expose could force a cleanup down to the grass roots. What happened in Jersey is what usually happens: a few heads roll, the law is pacified, the headlines die, and the system goes on.[21]

The unenthusiastic response to the committee's recommendations was anticipated by a Kefauver investigator: "There is a segment of public opinion in many cities that believes that gambling, in some cases, 'just a little gambling,' is good for business, and that strict enforcement of anti-gambling laws could be a mistake. This attitude on the part of law-abiding citizens can only come from a failure to comprehend the violence and racketeering which inevitably accompany gambling operations, and the extent of the resulting damage to the economic and social fabric."[22]

Fallout from the Kefauver committee temporarily hindered further legalization of gambling, as evidenced by a 1953 American Bar Association pronouncement that "professional gambling should not be under any circumstances or in any degree be licensed or legalized."[23] A Chicago crime commission member succinctly described the philosophical basis for antigambling sentiments: "Gambling as a business is wrong. That's the starting point for any proper discussion of this question. It is founded not only on morality but on the hard fact that gambling draws money from the regular channels of trade vital to the well being of a nation. Gambling is parasitic by nature."[24]

Ten years after the Kefauver hearings, another federal commission, the McClellan committee, presented evidence of the huge profits that organized crime garnered from gambling. Witnesses before the McClellan committee submitted estimates of the volume of illegal gambling ranging from a low of $7 billion to a steep $50 billion.[25] The latter figure was more than the U.S. defense budget for 1960. One of McClellan's investigators, Robert Kennedy, was firmly convinced of the baleful influence of gambling: "No one knows exactly how much money is involved in gambling in the United States. What we do know is that the American people are spending more on gambling than on medical care or on education; that, in so doing, they are putting up the money for corruption of public officials and the vicious activities of the dope peddlers, loan sharks, bootleggers, white slave traders, and slick confidence men."[26]

When Kennedy became U.S. attorney general, he was able to secure legislation that granted federal officials more authority to investigate gambling activities, an action taken because Kennedy and other justice officials had grown disillusioned with local efforts to combat illegal gambling. Kennedy however realized that "in the last analysis it depends on the business executive, the factory worker, and the housewife who have been financing big-time crime with their two-dollar bets and their ten-cent wagers. If they would stop patronizing the illegal bookie, the numbers runner, and the sports-pool operator, they could take the profit out of gambling and bring organized crime down to size quicker than all the combined efforts of the local law enforcement agencies."[27]

Other observers also attempted to link gambling with organized crime. Rufus King, another McClellan investigator, stated that "law enforcement officials agree almost unanimously that gambling is the greatest source of revenue for organized crime,"[28] while the title of Fred Cook's book says it all: *The $2 Bet Means Murder.* Despite law enforcers' assumption of a relationship between the mob and gambling, however, the American public never quite made the connection, finding it hard to believe that their friendly bookie was in reality an evil mobster. The public's inability to perceive the link between gambling and organized crime proved an important factor in the eventual legitimation of gambling.

Contemporary Legitimation

Events Facilitating Legitimation

In postwar America, a series of events enhanced the social acceptability of gambling. These events, coupled with the improving public image of gaming, helped to resolve America's ambivalence toward gambling. Recent events that have significantly boosted the legitimation of gambling include the following, in chronological sequence:

1955   Las Vegas develops the Strip.
1963   New Hampshire approves a state lottery.
1970   New York approves offtrack betting.
1978   Atlantic City casinos open for business.
1984   Five states pass gambling referendums.
1986   The California lottery takes in over $2 billion in one year.

In 1955, the nine-story Riviera Hotel opened on the Las Vegas Strip and ushered in the era of high-rise casino complexes. The twenty-four-story Sahara and twenty-nine-story Landmark were built soon after the Riviera's opening. After World War II, Las Vegas became an increasingly important gambling location. Spurred by tourists from Southern California, who arrived by recently completed freeways, and junketeers, who arrived en masse on new jumbo jets, Las Vegas expanded its facilities to meet the demand. The multistoried casinos that appeared on the Strip were tangible signs that gambling was a profitable business endeavor. The intimate, unsophisticated clubs of the 1940s were replaced by the pleasure palaces of the 1950s. Gambling had come of age, and the Las Vegas Strip, with its massive, neon-decked edifices, reflected that sophistication. With the development of the Strip, Las Vegas became America's ultimate resort.

Strapped for funds since its efforts to institute a state income tax had been deemed unconstitutional, the 1963 New Hampshire legislation approved a state-run sweepstakes; thus the lottery was revived in the United States after a seventy-year hiatus. Proceeds for the new lottery were earmarked for public education, a pattern that other states would also follow. New Hampshire's lottery consisted of two biennial sweepstakes, with winning numbers determined by the outcome of designated horse races. In 1966, New York State authorized a lottery with monthly drawings; the proceeds again were to aid education. These first two lottery systems were relatively unsuccessful, with sales falling below projected estimates. The long intervals between drawings caused interest to wane and participation to fall off. In addition, the waiting for drawings was passive; the lack of active participation further discouraged players. Although not spectacular financial successes, these first lotteries had broken legal ground, and other states followed with more marketable schemes. In 1970, New Jersey piqued players' interest by holding weekly drawings; two years later, operators introduced daily games. To increase player participation, Massachusetts lottery officials sold instant winner scratch-off tickets. These games have been termed "paper slot machines." Lotto and superjackpots offering prizes of several million dollars further advanced the popularity of lotteries. As of 1987, twenty-eight states and the District of Columbia offer legalized lotteries.

The advent of state-sponsored lotteries was a watershed in the American view of gambling. In effect, governments had moved from tolerance to active sponsorship of gaming in a significant policy shift. Instead of merely regulating gambling, states now aggressively marketed their own games. In order to run their lotteries efficiently and profitably, state governments have gone into partnership with high-tech lottery operators. The operators, or vendors, are part of large companies such as Scientific Games (a subsidiary of Bally's), Control Data, British American Bank Note, and General Instrument. These companies serve as powerful lobbies for the expansion of existing operations and the adoption of new lotteries. The fact that lotteries have been characterized as a highly regressive form of taxation because of their emphasis on lower-income demographics[29] has not deterred their acceptance by the public. Concern that workers will incur excessive gambling losses no longer appears to be an overriding social consideration.

In 1970, New York took the unprecedented step of getting into the bookmaking business by establishing a state-run Off-Track Betting (OTB) agency. Although prior to this move there had been considerable discussion of the possibility of offtrack betting, horse racing interests (fearing a loss of income) and moralists (opposed to gambling in principle) had successfully lobbied against legalization efforts. In 1970, however, circumstances combined to favor legalization. New York City's Mayor John Lindsey faced a $300-million budget deficit while Governor Nelson Rockefeller had command of the state legislature. Lindsey urged state action, and Rockefeller (powerful and independent of lobbying pressure) responded by drafting a statewide local-option offtrack betting bill. With almost no public debate, the bill was whisked through the state legislature (at the urging of the governor) in two days and promptly signed by Governor Rockefeller.

The rationale behind legalizing offtrack betting was twofold: to increase state and local revenues and to drive illegal bookmakers out of business. Neither of these goals has been fully achieved. Although offtrack betting has been substantial (over $2 billion in 1986), it has somewhat diminished attendance and betting handle at racetracks. The racing industry in New York has been restructured to accommodate offtrack betting, but after seventeen years, areas of disharmony still remain, as powerful institutional and private interests vie for their share of New York's horse bets. While illegal race bookies suffered an initial setback with the passage of OTB, they have adjusted and have made a substantial comeback by catering to customer needs through credit extension and improved services.

Although only Connecticut has followed New York's example by sanctioning offtrack betting, several states are seriously considering this step. Others, like Illinois and California, have set up intertrack wagering by which patrons at designated racetrack locations can bet on races at other tracks within the state. Clearly, the active involvement of the second most populous state in the United States in the bookmaking business has given gambling additional acceptability. Legalizing OTB effectively stifled much of the moral paternalism that previously had sought to protect working people from the wages of gambling.

In the wee hours of election night 1976, bar owners in Atlantic City treated their customers to free drinks, exuberantly celebrating voter approval of a social experiment. Faced with deteriorating buildings and infrastructure, declining employment, and a reduced tax base, Atlantic

City officials had openly courted casino gaming. After an earlier defeat in 1974, state voters, by a 3 to 2 margin, approved a referendum legalizing gambling within the city limits of Atlantic City. On May 26, 1978, Resorts International opened its doors and Las Vegas East was born. Ten years and eleven casinos later, gaming operators have reaped over $12 billion from a legion of bettors. In 1985, 29 million visitors (almost half arriving in buses) came to Atlantic City.[30] The casinos now employ forty-one thousand full-time workers and are a major contributor to state coffers; New Jersey has been able to balance its budget with the aid of gaming revenues.

Even though casino gaming has proved fantastically successful in generating revenue, as a social experiment it has proved a mixed blessing. While property values in the immediate casino area have skyrocketed and the Boardwalk has been refurbished, most of Atlantic City has not prospered. In neighborhoods just outside the casino compound, run-down, crumbling gray buildings stand in stark contrast to the glitter of high-rise gambling palaces. And although gaming has increased employment, most of the jobs have gone to out-of-towners; the number of permanent residents in Atlantic City has actually declined since 1978. In addition, although little actual evidence has been disclosed, organized crime is alleged to be deeply involved in Atlantic City gaming.

States and localities currently considering legalizing casinos are confused by the example of Atlantic City. On one hand, they covet gaming revenues, while on the other, they are dissuaded by the social costs. Most agree, however, that casinos are, in fact, legitimate businesses. It thus seems safe to assume that officials in other locales will reason that with better planning, they can take in casino revenues without paying the social costs. Notwithstanding the downside of Atlantic City gaming, legalization has dramatically increased the visibility and accessibility of gambling. The central location of Atlantic City— squarely in the densely populated mid-Atlantic metropolitan corridor—has exposed new population groups to gambling, and many seem to like what they have found.

In 1984, voters throughout the United States approved lotteries and horse racing while nixing casinos. Initiatives to legalize lotteries won convincingly in every state where they were on the ballot. Residents of California, Oregon, Missouri, and West Virginia can now participate in lotteries. Missourians gave their nod to legal betting on horse racing. Arkansas voters, however, defeated an initiative to approve casinos in Garland County, which includes the resort of Hot Springs; ironically, illegal gambling casinos have long flourished in this area. In Colorado, a proposal to allow construction of casinos near the depressed steel town of Pueblo was rejected. In both Arkansas and Colorado, the governor worked vigorously to defeat casinos, but for the initiatives to actually have gotten on statewide ballots, a solid base of support had to exist. Thus, with the support of influential politicians, new casino gaming initiatives may find a more receptive electorate. The elections of 1984 underscored the fact that horse racing and lotteries had the whole-hearted support of the American voters. This was reinforced in 1986 and 1987 when six more states approved lotteries and one (Texas), horseracing.

In 1984, California approved proposition 37, the lottery initiative, by a 2 to 1 margin. Proposition 37 provided for the distribution of lottery proceeds as follows:

> Fifty percent of lottery sale receipts shall be returned to the public in the form of lottery prizes. No more than 16 percent of lottery sales receipts shall be used for administrative-related expenses of operating the lottery including commissions to lottery retailers, advertising-related expenditures, lottery ticket purchases, and other types of expenses. Thirty-four percent of lottery sales receipts shall be allocated to various levels of public education, along with any unclaimed lottery prizes and any portion of the amount by which actual administrative expenses of the lottery fall short of 16 percent.[31]

After time-consuming start-up problems, the first California lottery began operation in October 1985. It was an instant and phenomenal success. In the first year of operation, the lottery generated over $2 billion in sales, with average daily sales varying from $5 to $12 million. With its addition of a lotto game in October 1986, the California lottery is expected to become the largest single gambling operation in the world.

The first winners of grand prizes in California's Big Spin lottery were members of minority groups (some were black welfare recipients, others itinerant Chicanos and Southeast Asian immigrants). Although the lottery has been criticized in newspaper editorials and (humorously) on late-night talk shows for encouraging the poor to gamble and for taking the milk money from unsophisticated players, the drastic changes in life-style experienced by the early winners were hard to overlook. Lottery advertisers have stressed that proceeds were going to education and that when patrons buy tickets, "our schools win too." This reminder has sufficiently deflected serious criticism, and Californians continue to purchase lottery tickets without guilt, sometimes doing so, in fact, with a sense of state pride—they are, after all, helping schoolchildren.

Gambling's New Image

After World War II, the public's image of gambling improved gradually. Some of the reasons for this improvement can be traced to gambling's continual contribution to charitable pursuits, the lessening of bookmakers' dependence on criminal syndicates, the incorporation of gaming operations, and the growing realization that gaming operators don't have to cheat their customers to realize substantial profits.

Bingo and church raffles, once thought to be minor diversions, became important sources of revenue for church groups in postwar America. Most states legalized church-related bingo—in 1987, forty-three states had approved such games—reflecting the view that gambling for charity is permissible. Several racetracks capitalized on this notion by requesting and receiving more racing dates after promising to give a share of the proceeds from the added races to designated charities. Church groups that had been in the forefront of antigambling movements found it hard to accept revenues from bingo while continuing to condemn other forms of gambling. As bingo games proliferated, charities turned to other games, such as punchboards, pulltabs, bazaars, and Las Vegas Nights as well. In 1981, North Dakota legalized two-dollar blackjack games, with revenues going to charity. Indian reservations throughout the United States have sanctioned nonprofit bingo and blackjack, with the gambling take going to tribal welfare funds.

By the 1960s, the race wire that had tied bookies to criminal syndicates, was no longer a significant factor in bookmaking. Timely racing and sports information was available from a variety of sources, and the race wire became superfluous. Broadcast media were under minimal restrictions concerning the results of sports events. Horse race results were broadcast on the radio with only a thirty-minute delay (fifteen minutes in some areas), while baseball, basketball, and football scores were available immediately. The UPI and AP wire services also carried up-to-date sports results. The growing popularity of National Football League games, prominently displayed on television, caused a shift in bookmaking away from horse betting to sports betting (wagering on football, basketball, and baseball).

With information on sporting events readily available in the media and the development of a uniform point spread for football games, bookies felt more comfortable taking betting positions and therefore were much less likely to use layoff services. Bettors grew accustomed to placing their bets by phone, and large betting parlors where gamblers came together to hear sports results were no longer necessary. This considerably lessened the need for police protection to "overlook" the presence of a betting establishment and effectively reduced a major source of local police corruption. All of these developments enabled individual bookies to break free of centralized control. Bookmaking in many instances became more of an independent business than an adjunct of criminal syndicates. The new style of bookmaking was noticeable and helped improve the overall image of gambling.

The profitableness of casino gambling was not lost upon corporate America. Starting in the 1960s, corporate involvement in gaming became increasingly apparent, and the historical connection between casino operators and criminal elements was no longer assumed. This trend accelerated after Atlantic City authorized gambling, and today many casinos are owned and operated by publicly traded corporations. Many of these, such as Bally Manufacturing Corporation, Hilton Hotels Corporation, Ramada Inns, and Holiday Corporation, are widely held companies with excellent reputations. State regulatory agencies in New Jersey and Nevada generally have encouraged corporate control as an effective method of removing mob influence. For example, Atlantic City regulations require that applicants for a casino license post a $1-million application fee and guarantee that they will construct a hotel complex with a minimum of five hundred rooms.

The incorporation of gaming has spawned a new type of casino management, one that is vitally concerned with broadening the base of gambling participation. Originally, many casinos were geared either for high rollers (premium business) or for small-time but steady losers (grind business). To garner new markets, corporate managers are targeting the middle class. Casino management in many cases is making a concerted effort to cater to middle-income play; this tactic appears to be working well. Holiday Inn significantly increased its casino revenues by aiming advertising, marketing, and promotion campaigns specifically at middle-class players. In another case, Henry Glueck took over as chairman of Caesars World in 1982. Indicating that Caesars could no longer rely on high rollers, he declared that under his leadership the company would "make a push to embrace middle-income players." Since taking this new approach, Caesars has shown steady growth and in 1986 reported record earnings.[32]

Gambling operations traditionally have been guided by a "carny philosophy": customers were suckers to be fleeced, and any technique that would accomplish this end was appropriate. This approach has caused bettors to assume that gambling operators (the *house*) will cheat customers "every chance they get." In many cases this was an accurate appraisal. The legendary George Canfield, at the turn of the nineteenth century, clearly demonstrated, however, that gambling operations can be both fair and profitable. Given the frailties of betting populations and a guaranteed statistical edge, an efficient gambling operation should prove profitable. Operators have learned that running clean, fair games, and thereby encouraging active and continued participation, is in their best interest.

Racetrack owners have taken broad measures to convince the public that racing is an honest game. They have initiated comprehensive drug testing, presented televised reruns of races, organized an efficient security force, and handed out draconian penalties to those involved in incidents of race fixing. Casino owners also have made concerted efforts to convince players that the games are being fairly run. The fact that state agencies oversee legalized gaming operations lends credibility to those operations. Gamblers are slowly becoming convinced that gambling is "on the square."

Summary

A review of gambling in the United States reveals that, until recently, periodic reform movements and congressional investigations attempting to link gambling with organized crime have limited the social acceptability of gambling. At the same time, philosophical inconsistencies that damned gambling in one context while praising it in another encouraged an ambivalence toward gambling. Recent developments, such as increasing legalization and an improved public image, have more than offset the effect of reform movements and ambivalence. Gambling participation, for all intents, has been legitimated; and although future reform movements may develop, they will not severely restrict gambling's acceptance. While resistance to casino gambling and state-sanctioned sports betting continues, gambling in many jurisdictions has become institutionalized. State budgets are increasingly dependent on gaming revenues, and it is unlikely that future reform movements will be allowed to disturb these revenues. Middle-class participants have embraced gambling, which has become an integral part of their leisure activities. Reform movements can thus no longer count on middle-class morality for support, nor can gambling be restricted to a favored social class or to a charitable purpose. In short, ambivalence of Americans toward gambling has been resolved in favor of accepting gambling participation.

Notes

1. Henry Chafetz, *Play the Devil* (New York: Potter Publishing, 1960), p. 343.
2. Herbert Asbury, *Sucker's Progress* (New York: Dodd, Mead, 1938), p. 455.
3. Ibid., p. 106.
4. Charles B. Parmer, *For Gold and Glory* (New York: Carrick & Evans, 1939), p. 163.
5. Chafetz, *Play the Devil*, p. 391.
6. U.S. House Committee on Interstate and Foreign Commerce, *Transmission of Bets on Races* (Washington, D.C.: U.S. Government Printing Office, 1920), pp. 24–25.
7. Chafetz, *Play the Devil*, p. 381.
8. Ibid., p. 386.
9. For an appreciation of the complicated maneuvering behind New York's attempt to maintain horse race gambling, see "Reformers March with Banners," in Parmer's *For Gold and Glory*, pp. 152–173.
10. Chafetz, *Play the Devil*, p. 395.
11. Ibid., p. 396.
12. Asbury, *Sucker's Progress*, p. 451.

13. One of the first surveys of the nation's gambling behavior was conducted by the American Institute of Public Opinion. The results of their research were reported in Chafetz, *Play the Devil,* pp. 449–450.

14. Another finding of the American Institute of Public Opinion. Chafetz, *Play the Devil,* p. 449.

15. John S. Ezell, *Fortune's Merry Wheel* (Cambridge, Mass.: Harvard University Press, 1960), p. 278.

16. Ibid., p. 279.

17. Mark H. Haller, "Bootleggers and American Gambling 1920–1950," in Appendix 1 of *Gambling in America: Final Report of the Commission on the Review of the National Policy toward Gambling* (Washington, D.C.: U.S. Government Printing Office, 1976), p. 123.

18. Mark H. Haller, "The Changing Structure of American Gambling in the Twentieth Century," *Journal of Social Issues* 35, no. 3 (1979), p. 110.

19. According to some Floridians, young children were squandering their lunch money on one-armed bandits. See Chafetz, *Play the Devil,* pp. 448–449.

20. John M. Findlay, *People of Chance* (New York: Oxford University Press, 1986), p. 121.

21. Fact Research, "Gambling in Perspective," in Appendix 1 of *Gambling in America: Final Report of the Commission on the Review of the National Policy toward Gambling* (Washington, D.C.: U.S. Government Printing Office, 1976), pp. 53–54.

22. Ibid., p. 52.

23. Ibid., p. 55.

24. Ibid., p. 55. For a detailed analysis of the Kefauver hearings see William Moore, *The Kefauver Committee and the Politics of Crime 1950–1952,* (Columbia: University of Missouri Press, 1974). Moore criticizes the committee for failing to conduct an actual investigation. He indicates that committee members did not undertake an independent inquiry but instead offered a forum for the unsubstantiated opinions of law enforcement officials.

25. For a full discussion of the volume of illegal gambling see Vicki Abt, James F. Smith, and Eugene M. Christiansen, *The Business of Risk* (Lawrence: University of Kansas), pp. 234–248.

26. Robert F. Kennedy, "The Baleful Influence of Gambling," in *Gambling,* ed. Robert D. Herman (New York: Harper & Row, 1967), p. 169.

27. Ibid., p. 177.

28. Rufus King, *Gambling and Organized Crime* (Washington, D.C.: Public Affairs Press, 1969), p. 192.

29. Abt et al., *The Business of Risk,* p. 65.

30. The growth in bus traffic to Atlantic City has been phenomenal. For example, in 1978, approximately 30,000 buses brought in 742,000 visitors, whereas in 1985, 400,000 buses brought in 12,600,000 passengers. James F. Smith, "Las Vegas East? Atlantic City Ten Years after the Referendum," in *Betting on the Future: Gambling in Nevada and Elsewhere* (Reno: Nevada Public Affairs Review, 1986), p. 53.

31. Jon D. Vasché, "The California State Lottery: Provisions, Performance and Policy Issues," in *Betting on the Future: Gambling in Nevada and Elsewhere* (Reno: Nevada Public Affairs Review, 1986), p. 43.

32. Jane A. Morrison, "Caesars Begins Catering to Middle-Income Crowd," *Reno Gazette Journal,* 31 August 1986, p. 1 F.

Explaining Gambling Behavior

Analysis of gambling practices, age-old and world-wide as they are, suggests that we are dealing here with some of the most profound and complex features of the human mind. Repercussions extend far beyond the gaming table or the pack of cards into risk-taking and decision-making in all walks of life.

John Cohen*

Attempts to explain the ubiquity and persistence of gambling have been only partially successful; the complex set of behavior patterns involved in gambling participation remains elusive. Researchers have examined gambling using methodologies that include clinical, survey, historical, experimental, and ethnographic perspectives. However, their efforts typically have concentrated on the deviant aspects of gambling while ignoring its normative dimensions. Consequently, gambling research has lacked both an integrative, unified theme and a firm theoretical base.

The vast majority of gambling research has been conducted by professionals in four disciplines: (1) psychiatry, (2) sociology, (3) economics, and (4) psychology. This chapter will examine the major studies done within each of these disciplines and end by suggesting new avenues of research that could lead to a more comprehensive understanding of gambling.

Psychiatry

Most of the early gambling studies investigated the psychiatric aspects of participation, a trend that significantly influenced the course of gambling research in the United States. The prevalence of psychiatric studies led to a research emphasis on the pathological characteristics of gambling. Using a clinical approach and generalizing from a limited sample of troubled gamblers, psychiatric researchers concentrated on the problematic dimensions of gambling. Only recently have research-

* From "The Nature of Gambling," by John Cohen, *Scienta* 40 (1970), p. 445.

ers begun to seriously question psychiatric explanations for gambling behavior. Familiarity with the major psychiatric studies is essential to understanding the course of gambling research.

The first known psychoanalytic study of gambling was conducted by H. Von Hattingberg in 1914.[1] After studying one of his patients, Von Hattingberg generalized that psychosexual inadequacies are at the core of gambling behavior. The contention that gambling has definite sexual referents was to become a theme of subsequent psychiatric research. In 1920, Ernst Simmel expanded upon Von Hattingberg's finding of sexual inadequacy, specifying that the lure of gambling could be located in a gambler's desire to achieve autoerotic gratification.[2] Simmel based his conclusions on observations of a young patient who had been sentenced to prison for stealing money to obtain gambling funds. Simmel contended that gambling is an expression of a narcissistic preoccupation with birth fantasies and the wish to inseminate oneself, bypassing both parents and thereby serving a bisexual aim. He further observed that financial gain is not a prime motivating factor in the passion to gamble. The idea that unconscious motivation rather than economic gain drives individuals to gamble was taken for granted in later psychiatric studies.

In 1928, Sigmund Freud, at the urging of a colleague, analyzed the published writings and personal correspondence of the writer Fyodor Dostoyevsky, an acknowledged compulsive gambler.[3] Freud concluded that for Dostoyevsky gambling was a form of self-punishment that stemmed from oedipal conflict. He argued that the Russian author's gambling addiction signified an adult manifestation of childhood masturbatory urges. The gambler's frantic gambling play, accompanied by hand movements, was essentially an autoerotic activity. Freud theorized that Dostoyevsky's fascination with masturbation stemmed from a desire to supplant his authoritarian father and possess his mother. This incestuous fantasy drove Dostoyevsky to punish himself by losing all at the roulette wheel. Through a recurring cycle of loss and recrimination, Dostoyevsky could temporarily assuage guilt for his oedipal urges. Although Freud did not attempt to generalize beyond Dostoyevsky, his students extended the concept that gambling is essentially masochistic, neurotic behavior to larger gambling populations.

In 1930, Robert LaForgue argued that gamblers find pleasure in the pain of losing and that psychic masochism is a prime ingredient in the decision to gamble regularly.[4] In 1935, E. Kris described a sequence of events that led gamblers from playful experimentation to increasing ego involvement, to a ritualistic circle of mounting losses, to a need for reassurance, and finally to a dangerous escalation of tension.[5] According to this scenario, gambling progresses from harmless recreation to a matter of life and death. Theodor Reik, in 1940, also linked gambling to an obsessive concern with oedipal desires, but added that participation serves an oracular function as well.[6] Gamblers frequently test their fate to ascertain whether or not they will be punished for their oedipal lusts. Winning is symbolic of forgiveness, whereas losing represents punishment.

Otto Fenichel, writing in 1945, also viewed gambling as fulfilling an oracular function.[7] Since oedipal guilt can never be fully expiated, however, Fenichel concluded that true gamblers must inevitably be ruined. Their endless quest for forgiveness can never be realized. R. Greenson, drawing on clinical data from five patients, in 1948 identified gamblers as being orally fixated.[8] He observed that gamblers seek from "Lady Luck" the favorable treatment that they haven't received from their parents. Greenson concluded that the impulse to gamble cannot be satisfied by fantasizing but must be acted upon; that is, the gambler must continue to play. Robert Lindner, noted author of *The Rebel without a Cause* and *The Fifty Minute Hour*, presented an important psychoanalytic study in 1953. After analysis of a single patient, Lindner theorized that gamblers are caught in an unsatisfactory appeal to destiny as they wrestle with such questions as: "Did I kill my father by wishing his death?" (or in the case of gamblers with living male parent: "Are my wishes powerful enough to cause the death of my father?") and: "Will I be punished or rewarded for my secret sexual desires (incest)?"[9] Lindner portrayed the gambler's dilemma as unresolvable. On the one hand, winning serves to revive guilt for oedipal desires; on the other hand, losing is tangible proof of punishment for those desires.

Early psychoanalytic studies cluminated in the research of Edmund Bergler. His investigations were the most carefully documented work undertaken by a psychoanalyst and represent a veritable compendium of psychiatric observation. Bergler's theoretical statements have attained widespread recognition among both academicians and the general public, and he remains one of the most widely quoted sources on gambling. In 1957, Bergler published *The Psychology of Gambling*, which described his thirty-year career treating troubled gamblers. His research was based on sixty gamblers he personally treated and on the brief contacts he had with several hundred more. Bergler's major contention was that compulsive gamblers are neurotics driven by an unconscious wish to lose. Their repeated gambling represents a self-destructive desire to punish themselves by rebelling against the rationality of adult authority. The anguish of losing is eroticized into a chronic masochism that the compulsive gambler craves with uncontrollable passion, becoming unable also to control his or her gambling. Bergler contended that such gamblers are in the grips of an illness and should be accorded medical treatment rather than moral condemnation.

Like other psychiatrists, Bergler did not believe that economic gain was a determining factor in the decision to gamble. Bergler felt that gamblers are orally fixated, unconsciously provoking situations in which they will be defeated and then self-pityingly blaming their plight on a cruel fate. Bergler concluded that a gambler's "chronic masochism" manifests itself in six behavior patterns:

1. The gambler habitually takes chances.
2. The game precludes all other interests.
3. The gambler is full of optimism and never learns from defeat.
4. The gambler never stops when winning.
5. Despite initial caution, the gambler eventually risks relatively too large sums.
6. "Pleasurable–painful tension" (thrill) is experienced between the time of betting and the outcome of the game.[10]

The assumption that problem gamblers are neurotics with unresolved sexual desires was accepted by the psychiatric community of the 1950s and 1960s. Iago Galdston, in 1960,[11] H. Harris, in 1964,[12] and Jon Halliday and Peter Fuller, in 1974,[13] reported findings that substantiated that assumption. In 1968, Darrell Bolen and William Boyd delineated the classic psychoanalytic view of gambling:

> Gambling is forbidden and an unconscious transgression because of the indirect, intrapsychic satisfaction of multiple aggressive and libidinal determinants. Here is the origin of the abundant, pervasive guilt feelings which plague the gambler, as well as the origin of anticipated, desired punishment in the form of gambling loss. Gambling is a unique situation with inherent infallible mathematical machinery . . . which insures guilt-alleviating loss such that the unconscious books are balanced and restored to psychic equilibrium. Gambling represents an activity of unconsciously forbidden nature which activates guilt and contains its own system of probabilistic loss and guilt cancellation.[14]

In recent years the traditional psychoanalytic position that gamblers are neurotic masochists has been questioned by practicing psychiatrists. After studying fifty troubled gamblers in England, E. Moran concluded that problem gambling develops primarily from a host of social and environmental factors. He found that only 20 percent of his subjects could be termed neurotics, and even fewer exhibited a masochistic desire to lose. Moran contended that the term *compulsive gambling* was inappropriate and inaccurate, since gamblers do not exhibit signs of true compulsion, that is, "pursuing an activity which is felt to be alien and is therefore persistently dreaded and resisted."[15] He suggested that the term *pathological* replace compulsive as a descriptor of this behavioral syndrome. Moran stressed the importance of subcultural gambling that arises out of the individual's familiarity with gaming and acquaintance with other gamblers, reporting that in some working-class neighborhoods the nongambler would be considered an outsider.

In the United States, Sanford Chapman, after analyzing gambling experiences, concluded that Bergler's unconscious-wish-to-lose theory is not applicable to actual gaming situations. The psychiatrist observed that problem gamblers typically are impatient players who crave action more than gambling losses. Chapman warned that gambling is difficult and that participants inevitably lose money and suggested that the problem is not that gamblers need to lose but that they need to gamble.[16]

One of the leading contemporary authorities in the field of compulsive gambling is Robert Custer, a psychiatrist with the Veterans Administration in Washington, D.C. After treating hundreds of compulsive gamblers in and out of hospital settings and consulting on numerous other gambling cases, Custer concluded that only a small percentage (10 to 20 percent) exhibit neurotic symptoms. He found no substantial evidence that gamblers exhibit an unconscious wish to lose. For Custer, the compulsive, or pathological, gambling syndrome represents a "confluence of numerous psychological, social, cultural, and even biological factors."[17] In 1980, Custer was instrumental in convincing the American Psychiatric Association to include pathological gambling in its *Diagnostic and Statistical Manual III*. Custer believes that problem gamblers closely resemble substance addicts, becoming heavily dependent on gambling to provide them with stimulating experiences. In the 1985 book, *When Luck Runs Out*, Custer wrote: "Compulsive gambling is an addictive illness in which the subject is driven by an overwhelming, uncontrollable impulse to gamble. The impulse persists and progresses in intensity and urgency, consuming more and more of the individual's time, energy, and emotional and material resources. Ultimately, it invades, undermines and often destroys everything that is meaningful in a person's life."[18]

Moran and Custer have been influential in altering the classic psychoanalytic view of gambling. They have clearly documented, through empirical research, that neurotic behavior and gambling participation are not directly linked, and that gambling is much more than a substitute for masturbation or an expression of unresolved oedipal conflict. The contemporary psychiatric establishment has generally rejected Bergler's unconscious-wish-to-lose theory in favor of an addiction model that retains the concept that some individuals are compelled to gamble.

Psychiatric researchers were the first to seriously examine gambling behavior. Although they studied patients seeking treatment to stop gambling, their findings were generalized to other gambling populations. Bergler's unconscious-wish-to-lose theory was adopted by media figures and received widespread publicity in the lay community. Many gambling participants are familiar with Bergler's concept and often invoke it after disheartening losses. Although psychiatrists were studying only problem gamblers, their clinical conclusions frequently were applied to other contexts. Until quite recently, the psychiatric perspective set the agenda for gambling research in the United States.

Researchers studied gambling dropouts—losers who needed help to abstain from further participation. The normative, nonproblematic aspects of gambling were often overlooked in the haste to chronicle the woes of compulsives. Gambling participation was viewed as abnormal, deviant, and qualitatively different from conventional behavior.

Sociology

Early sociological studies, like their psychiatric counterparts, viewed gambling as deviant behavior and explained participation in that context. Later, sociologists tried to "prove" that gambling was nondeviant and therefore a "normal" activity. More recently, sociologists have taken gambling's normalcy for granted and have begun to examine it as conventional mainstream behavior. The shift in sociological research has thus followed the increasing legitimation of gambling.

The first important sociological study of gambling was reported by Edward Devereux in 1949. He presented a nine hundred-page dissertation to Harvard University entitled "Gambling and the Social Structure: A Sociological Study of Lotteries and Horse Racing in Contemporary America." His work, unfortunately never published, remains one of the most comprehensive studies of gambling ever conducted. Devereux, a student of the functionalist Talcott Parsons, rejected individualistic views of gambling and attempted to explain how "deviant behavior patterns and sub rosa organizations fitted into the general framework of the social structure."[19] He concluded that gambling serves as a safety valve for the contradictions, inconsistencies, and strains inherent in the social value system. Devereux theorized that the prevailing social structure is in conflict with its value system. Gambling serves to relieve some of these tensions without altering the basic structure and thus enhances societal equilibrium. Participation in gambling provides a safe outlet for divergence. Unable to attack the basic institutions directly, malcontents can instead work out their frustrations by gambling.

Although Devereux contended that gambling serves an important societal function, he was insistent that it represents a reversal of dominant values and as such must be considered deviant behavior. The existence of gambling challenges the prevailing ethical system and therefore can be tolerated only in small doses and in segregated settings. Devereux stated that "potentially disruptive speculative urges and ethically deviant economic motivations may be deflected more or less harmlessly within the segregated contexts of gambling. With his gambling thus rationalized and kept within bounds, he may be able to 'drain off' potentially dangerous energies and thus, indirectly, to bolster and protect the precarious equilibrium of the dominant personality organization."[20]

In a 1951 study, Herbert Bloch contended that gambling is a retreatist adaptation to the routine and boredom of modern industrial life: "Taking a chance destroys routine and hence is pleasurable, particularly in a culture where the unchanging and predictable routines of employment are sharply separated from leisure."[21] In this and later studies, Bloch emphasized that gambling is both deviant and dysfunctional behavior, since it disrupts family life, facilitates criminal activities, and interferes with worker productivity. Virgil Peterson, also in 1951, after examining the merits of legalized gambling, emphatically concluded that legalization would be detrimental to society. He considered gambling a frivolous activity whose participants are motivated by a desire to "get rich quick" without putting forth the necessary effort.[22] In 1960, Kirson Weinberg reported that gambling is both deviant and criminal, and concluded that it had become "an important contemporary problem."[23] In 1964, in a widely used introductory sociology text, Paul Landis called gambling disruptive, saying it represents "the very heartbeat of organized crime."[24]

Irving Zola conducted an important study of gambling behavior in 1963 called "Observations of Gambling in a Lower-Class Setting." His research represented a sociological landmark, since the findings were generated from firsthand observations of an ongoing gambling group. He was one of the first researchers to investigate the practices of regular gambling participants in an actual gaming situation. Although impressed with the rational betting practices of horse race gamblers, Zola considered gambling a lower-class behavior pattern and implicitly a deviant activity. He described the social setting of a tavern that, segregated from conventional society, represented a safe haven where its gambling patrons could take control of their lives through offtrack betting, however illusory that control might be: "By 'beating the system,' outsmarting it by rational means, these men demonstrated they can exercise control and that for a brief moment they can control their fate. Offtrack betting is thus a kind of escape. It denies the vagaries of life and gives these men a chance to regulate it."[25]

In the 1970s, social psychologist Jay Livingston and sociologist Henry Lesieur, working separately and using Gamblers Anonymous members as subjects, analyzed the processes whereby gambling becomes a compulsive addiction.[26] Livingston described a process of entrapment wherein gamblers are inexorably drawn into escalating participation and disastrous betting practices. Lesieur identified the phenomenon of chasing after money in an attempt to remain in action.

These two studies were testimonials to the potential deviancy of gambling.

Not all sociologists perceived gambling as deviant behavior; some were careful to point out its socially adaptive and nondeviant dimensions. Sociologists who adopted this perspective typically conducted ethnographic or participant-observation studies. In 1967, after studying racetrack patrons, Robert Herman rejected the idea that gambling is either deviant or a form of escapism. Observing members of several social classes betting on horse races, he was impressed with the bettors' disciplined composure and rational decision making. Herman concluded that horse race gamblers emulated traditional entrepreneurial practices: "In short, commercialized gambling offers to many people efficient means of enhanced self-esteem and gratification in a culture in which satisfactions are increasingly likely to be found in enterprises of consumption rather than production."[27]

In 1968, Marvin Scott published a fascinating study of the racetrack.[28] Drawing upon a lifetime of personal experience, Scott reported that the world of horse racing centers on problems of information. Trainers of horses seek to withhold information concerning their horses in order to perpetuate betting coups, whereas bettors seek to uncover the horses' capabilities and the trainers' intentions. He analyzed racing from a games theory framework, with the information game taking center stage. Scott emphasized that horse race bettors, in their study of form and betting patterns, are engaging in a rational activity. Although he acknowledged that some deviant types such as touts (who contact several racing patrons before a race and for a fee "give" each patron a different horse as the sure winner), and unethical horse trainers can be found at the racetrack, the vast majority of gamblers are not deviants but ordinary people searching for the right horse to bet. Gamblers are adhering to the same norms of rationality that guide everyday situations.

In a 1982 work, written after a study of racetrack patrons, I noted that "once psychiatric models and deviance labels are set aside the behavior of the vast majority of regular horse players can be accepted as normal, functional, and rational."[29] Participant observation revealed that the racetrack was frequented mostly by ordinary people rather than by the colorful, Runyonesque characters of popular stereotypes.

In 1970, Louis Zurcher, observing participants in friendly poker games, introduced the concept of an "ephemeral role" to describe behavior patterns that exist only within a gambling situation.[30] Poker playing provides the participants with temporary satisfactions, unavailable in the more lasting roles of their everyday-life positions. The subjects of the study were not gamblers on the fringes of society but professional workers and college professors. Zurcher didn't study gambling from a social problem perspective, but instead sought to identify some of the social–psychological benefits that derive from the widely played game of poker.

David Hayano, a part-time poker player, chronicled the life and work of professional poker players, reporting that professional poker playing had evolved from "a profession composed largely of self-admitted cheaters to one in which public elite professionals are negotiating for respectability and public acceptance."[31] Hayano concluded that increasing media coverage of poker tournaments and more favorable public opinion has enhanced the image of professional poker playing.

In 1977, Ivan Light clearly demonstrated that numbers gambling among blacks is not a deviant activity but instead an alternative form of investment: "Banks combine the savings of depositors to create a capital fund for business, mortgage and consumer investments. Numbers banks mimic this rhythm, first taking in the 'savings' of the poor, then returning capital to the poor community in the form of usurious loans, free loans, philanthropy and direct business investments by racketeers. Therefore, numbers gambling banks are an irregular financial institution."[32] Considered in this light, playing the numbers is a form of forced savings. Rather than waste their money on frivolities, numbers players are putting something away for a rainy day.

Probably the most famous sociologist to study gambling was Erving Goffman. He worked as a blackjack dealer and croupier in the Nevada casinos to develop an intimate knowledge of gaming. Goffman concluded that gambling participation serves as a surrogate for risk taking that has been effectively removed from modern life by the bureaucratization of social and economic arrangements. By engaging in voluntary risk taking, the gambler can demonstrate character strength; such demonstrations, although culturally valued, generally are unavailable in ordinary life situations. Players who engage in gambling action can exhibit valued traits such as courage, gameness, integrity, and composure. Goffman viewed gambling as reaffirming rather than deviating from conventional values, and noted that gamblers "subscribe to a normative code no less stringently disciplined than that required of the captain of industry, the political leader, or the hero of popular fiction."[33]

In 1975, a sociological study was undertaken that significantly changed the way academicians, politicians, gaming operators, and the general public viewed gambling. The Survey Research Center at the University of Michigan was given a grant by the Commission on the Review of the National Policy toward Gambling to (1) study the extent of gambling in the United States, (2) estimate government revenues from changes in gambling laws, and (3) examine the social consequences of gambling legalization. While the project did not attempt to explain motivation or to test theoretical propositions, it did provide a macroscopic profile of gambling. The study, although fraught with methodological, political, and philosophical problems,[34] represents by far the most comprehensive effort undertaken in the United States to obtain reliable data on gambling. A national sample of two thousand subjects was surveyed, three hundred of whom were Nevada residents.

The results of the survey clearly demonstrated the widespread prevalence of gambling: 61 percent of those interviewed reported they had placed some kind of bet during the previous year. The general acceptance accorded gambling was also demonstrated: over 80 percent approved of legalizing various gambling games and 70 percent said they would not be deterred from betting even if it were to become illegal. Other findings showed that

1. men gamble more than women;
2. whites gamble more than blacks;
3. the young (eighteen to twenty-four) gamble much more than people over sixty-five;
4. gambling rises sharply with income;
5. gambling likewise rises with education;
6. Catholics, Jews, and liberal Protestants are the most likely of religious groups to gamble, whereas Baptists, atheists, and fundamentalist Protestants are the least;
7. people with East European and Italian backgrounds have the highest rate of gambling among ethnic groups, whereas those from Spanish-speaking backgrounds have the lowest; and
8. participation is greater in the suburbs than in the city and least in small towns and rural areas.[35]

The study also found that gambling participation (both legal and illegal) increases with legalization; that most gamblers bet small amounts during the year (50 percent bet less than $50, 30 percent between $50 and $100, and the remaining 20 percent over $100); and that approximately 1 percent of the sample could be considered compulsive gamblers. The survey findings revealed that gambling is an almost universal phenomenon engaged in by members of all social categories. Gambling could no longer be considered primarily a lower-class activity and, considering its ubiquity, could hardly be labeled deviant. The survey concluded that "gambling is inevitable. No matter what is said or done by advocates or opponents of gambling in all its various forms, it is an activity that is practiced, or tacitly endorsed, by a substantial majority of Americans."[36]

After the survey findings were released, researchers could stop focusing on the deviant aspects of gambling. Felicia Campbell, in a controversial 1976 report advocating the placement of slot machines in nursing homes, took a positive view of gambling, calling it a normal part of human behavior that provides the participants with important sources of stimulation that often are lacking in their mundane lives.[37] In 1985, Vicki Abt, James Smith, and Eugene Christiansen, the authors of an important sociological study, *The Business of Risk*, began their investigation with the premise that gambling is "conventional behavior practiced by most Americans."[38] In 1986, sociologist Jim Frey observed that "people don't want to admit it, but a great part of gambling is consistent with the American way. We admire people that take risks."[39] His comment appeared in a *Sports Illustrated* article, the title of which is perhaps indicative of the acceptance that gambling has received: "Gambling: America's National Pastime?"

Economics

Economic explanations of gambling behavior maintain that people gamble for monetary gain. Since economic theories assume that individuals generally are rational, they must address the phenomenon of persistence at gambling despite financial loss. In other words, why do people continue to gamble when the odds of winning are obviously not in their favor? A review of the economic literature reveals three central arguments for gambling participation: (1) bettors are not aware of their chances of winning, (2) the potential utility of wealth outweighs the unfavorableness of the true odds, and (3) members of affluent classes gamble to demonstrate their social standing.

In the eighteenth century, economist Adam Smith advanced the concept that gamblers don't understand their chances of winning. According to Smith, gamblers are affected with conceit, and "a risk-aversive individual will incorrectly compute the true probability of winning by underestimating the chance of a loss and overestimating the chance of a winning."[40] One of the first contemporary researchers to test Smith's concept was Robert Griffith, who in 1949 studied the betting patterns of horse race gamblers. After analyzing the results of over ten thousand races, he concluded that horse players are essentially a rational, sophisticated group, and that "the socially determined odds on horses in races are on the average correct reflections of the horses' chances."[41] Although he found a slight but consistent bettor bias, undervaluing the low-odds horses and overvaluing the high-odds horses, the final odds are fairly accurate: the lower the odds on a horse the higher its probability of winning. The finding that horse players, overall, are good estimators of probabilities was replicated by several subsequent studies. Wayne Snyder, in 1978, after assessing the results of thirty-five thousand races concluded that horse race betting is an effective speculative market because it offers (1) ease of entry, (2) a large number of participants, (3) extensive information, and (4) prices that reflect all available information.[42] He suggested that in terms of efficiency there were distinct parallels between horse race gambling and the stock market. Such research belies the notion that gamblers are unaware of the odds against their winning.

In 1948, Milton Friedman and L. J. Savage introduced the utility-of-wealth concept and theorized that rational individuals will gamble if they place high value on the chance of achieving a major increase in wealth that will allow them to markedly improve their socioeconomic position. Within this context, a gambler could logically choose to purchase a small chance (with extremely long odds) in the hope of winning a large amount of money. In essence, "increases in income that raise the relative position of the consumer unit in its own class but do not shift the unit out of its class yield diminishing marginal utility, while increases that shift it into a new class, that give it new social and economic status, yield increased marginal utility."[43]

There have been two major studies designed to test the Friedman–Savage model of utility. In 1976, F. L. Pryor studied gambling from a cross-cultural perspective and found a "positive correlation between socio-economic inequality and the presence of gambling."[44] In 1981, Gregory Brunk tried to test the Friedman–Savage model with reference to gambling in the United States by analyzing cross-indexed survey data collected by the 1976 Survey Research Study. He concluded that dissatisfaction with current income was significantly related to the purchase of lottery tickets. For other forms of gambling, however, he found no significant correlation: "In fact, for three types of social gambling (poker, sports, and bingo), the more satisfied the individual was with his income, the more he tended to gamble."[45]

Thorstein Veblen's (1899) theory of conspicuous consumption by members of the upper class has been used to explain gambling motivation. This perspective holds that gamblers display their affluence through gaming. Veblen maintained that gambling is primarily an activity of the leisure class. After conducting a study to test Veblen's position, Wen Lang Li and Martin Smith found that in general "the higher the social class, the higher the propensity to gamble."[46] However, upon closer statistical analysis, they discovered that neither Veblen's leisure-class nor his conspicuous-consumption theory taken by itself could explain gambling behavior. In 1984, Ronald Smith and Frederick Preston reexamined Veblen's theories and succinctly concluded, "Obviously Veblen's theory of gambling goes beyond the idea of people desiring economic profit and suggests that the wager won or lost also serves some larger purpose."[47] Thus economic explanations of gambling, though insightful, cannot fully explain this phenomenon.

Psychology

Psychologists typically have studied gambling by testing risk taking under experimental conditions. The vast majority of these studies have been based on questionnaires administered to volunteer subjects or on observations of subjects under simulated gaming conditions. Many of these experiments have used college students as subjects. One of the earliest psychological studies was conducted by J. Hunter and R. Brunner in 1928. They identified several hundred college students "with an excessive indulgence in games of chance,"[48] compared them with a group of nongamblers, and concluded there was no significant difference in terms of intelligence, neurotic tendencies, or introversion–extraversion characteristics. In 1957, Robert Morris administered a battery of personality tests to Harvard undergraduates. The test results revealed that students who gambled regularly were more secure, more dominant, more masculine (all were male), less socially responsible, and about as happy as nongamblers. Nevertheless, Morris concluded (and most subsequent studies confirmed) that although "some marked differences were found, both between gamblers and nongamblers and among subgroups of gamblers, differential patterns did not reach statistical significance."[49]

In 1962 and 1964 studies, Paul Slovic administered standardized personality tests to a variety of college students but could not locate a distinctive type of personality prone to gambling.[50] This finding was replicated by Malcomb Weinstein in 1969. He gave a wide range of tests to 173 graduates and concluded that the results argued "strongly against a general organismic risk-taking propensity."[51]

One of the most sophisticated studies of simulated gambling was undertaken by J. Blascovich, T. L. Veach, and G. P. Ginsburg in 1973 at the University of Nevada at Reno.[52] The researchers established a miniature casino within university confines. Seventy-five college students were given casino chips to play blackjack, and their subsequent betting patterns were analyzed. The results lent support to the concept of *risky shift,* which holds that gamblers take greater risks in the presence of other players. At Laval University in Quebec, Canada, Robert Ladouceur and other psychologists set up a casino-type roulette game. In 1984, after studying college students and their bout with the wheel, they reported that "exposure to gambling activities increases the level of risk-taking behavior in gamblers and nongamblers." Ladouceur also concluded that "most psychological studies have attempted to explain and/or modify pathological or compulsive gambling. Very few researchers have tried to identify various factors responsible for the acquisition of gambling as a normal behavior."[53]

Psychologists familiar with actual gaming situations have also criticized traditional psychological studies of gambling. When William McGlothin (1956) used a racetrack setting, he failed to replicate well-established laboratory findings regarding stability of choices. He blamed the significant discrepancy on "the difference between college and horse betting populations."[54] Igor Kusyszyn, an internationally recognized psychologist and avid gambler, has long been critical of experimental studies dealing with risk taking and decision making under simulated conditions of risk. In a 1977 masterpiece on gambling entitled "How Gambling Saved Me from a Misspent Sabbatical," Kusyszyn listed several criticisms of experimental research:

> First, although some type of risk is usually involved in the experimental studies, their purpose is rarely the study of gambling. Second, usually very small or even imaginary amounts of money are used in such studies. Third, the money is almost always provided by the experimenter: the subject is not allowed to risk his or her own money. Since the subject never gambles, he or she may be responding more to a threat of failure at the task than to a threat of financial loss. Fourth, the subjects are almost always college students, and college students are more conservative and less proficient at interpreting payoff probabilities than are gamblers. Fifth, the tasks in these experiments are usually trivial with many trials allowing for little ego involvement and much boredom. Sixth, the subjects have no freedom of choice as to the nature of the game unlike gamblers who are free to display individual differences through game and bet preferences. Seventh, the experimental tasks and payoff probabilities rarely resemble those of real gambling games.[55]

Kusyszyn has conducted several naturalistic (field) studies of gambling groups, including horse race bettors, poker players, football afficionados, and casino plungers. He advocates an existential perspective and views gambling as functional play that confirms the participants' existence and affirms their worth. The risk taking involved in gambling enhances one's self-worth, and the excitement of the game confirms one's aliveness. Kusyszyn maintains that gambling is a positive, fulfilling activity, and his research demonstrates that gamblers are more self-actualized than nongamblers.[56]

Some psychologists have attempted to analyze gambling from a functional perspective, seeking to identify the environmental conditions under which gambling behavior occurs. According to Terry Knapp, a leading proponent of this approach, "the fundamental question posed by a functional analysis of gambling behavior is not Why do people gamble? but Under what circumstances will people gamble?"[57] One of the first psychologists to attempt a functional analysis of gambling was B. F. Skinner. Skinner stressed the importance of a varied pattern of rewards, termed a schedule of reinforcement, and, in 1953, described how these schedules could determine gambling behavior:

> The efficacy of such schedules in generating high rates has long been known to the proprietors of gambling establishments. Slot machines, roulette wheels, dice cages, horse races and so on pay off on a schedule of variable-ratio reinforcement. Each device has its own auxiliary reinforcements, but the schedule is the important characteristic. Winning depends upon placing a bet and in the long run upon the number of bets placed, but no particular payoff can be predicted. The ratio is varied by any one of several "random" systems.[58]

One of the promising aspects of functional analysis is the importance placed on the study of gambling in natural environments. However, few psychologists have undertaken actual field studies using this perspective, and functional analysis of gambling remains an underresearched area.

An excellent summary of the many psychological investigations into gambling has been put together by D. B. Cornish, who provides a comprehensive view of the psychological studies done before 1978.[59] More recently, Terry Knapp and C. Petrie have compiled an excellent summary of the psychological view of gambling behavior.[60]

New Areas of Research

Although gambling has been probed and dissected using a variety of perspectives and methodologies, one important area has not been adequately researched. Psychoanalytic, sociological, economic, and psychological researchers alike have neglected the fact that most gambling occurs in group settings. The social rewards that are part of this activity remain largely unidentified. A common misconception (often subscribed to by gamblers themselves) is that gambling is done alone. Racetracks and casinos are filled with individuals apparently engaged in solitary endeavors. On scrutiny, however, it is clear that the participants are in fact interacting with others, and in reality have established networks of association with other gamblers. These associations often represent important sources of human contact and enduring social relationships. The social rewards of these relationships can be sustained only by maintaining gambling participation.

Much of gambling is conducted within boundaries, in self-contained settings that can be termed social worlds. Racetracks, casinos, bookie joints, poker rooms, lottery purchasing outlets, bingo parlors, offtrack betting shops, taverns, and other activity-specific arenas foster the development of distinct social worlds. The significance of membership in these social worlds is enhanced by the impersonal, bureaucratic character of modern life. In chapter 5, I will explore some of the social rewards found within the many social worlds of gambling.

Summary

Most gambling research has been conducted by psychiatrists, sociologists, economists, and psychologists. Although the various disciplines have looked at gambling from different perspectives, a comprehensive understanding of gambling behavior remains elusive. Until recently, most studies concentrated on problem gamblers, ignoring the vast majority of participants.

Psychiatric investigators using patients as their data base developed the first "scientific" explanations of gambling behavior in studies that examined the pathological behavior of troubled gamblers. The first sociologists to study gambling also looked upon it as a social problem. This perspective was revised after the 1976 Survey Research findings, which demonstrated clearly that gambling is a widespread American activity. Most contemporary sociologists have accepted the concept that gambling is, in fact, conventional behavior. Economic explanations for gambling have focused on monetary decision making. Although this is an important part of the activity, most observers agree that several other factors are also involved in gambling behavior. Psychologists typically have examined the risk-taking dimension of gambling and have usually done so in a laboratory setting. Such an approach has been questioned, since bettors in actual gaming situations act differently than subjects in experimental settings. The social rewards of gambling, as found within its distinct social worlds, appear to be an important but underresearched area.

Notes

1. H. Von Hattingberg, "Analerotik, Angstlust und Eigensinn," *Internationale Zeitschrift für Psychoanalyse* 2 (1914): 244–258.
2. Ernst Simmel, "Psychoanalysis of the Gambler," *International Journal of Psychoanalysis* 1 (1920): 352–353.
3. Sigmund Freud, "Dostoevsky and Parricide," in *Complete Psychological Works of Freud*, ed. James Strachey, vol. 21 (London: Hogarth Press, 1928), pp. 177–194.
4. Robert LaForgue, "Über Erotisierung der Angst," *Internationale Zeitschrift für Psychoanalyse* 16 (1930): 420–429.
5. Ernst Kris, "Ego Development and the Comic," *International Journal of Psychoanalysis* 19 (1938): 77–90.
6. Theodor Reik, *From Thirty Years with Freud* (New York: International University Press, 1940).
7. Otto Fenichel, *The Psychoanalytic Theory of the Neuroses* (New York: Norton, 1945).
8. R. Greenson, "On Gambling," *The Yearbook of Psychoanalysis*, 1948, pp. 110–123.
9. Robert Lindner, "The Psychodynamics of Gambling," in *Explorations of Psychoanalysis*, ed. Robert Lindner (New York: Julian Press, 1953), p. 197.
10. Edmund Bergler, *The Psychology of Gambling* (New York: Hill & Wang, 1957), pp. 2–7.
11. Iago Galdston, "The Gambler and His Love," *American Journal of Psychiatry* 117 (1960): 553–555.
12. H. Harris, "Gambling Addiction in an Adolescent Male," *Psychoanalytic Quarterly* 33 (1964): 513–525.
13. Jon Halliday and Peter Fuller, eds., *The Psychology of Gambling* (London: Allen Lane, 1974).
14. Darrell W. Bolen and William H. Boyd, "Gambling and the Gambler," *Archives of General Psychiatry* 18 (1968): 626.

15. E. Moran, "Varieties of Pathological Gambling," *British Journal of Psychiatry* 116 (1970): 593–597.
16. Sanford R. Chapman, "An Argument against the 'Unconscious Need to Lose' Concept in the Compulsive Gambler" (Paper presented at the Second Annual Conference on Gambling and Risk Taking, Lake Tahoe, 1975).
17. Robert L. Custer is quoted in Harvey Greenberg's "Psychology of Gambling," in *Comprehensive Textbook of Psychiatry* 3, ed. Harold Kaplan, Alfred Freedman, and Benjamin J. Sadock (New York: Williams & Wilkins, 1980), p. 3281.
18. Robert L. Custer and Harry Milt, *When Luck Runs Out* (New York: Facts on File Publications, 1985), p. 40.
19. Edward C. Devereux, "Gambling and the Social Structure: A Sociological Study of Lotteries and Horse Racing in Contemporary America" (Ph.D. diss., Harvard University, 1949), p. 4.
20. Ibid., p. 109.
21. Herbert Bloch, "The Sociology of Gambling," *American Journal of Sociology* 57 (November 1951): 216.
22. Virgil W. Peterson, *Gambling: Should It Be Legalized?* (Springfield, Ill.,: Charles C Thomas, 1951), p. 49.
23. Kirson S. Weinberg, *Social Problems of Our Time* (Englewood Cliffs, N.J.: Prentice-Hall, 1960), p. 285.
24. Paul H. Landis, *Sociology* (Boston: Ginn, 1964), p. 279.
25. Irving K. Zola, "Observations on Gambling in a Lower-Class Setting," *Social Problems* 10 (Spring 1963): 360.
26. Jay Livingston, *Compulsive Gamblers* (New York: Harper & Row, 1974), and Henry R. Lesieur, *The Chase: Career of the Compulsive Gambler* (Cambridge, Mass.: Schenkman, 1984).
27. Robert D. Herman, "Gambling as Work: A Sociological Study of the Race Track," in *Gambling*, ed. Robert D. Herman (New York: Harper & Row, 1967), p. 104.
28. Marvin B. Scott, *The Racing Game* (Chicago: Aldine, 1968).
29. John Rosecrance, "The Regulars: A Study of Inveterate Horse Players" (Master's thesis, University of California, Santa Barbara, 1982), p. 103.
30. Louis A. Zurcher, "The Friendly Poker Game: A Study of an Ephemeral Role," *Social Forces* 49, no. 2 (1970): 173–186.
31. David M. Hayano, *Poker Faces* (Berkeley: University of California Press, 1982), p. 131.
32. Ivan Light, "Numbers Gambling among Blacks: A Financial Institution," *American Sociological Review* 42 (December 1977), p. 901.
33. Erving Goffman, *Interaction Ritual* (Garden City, N.J.: Doubleday, 1967), p. 218.
34. For a frank appraisal of the "problems" that arose during this study, see Peter Reuter, "Easy Sport: Research and Relevance," *Journal of Social Issues* 35, no. 3 (1979): 166–182.
35. Raymond N. D'Angelo summarized these findings in "The Social Organization of Sports Gambling: A Study in Conventionality and Deviance" (Ph.D. diss., Bryn Mawr University, 1983), p. 15.
36. "Survey of American Gambling Attitudes," in *Gambling in America: Final Report of the Commission on the Review of the National Policy toward Gambling*, app. 2 (Washington, D.C.: U. S. Government Printing Office, 1976), p. 1.
37. Felicia Campbell, "Gambling: A Positive View," in *Gambling and Society*, ed. William R. Eadington (Springfield, Ill.: Charles C Thomas, 1976), pp. 218–228.

38. Vicki Abt, James F. Smith, and Eugene M. Christiansen, *The Business of Risk* (Lawrence: University of Kansas Press, 1985), p. 1.
39. Jim Frey, quoted in "Gambling: America's National Pastime?" *Sports Illustrated*, 10 March 1986, p. 56.
40. Elizabeth Elmore, "Economic Aspects of Gambling," in *Gambling Today*, ed. David Lester (Springfield, Ill.: Charles C Thomas, 1979), p. 13.
41. Robert M. Griffith, "Odds Adjustments by American Horse Race Bettors," *American Journal of Psychology* 62 (1949): 294.
42. Wayne W. Snyder, "Horse Racing: Testing the Efficient Markets Model," *American Journal of Psychology* 91 (1978): 1109–1118.
43. Milton Friedman and L. J. Savage, "The Utility Analysis of Choices Involving Risks," *Journal of Political Economy* 56 (1946): 288.
44. F. L. Pryor, "The Friedman–Savage Utility Function in Cross-cultural Perspective," *Journal of Political Economy* 84 (1976): 823–824.
45. Gregory G. Brunk, "A Test of the Friedman–Savage Gambling Model," *Quarterly Journal of Economics* 95 (May 1981): 345.
46. Wen Lang Li and Martin H. Smith, "The Propensity to Gamble: Some Structural Determinants," in *Gambling and Society*, ed. William R. Eadington (Springfield, Ill.: Charles C Thomas, 1976), p. 191.
47. Ronald Smith and Frederick Preston, "Vocabularies of Motives for Gambling Behavior," *Sociological Perspectives* 27 (July 1984): 326.
48. J. Hunter and R. Brunner, "The Emotional Outlet of Gambling," *Journal of Abnormal Social Psychology* 23 (1928): 38–39.
49. Robert P. Morris, "An Exploratory Study of Some Personality Characteristics of Gamblers," *Journal of Clinical Psychology* 13 (1957): 191–192.
50. Paul Slovic, "Congruent Validation of Risk-Taking Measures," *Journal of Abnormal and Social Psychology* 65 (1962): 68–71, and "The Assessment of Risk-Taking Behavior," *Psychological Bulletin* 61 (1964): 220–233.
51. Malcolm Weinstein, "Achievement Motivation and Risk Preference," *Journal of Personality and Social Psychology* 12 (1969): 170.
52. J. Blascovich, T. L. Veach, and G. P. Ginsburg, "Black Jack and the Risky Shift," *Sociometry* 36. (1973): 42–45.
53. Robert Ladouceur, "Risk Taking Behavior in Gamblers and Non Gamblers During Prolonged Exposure" (Paper presented at the Sixth National Conference on Gambling and Risk Taking, Atlantic City, November 1984).
54. William H. McGlothin, "Stability of Choices Among Uncertain Alternatives," *American Journal of Psychology* 69 (1956): 615.
55. Igor Kusyszyn, "How Gambling Saved Me from a Misspent Sabbatical," *Journal of Humanistic Psychology* 17 (Summer 1977): 21–22.
56. Igor Kusyszyn, "The Psychology of Gambling," *Annals of the American Academy of Political and Social Sciences* 474 (July 1984): 133–145.
57. Terry J. Knapp, "A Functional Analysis of Gambling," in *Gambling and Society*, ed. William R. Eadington (Springfield, Ill.: Charles C Thomas, 1976), pp. 276–294.
58. B. F. Skinner, *Science and Human Behavior* (New York: Appleton-Century-Crofts, 1953), p. 103.
59. D. B. Cornish, *Gambling: A Review of the Literature and Its Implications for Policy and Research* (London: Her Majesty's Stationery Office, 1978).
60. Terry J. Knapp and C. Petrie, *Gambling Activity Inventory* (Work in progress, 1987). Copies available from the Psychology Department, University of Nevada at Las Vegas.

The Social Worlds of Gambling

At the racetrack I feel at home.

An inveterate horse player

Gambling in the United States can be divided into five basic types: (1) horse race gambling, (2) sports betting, (3) poker playing, (4) casino gaming, and (5) lottery ticket purchasing. Almost all gamblers specialize in one of these five types. Contrary to the common perception that gamblers will bet on anything, most concentrate their efforts in one specific area. Although they may experiment with a variety of games, once gamblers find a game they favor they tend to stick with it. The comment of a longtime gambler reflects the game loyalty that characterizes gambling behavior: "I've played all the table games, bet on sports teams and horses, and even bought a few numbers and lottery tickets, but that's just a diversion. My game is poker. That's what I take seriously. That's where I go for action. For me it's poker; the rest is just fooling around." Several demographic studies of gambling participation lend empirical support to the contention that gamblers typically specialize in one gaming activity and that the various games are not interchangeable.[1]

The major gambling games have all fostered the development of activity-related social worlds. Within these worlds, gambling holds center stage; more accurately, it is the stage. Relationships that develop in these contexts provide the participants with important sources of social interaction. In this chapter I will describe the five types of gambling and give examples of their discrete environments or social worlds. I will also present some of the social rewards of gambling participation and will analyze the significance of social relationships that develop among gamblers. In order to understand the material in this chapter, three concepts—occasional, regular, and social worlds—must be grasped.

71

Gamblers can be divided into two broad categories: *occasionals* and *regulars*. Although these categories are based to some extent on frequency of participation, they are essentially self-designated groupings. Regulars would agree that their lives have been changed and influenced by their gambling; occasionals would not. Obviously, within the two categories there are various stages and levels; these general terms can nonetheless be useful.

The categories are fluid, and movement between them is possible. Advancing from an occasional to a regular is the most common move. Occasionals are basically recreational players who don't form significant relationships with other gamblers; regulars are serious players who often develop significant relationships with other participants. In the move from occasional to regular, the social rewards derived from gambling relationships become an important part of continued participation.

The concept of *social worlds* has been advanced by social psychologists to identify "those groupings of individuals bound together by networks of communication or universes of discourse and who share perspectives on reality."[2] According to this concept, mass society breaks down into individual units or worlds as people define who they are and what they do. Anselm Strauss, a leading proponent of the concept, contends that all social worlds are organized around a specific activity and recognizes "countless worlds—those of opera, baseball, literature, surfing, stamp collecting, medicine, law, science, and Catholicism."[3] Some of these worlds are small, others huge; some are international, others local. Some are highly public and publicized, while others are barely visible.

In order to add authenticity to this discussion of gambling social worlds, I examined wherever possible those worlds to which I had some access. This effort was facilitated by my living in Lake Tahoe and having thirty-two years of participation in gambling activities. Because of their Nevada location, the gambling social worlds of Lake Tahoe are relatively open to observation. Given the growing acceptability of gambling in the United States, the legalized gaming available at Lake Tahoe may, in fact, reflect and portend societal developments. In any case, on the basis of my observations of other gambling locales and on a review of pertinent literature, the social worlds developed around gambling at Lake Tahoe appear to be typical of those found in other areas.

The Social World of Horse Race Gambling

In Lake Tahoe, there is a group of dedicated local residents who regularly wager on horse races. (I have gambled on horse races at Lake Tahoe for twenty years and consider myself a regular.) These regulars are joined by occasional patrons and by horse players from throughout the country, who combine vacations with betting, to form social worlds focused on horse racing. The majority of players are males with no particular skill for winning consistently.[4] While offtrack horse betting differs slightly from wagering at the racetrack, the two activities and their participants, for all intents and purposes, are interchangeable.[5]

Three of Lake Tahoe's largest casinos (Harrah's, High Sierra, and Caesars) offer offtrack betting on leading tracks in New York, Maryland, Pennsylvania, New Jersey, Florida, and California, with many of the races televised. Horse race wagering and sports betting are combined in an area of the casino called a *race and sports book,* where information on races and sports events is available and bets are taken and paid off. The books have separate betting windows for horse racing and sports; horse players and sports bettors congregate at long tables with comfortable seating near their respective wagering areas, thus separating themselves into two groups. Though in close proximity to each other, the two groups interact little. Books are also separate from other casino areas.

The description of a "typical" day at Harrah's race book illustrates the social world of offtrack gamblers. The following account of actual events and verbatim conversations, taken from my field notes,[6] will show the social structure in which the participants' relationships develop and flourish.

At 8:30 A.M., several men were congregated outside the entrance to Harrah's race book. Although the book would not open until 9:00, the self-proclaimed early birds were already discussing the day's races.

One inveterate player commented, "I see where Frankel's [a trainer] putting the Prince horse in the fifth at Hollywood; do you think he can run on the grass [a special kind of track surface distinct from the normal dirt track]?"

His companion replied, "Never really know until he tries it, but he's sure bred for the grass. Say, check out the third at Aqueduct; Syndicator's going for three straight, but's picking up 122 [pounds of weight]."

As new arrivals thronged the entrance, they greeted one another in a bantering manner. "Hi, Charlie, see you're back for more money; didn't get enough yesterday, huh?" "Shit, Bob, saw you cashing more tickets yesterday than I have in the last month. Hey, look who's here, the Stud—your woman let you come today?" "Hey, you guys know women are fun, but horses are serious business. Besides, you'd miss me— who'd brighten up your day?"

When the book opened, the men quickly lined up to get a copy of the *Daily Racing Form* [a newspaper devoted exclusively to horse racing activities]. The steady patrons—known to the management as regulars—were given the *Form* while others had to pay for it. Upon receiving the paper, the men broke up into small clusters and began intently scanning the past performances of the horses entered in the day's races. The entries were posted on large boards inside the race book. A "boardman" recorded changes such as scratches, overweights, or jockey changes, given to him by a national wire service. Although engrossed in studying the *Form*, regular patrons carried on running conversations with one another.

One racing fan mused, "You know, the first part of the day is the best. Anything's possible. You never know which horse might pop up or what new angle might appear." His track buddy added, "Yeah, remember back two years ago? We doped out that three-horse round-robin [three consecutive winners] and split four grand. Say, who do you like in the double at Monmouth?"

The first race at Aqueduct Race Track in New York began at 10:00 A.M. As post time neared, the men talked animatedly among themselves and exhibited varying degrees of indecision. When the gamblers arrived at their decisions they placed bets with ticket sellers located behind a large counter. A casino worker intoned, "Last call for New York. We're closing the first." A few last-minute players hurriedly placed their bets to avoid being "shutout."

One bettor jokingly remarked, "You can't start the race without me. You gotta let me lose! Please take my money."

After getting their bets down, the men returned to their cliques and resumed studying the *Racing Form* while continuing to discuss later races. When a voice came over the public address system to report that the call of the first race would begin, conversation hushed, and all faces turned toward the television monitors. During the first part of the race, the gamblers generally remained passive, glancing at one another with a raised eyebrow or tilted head to signify their horse's progress. When the horses entered the stretch, some gamblers clenched their fists and raised their hands in silent entreaty while others chanted: "One time." "Hang in there, baby." "Keep 'em going." "Don't stop now."

When the race call was completed, many of the losing gamblers angrily threw their now worthless tickets on the floor. The winning bettors slapped the tables, clucked to one another, punctuated the air with their fists, and lined up at the cashier's window to collect on their wagers. Losing gamblers offered plausible excuses: "The trainer stiffed 'em [did not adequately prepare the horse]. "The jock screwed up." "The horse just doesn't have it anymore." "The pig was in over his head." Occasionally the regulars offered commiserations." "That's a tough beat—you should've won." "Man, your luck is bad." "You had the best horse—if that's any consolation." After such exchanges, the gamblers took up the task of picking a winner in the next race.

Throughout the day, other regulars appeared in the race book and were greeted by name, usually with an accompanying quip. "Here's Ed the horse player. Tell us who you like so we know who to throw out [disregard]." "Hey John, you look hungover; maybe it'll improve your handicapping." Some of the gamblers were employed during the day and came in before work, during their lunch breaks, or on their days off. Typically, work discussions were oriented around how the jobs affected their ability to attend the race book: "I'm working swing this week so I'll be in early." "Shit, I'm back on days and won't be able to get in till Saturday." "Got most of my patients scheduled in the afternoon so I can catch the doubles."

When the races were over in New York, they were just starting in California. As the day wore on, the betting area was littered with losing tickets and discarded newspapers. For many, the promise of morning had been replaced by the reality of a losing day. After a particular displeasing loss, an inveterate gambler systematically tore his *Form* in shreds and shuffled toward the exit proclaiming, "I hate this shit!" He turned to a companion, winked, and whispered, "But I really love it." Regulars frequently discussed their losing streaks with each other and offered remedies: "Man, you're salty as hell [can't pick a winner]. Why don't you take a break? Stay at home for a while, go for a hike—anything, but stay out of here." "Stop betting those cheap sprints [races less than seven furlongs in length] and concentrate on distance races." "Hang in there, you're doing the right things; your luck will break."

Losing gamblers occasionally replenished their gambling funds by borrowing money from companions who responded to queries such as "Give me a hundred till my wife gets here in a couple of hours." "Loan me twenty till tomorrow." "Let me have fifty till next week."

The following incident occurred after the running of the seventh race at Hollywood Park. A veteran player jumped up, turned to his buddies, and exclaimed: "I got that one! Five bills on the nose; should get five or six to one. Whew! I really needed that one." The gambler's buddies slapped him on the back, ruffled his hair, gently punched his arm, and seemed pleased with his good fortune.

However, his pleasure was short-lived as the announcer indicated: "Hold all tickets. The stewards have called for an inquiry [into the outcome of the race]—the winner is involved."

The player anquished, "I'll never win. The winner's coming down. I know it." He paced towards the exit with a wild look in his eyes and stormed out, slamming the race book door behind him.

His buddies looked at one another until one of them with a shrug said, "Guess I better baby-sit the shithead—he might damage himself." He found the disconsolate gambler in the parking lot berating a security guard for asking him to quiet down. The good samaritan placated the perturbed guard and at the same time wrestled the distraught gambler to the side of the race book.

One of the regulars emerged from the book and yelled, "No change! The winner stands." The winning gambler slumped, his anger dissipated, and he looked at his companion with unbridled gratitude. The samaritan nodded in understanding.

After the last race at Bay Meadows in San Francisco, a cashier told the remaining patrons, "We're closing in five minutes." The players gathered up their belongings and made their way out. Several of them indicated they would return the following day: "See you tomorrow." "Sure, I'll be here unless I get smart overnight." "You guys study up; we'll get 'em tomorrow." As the patrons left, a group of sweepers arrived to clean the room and prepare the arena for another day of racing.

The Social World of Sports Betting

Three of Lake Tahoe's biggest casinos offer sports betting. As mentioned earlier, sports betting is combined with horse race wagering at race and sports books within the casinos. The three Lake Tahoe casino books take bets on all professional major league baseball, basketball, and football games, as well as on major college football and basketball contests. Although odds are quoted on National Hockey League contests, these games get little action.

Sports bettors at Lake Tahoe are predominately male, white, and between thirty and fifty-five years old, have been gambling since their teens, and come from diverse socioeconomic backgrounds. The vast majority are not professionals and depend on nongambling earnings for their livelihood. Sports bettors generally maintain active participation in spite of economic and social costs. As among horse players, there is a hard core of sports patrons who attend frequently and who consider themselves regulars.

All the casinos have large satellite dishes that can pick up televised games broadcast from locations throughout the United States. According to the casino personnel with whom I talked, the wholesale televising of games has stimulated sports wagering. Most of the Lake Tahoe bettors indicated that they prefer to wager on TV games because they like to see what actually occurs on the field. Watching televised games allows bettors to feel more personally involved with the action. Bettors are kept up to date on virtually all major sporting contests by a CQI sports ticker, an electronic strip that displays pertinent information. Generally the scores of baseball games are provided each half inning, football scores are given each quarter (more often for pro games), and basketball contests are updated every quarter. The ticker also provides a variety of other sports information, such as statistical averages, weather data, player trades, attendance figures, sport association meetings, and personnel changes. The sports ticker serves essentially the same function as the Dow Jones stock ticker.

The primary activity in this social world is obviously betting on sports events. Virtually every day of the year there are contests on which Lake Tahoe bettors can wager. The daily gambling sessions are governed by the starting times of the contests and therefore take on a regular character. On a typical weekday during baseball season, for example, the opening line is put up between 9:00 and 10:00 A.M. to correspond with a 1:00 P.M. starting time for East Coast day games. Bettors frequently get together at this time to compare numbers (odds or points offered by the various sports books) and to discuss wagering opportunities with other regulars. Some call acquaintances in Las Vegas or Reno to check the numbers being offered in those locations. The bettors generally divide into subgroups or cliques consisting of two to six people who sit together and talk sports, but some "lone wolves" (approximately 25 percent of the regulars) don't join any cliques. Though these bettors are usually approachable and responsive to questions, they prefer to remain separate from other bettors; often this distance allows them to concentrate fully on their betting.

After placing wagers on the early East Coast games, most of the bettors leave the book, returning later in the day. If, however, they have the time and inclination, they can watch televised games on monitors in the book. When there are West Coast day games, a flurry of activity occurs at 1:30 P.M. The next important starting time is at 4:30 P.M., when East Coast night games are scheduled to begin. Bettors once again congregate at the book, to wager on these games and to consider the odds on West Coast contests. Activity at the sports book then slows until just before 7:30 P.M., when many West Coast night games are scheduled to begin. Sports regulars frequently wait for the results of the East Coast night games before wagering on West Coast contests. After these night games start, the betting action is over until 9:00 A.M. the next day, when new numbers on new games are put up. During football and basketball season, of course, the time frames around which sports bettors orient their activities change.

Norms and hierarchies have developed to govern the behavior of sports bettors. Gamblers are expected to be well-behaved; loud talking, heated arguments, drunkenness, and unruly behavior are generally not tolerated. Blatant displays of emotion concerning the outcome of sporting events are discouraged, and losing bettors are expected to maintain a fairly neutral facade. Bettors form a hierarchy based on the amount of money they wager and the expertise they demonstrate. Individuals are categorized as dime ($1000) bettors, nickel ($500) gamblers, dollar ($100) players, or twenty-buck plungers, according to the amount they usually wager.[7] Dime bettors rarely associate with twenty-buck players. The bettor's general knowledge also affects his or her rank, with "wise guys" at the pinnacle and "bust-outs" at the bottom.

Interaction between sports bettors is regulated by established norms. Discussions between gamblers are expected to remain focused exclusively on sports. An individual's personal problems are not relevant within the context of sports betting. Typically bettors are expected to discuss with other regulars the criteria they used in deciding their selection. However, bettors are not obliged to reveal the exact amount of money they have wagered. Sports bettors usually share covert information such as player injuries, rumors of team dissension, and allegations of drug use. If financially able, regular sports bettors are expected to make juice-free (no interest) loans to fellow clique members. Loan recipients are required to repay in full as soon as possible or to arrange an appropriate payment schedule. Those who violate norms are subject to sanctions ranging from verbal rebukes to shunning. The latter is particularly serious, since Lake Tahoe is a small town and establishing new social networks is difficult. On occasion, gamblers who have been informally declared persona non grata (often for not paying loans) leave town to escape the disapprobation of their peers.

While most sports betting in America is done illegally, with wagers taken over the phone by bookies in a considerably less localized setting than a casino, many of the same social patterns shown by Lake Tahoe bettors have been identified in sub rosa sports betting groups outside of Nevada. Raymond D'Angelo, one of the first social scientists to study the world of illegal sports betting, described social dynamics markedly similar to those I observed among Lake Tahoe bettors. He, too, emphasized the significance of the long-standing relationships that develop among regular participants.[8]

The Social World of Poker Playing

Approximately forty players regularly participate in poker games in Lake Tahoe casinos. They typically play between three and five times per week and consider themselves regulars, frequently taking part in long-running games that may last several hours. Demographically, these regulars are comparable to offtrack bettors; they are generally over thirty-five, come from varying socioeconomic backgrounds, and have long histories of participation. Four or five women belong to the group of regular poker players. Most of the poker group don't depend on card winnings for their main income and thus fit the category of "outside-supported" players.[9] Between 15 and 20 percent (six to eight players) consider themselves professionals; that is, they derive most or all of their income from gambling. The occasionals and tourists who play at Lake Tahoe have similar backgrounds, with about 10 to 15 percent being women.

My lack of expertise in playing poker make it impractical for me to participate with the regular players of Lake Tahoe as I had with sports bettors and horse players. In order to investigate this group, therefore, I assumed an observer's role, spending many hours "hanging on the rail," an area set aside for spectators to watch the games.

Over the years, I had developed friendships with two regular poker players, who agreed to let me attend poker games with them and act as their "backer." This meant that I put up a share of their gambling funds in exchange for a percentage of the winnings. If one of them ran out of money (as happened on several occasions), I would supply further funds. As a backer, I was allowed to sit near the playing table when the poker room was not crowded. While observing the poker action, I was expected to remain unobtrusive and not disrupt the game; I could not talk to the participants while they were playing. Had I disrupted the players' concentration, my presence would not have been tolerated.

I made no attempt to conceal the fact that I was conducting a research project. The poker players soon became accustomed to me, and my observations did not seem to affect their behavior. My role as observer for much of the poker player investigation was that described by Raymond Gold, a leading qualitative methodologist, as one that "entirely removes a field worker from the social interaction with informants; here a field worker attempts to observe people in ways which make it unnecessary for them to take him into account."[10]

The structure of poker playing is very different from that of sports or horse race gambling. Participants don't play against the house but compete with one another; winning players profit directly from their tablemates' losses. Even in the competitive atmosphere of a poker room, however, regulars routinely share information among themselves. Poker players pride themselves on not being "tight-assed chickenshits" who are afraid to help other regulars. They openly discuss matters of mutual concern, calling such talk "weather reports," "scorecards," or "the daily news." Poker players frequently commented that they never entered big games without first checking out the competition with their poker pals.

Although poker players compete with one another, their goal is not to destroy other regulars but rather to "beat up" on outsiders. Poker players thrive on "live ones," newcomers who have money to lose. Poker regulars don't share information with nonregulars and consider them fair game for ruthless, competitive tactics. A veteran poker player described this attitude: "When I'm playing with a bunch of locals, I play soft and don't try to hammer them. But let a live one walk in and I pull out all the stops; I'll beat the shit out of him or her. I show no mercy."

Poker players are called upon to lend money more often than either horse or sports bettors. The ebb and flow of poker fortunes, combined with the irregular hours of many table games, increases the scope of lending. Poker players can be both borrowers and lenders in the span of a few hours. Playing against someone to whom money has been lent can decrease an individual's competitive zeal and result in soft play, that is, not raising or bluffing an opponent. Hayano observed a similar noncompetitive tendency when professional poker players were involved in games with close associates.[11] Refusing to extend a gambling loan if financially able is considered a serious breach of normative expectation. Social pressure also constrains players to repay their loans: those who develop a reputation for welching (not repaying debts) have a difficult time finding new loan sources and often find social relationships with other gamblers severely strained. In some cases, the debtor is forced to seek social networks in new areas.

Poker players typically believe that only other regulars can appreciate and understand their social world. They view themselves as being engaged in a highly specific activity, the intricacies of which are unknown outside the poker milieu, and find it difficult to discuss gambling experiences with persons unfamiliar with their activities. Communication with those who don't share a common perspective on poker is further complicated by the existence of a gambling argot, which creates specialized communication channels to which only other poker players have full access. The specialized nature of communication among players is reflected in the following quote from a poker devotee: "I know you degenerates heard it all before but one more time won't hurt. I was in a game with a live one. Had all the percentages figured perfectly; every angle was covered. I couldn't lose. Naturally I raise my ass off—I'm all in! Well, the idiot fills an impossible straight and my nuts are busted."

The Social World of Casino Gaming

For the purposes of this study, casino gaming includes those games that need a casino setting to achieve a significant level of continuing participation. Included in this category are blackjack, craps, roulette, and baccarat. Since significant participation in keno, bingo, slot machines, and policy occurs outside a casino environment, these games are excluded from this category and discussed instead with lotteries.

One of the main attractions of casino gaming is the fact that it is conducted in a totally self-contained environment—one that is clearly separate from ordinary life activities. Casino gaming typically attracts occasional players who come to casinos for periodic flings and who often look upon losses as an entertainment cost. Gambling meccas like Las Vegas and Atlantic City are frequently called adult Disneylands. For many occasional participants, the casino is a brief escape from real-life concerns. Casino gamers often believe that excursions to the tables relieve tensions brought on by stressful modern life-styles. The comments of an occasional casino player reflect a widely held viewpoint:

My job is tough. I'm well paid, but I have to always be on my toes. I can't let down, it's real competitive at the office. What I mean—it's a shitload of stress. So I take off a couple times a year and head for Vegas or Lake Tahoe. When I'm in the casinos I forget all about my job problems and, for that matter, any personal problems as well. For two, three days I'm in another world. No clocks, no routine, just the tables or an occasional show. Once in a while, I actually come out ahead. I soon get my fill of the gambling and head back home to take up my real life. I'm usually refreshed and recharged for another go at the real world. These gambling binges are cheaper than seeing a shrink—and a lot more fun. When I'm back in Fort Wayne hassling with the union rep, I keep thinking about getting back to the casinos.

Although the majority of casino gamers are occasionals, there is a hard core of regulars who find ways to sustain their participation. Most of these regulars live in close proximity to casinos. Lake Tahoe has a group of approximately fifty regulars who play casino games at least three days per week and a loyal cadre who do so every day. In general, regular casino gamers tend to be wealthier than participants in other forms of gambling. In Lake Tahoe, the regulars tend to be self-employed or retired, or they work for casinos; gambling activities do not seriously interfere with their employment routines. All of the regulars have developed some form of money management that allows them to remain in action for long periods of time. Many of these management practices involve restricting losses to set amounts or cutting back during losing streaks. Based on my observations of casino gaming in Lake Tahoe, I concur with the comments of sociologist David Oldman, who worked part-time in a gambling casino:

It is by no means automatic that a person who gambles regularly will eventually find himself in an economic mess. There are regular punters at the casino at which I worked for whom gaming is a way of life in that even their bread winning is organized so as to allow the maximum amount of time in the club and yet who have adopted strategies of play which involve regular but manageable expense. . . . One rather exceptional regular contented himself with playing one 10 p[ence] chip at a time at odds never greater than five-to-one and, moreover, he would only bet on about one spin of the wheel in five. His nightly entertainment cost him very little, but since he was a clerk in a local government office, he could afford very little. However, he was in no immediate danger of reaching economic crisis.[12]

While at the casino, regulars typically associate with one another and with casino employees such as dealers, croupiers, or pit bosses. Casino gamblers often learn the working schedules of these employees and play when their favorite dealer or croupier is on duty. Many regulars said they are treated royally by casino workers, who take their money "with a smile." Being known by name in a casino environment is an important sign of status. The casino gamers are spread throughout the casino and cannot be as easily identified as sports, horse, or poker bettors, who typically stay in one area. Regulars are most visible late at night and on weekdays during slow tourism periods (May, November, and February). At these times, they are often the only ones playing, and they banter good-naturedly with one another.

While occasional players view the casino as a place of temporary escape, regulars see it as a social haven where they can feel in complete control. The casino environment is predictable, and regulars can plan their activities accordingly. This viewpoint was expressed by a Lake Tahoe casino regular: "I know exactly what to expect when I go into the clubs. The games never change, the place is so predictable. I decide when to play and how much to put down. Nobody forces me into anything. I can quit any time I want, just cash in my chips and take off. At the clubs I'm in charge. I call the shots."

Regulars view the social world of the casino as a familiar place where they can feel at home. This perspective seems to follow established sociological principles. Sociologist Tomatsu Shibutani described the security of social worlds in a way that can be directly applied to the world of casino gaming: "Each is an arena in which there is some structure which permits reasonable anticipation of the behavior of others, hence an arena in which one may act with a sense of security and confidence."[13] Within the casino world, the actions of regular participants are not judged harshly. Failure at the tables will not result in rejection. One Lake Tahoe gambler commented, "No one ever gets kicked out of here for losing; in fact, this is a company of losers. It may sound strange but it gives one a secure feeling." Oldman found a similar sense of security among English casino regulars, who, even while losing, indicated that they felt a sense of belonging. One losing player in Oldman's study described his feelings about the casino as follows: "There I felt secure and comfortable. No great demands were made upon me. I knew I was destroying myself, yet at the same time, I had a certain sense of security." Oldman himself described similar feelings: "As a croupier, I also experienced this phenomenon. After working at the club for a few months, in spite of the fact that my class and regional and occupational identities were alien to other staff and punters, I found that to enter the club was to escape immediately and gratefully from all other problems of my existence into an entirely controllable world."[14]

Occasionals and regulars share a tendency to concentrate on one particular casino game and to perceive their favorite game as requiring skill. Once casino patrons find the game at which they feel most comfortable and knowledgeable, they show a demonstrable loyalty, devoting most of their gaming time to participation in that one game. For example, a confirmed crap shooter rarely plays twenty-one, a baccarat devotee will not often be found at the craps table, a twenty-one special-ist generally will not play roulette, and a roulette aficionado shows little interest in baccarat. Even while losing consistently, casino gamers demonstrate amazing game loyalty, as the following anecdote shows. A wealthy gambler lost $40,000 playing twenty-one. On the way out of the casino, his wife suggested that he play their last $500 at the roulette wheel. Aghast at such a suggestion, the gambler indignantly replied, "Why, I couldn't gamble our money on a game where I didn't have the edge."

Although casino games are commonly considered games of pure chance, players of casino games disagree. Instead they develop system-atic strategies of play and charts on which they base predictive theo-ries. Casino gamers do not passively deliver their money into the hands of blind fate but instead actively develop means of coping with the exigencies of gaming. They use rational methods to reduce the aleatory (chance) aspects of their gambling procedures. Twenty-one players de-velop counting strategies, craps players look for patterns that will indi-cate when the shooter is on a roll, roulette players keep intricate re-cords of numerical sequencing, and baccarat players tally the cards that have been shown.[15] The perception that casino games are a matter of rational skill rather than of chance is evident in the observation of an occasional casino patron: "The idea of 'playing' at casino games is inaccurate. They require a lot of hard work. I don't just sit back and watch while some hand of fate manipulates my cards. I try and figure out when to bet, how much to bet, when to quit, etc. What I'm trying to do is use my intelligence to increase the probability—notice I say prob-ability—of winning. I'm looking for an edge to exploit, but it takes a lot of effort to find it. I wouldn't call what I do 'playing.' "

Some twenty-one players, through great effort, are able to consist-ently profit from their gaming. This is accomplished through a strategy called "counting," in which players attempt to memorize the cards that have been dealt. When the cards remaining in the deck are favorable to the players, wagers are increased accordingly. Through skillful applica-tion of counting techniques and patient betting, players gain a slight statistical edge over the house.[16] Probably the most famous card counter is Ken Uston, a former executive of the Pacific Stock Exchange who formed blackjack teams that won millions of dollars from casinos throughout the world.[17]

Casinos have attempted to discourage card counting by increasing the number of decks used by twenty-one dealers and requiring frequent shuffles. These practices make it more difficult for players to keep an accurate count of the cards. However, skilled counters have adapted to these methods and are able to retain their statistical edge. Many casinos have therefore banned card counters from the premises. Some counters have donned disguises, or "beards," in an effort to continue their activities, while others have decided to sue. Several suits are pending in New Jersey to prohibit the exclusion of card counters from twenty-one games. Other successful twenty-one players have published their winning systems. There is a brisk market for such publications; two of the most popular are *Beat the Dealer* by Edward Thorp and *Professional Black Jack* by Stanford Woug.[18] It must be stressed, however, that only a few twenty-one players are able to make a living from their gaming. Still, the fact that professional blackjack players do exist encourages other players to apply rational techniques to their gambling at twenty-one.

The Social World of Lottery Ticket Purchasing

The final group of gamblers consists of participants in lotteries and related games, including keno, slot machines, numbers or policy, and bingo. This category includes diverse groups and environments, ranging from well-heeled players pulling the handles of $100 slot machines in a lavish casino, to welfare recipients buying fifty-cent numbers on a downtown street corner, to senior citizens playing bingo in a church basement. The common denominator in this varied category is that participants are all trying to win a large prize with a relatively small investment. Since these games are aimed at large audiences, the cost of individual participation is generally affordable and the level of risk is low. Most gamblers in this category do not perceive their participation as work-like and therefore do not develop elaborate game-playing strategies. Participation in this type of game does not involve lengthy learning, and as a rule players are less sophisticated than other gamblers.

The social rewards of participation vary considerably, from the close ties players may develop with one another in bingo to the relative isolation of lottery games, where solitary players buy tickets wherever it is convenient. In all these games, however, some interaction occurs between buyer and seller, and there is usually some discussion between participants as well. For example, the seemingly isolated and anonymous lottery ticket buyer often develops a continuing relationship with the clerk who sells the tickets and commonly talks about lottery experiences with other participants.

To some degree, the games within this category are interchangeable. Those who buy lottery tickets will tend to play slot machines, keno, or bingo if given the opportunity. Many avid lottery participants, before legalization, were numbers or policy players. In contrast, gamblers in the lottery and related games category rarely participate in sports betting, poker games, horse playing, or casino gaming. The majority of players in this group are occasionals whose lives are not significantly influenced by their gambling activities. Gambling for them is a recreational diversion and not a central life-concern. There are, however, some regular participants in this category for whom gambling takes on an added significance.

Bingo attracts a sizeable number of regulars who play several times per week. In attending bingo games at casinos, VFW halls, and churches, I have observed relationship patterns similar to those exhibited by horse players. Bingo players generally know one another by name and carry on lively conversations both before games and after closing. Conversations remain focused on their common activity, centering on the games being offered, where they are being held, who has won, and plans to meet at future games. Similarly, slot machine players who participate regularly often develop associations with other players as they share confidences and information about machines that are ready to pay off. Numbers and policy players associate continually with sellers and runners, also developing ongoing relationships with one another. Lottery clubs have emerged where participants pool their money in order to purchase large blocks of tickets. Club membership gives individuals opportunities to associate with other lottery ticket buyers. Small groups and partnerships for sharing and combining lottery ticket purchases have also developed. These relationships are all predicated on continuing lottery participation.

Though perhaps to a lesser degree than in other gambling categories, regular players in this category also attempt to use rational methods to increase the probability of winning. Slot machine regulars can be observed monitoring machines and carefully recording how much money has been played since the last large jackpot. Computer systems and sophisticated tables of random numbers are being used by regular lottery players in an effort to locate "hot numbers."[19] Policy and numbers players rarely have access to computers, but they do consult dream books and assorted charts to find numbers "due to hit." Bingo players practice mental games to increase their acuity so that they can play multiple cards and thus increase their chances of yelling "Bingo."

The Significance of Social Relationships

The relationships that develop within gambling worlds are especially significant for regular participants. Because interactions among regulars remain focused on gambling activities, relationships among these group members cannot be considered diffuse primary ties. Nevertheless, although gambling relationships are segmented and compartmentalized, retaining membership in betting groups is vitally important to regular participants. In many cases, through a process of socialization, gamblers have disengaged from other social groupings and maintain only a limited number of relationships outside of the gambling milieu.

Because membership in betting groups can be maintained only by continuing to participate, quitting gambling can be extremely disruptive.

Following is a brief synopsis of the process experienced by participants as they escalate their commitments to gambling and to other gamblers. Not all participants follow this progression; some (especially occasionals) never move beyond an early level of commitment. However, enough serious or regular players have had similar experiences to label the following a typical progression.

1. The stimulations of gambling are discovered.
2. Some financial success is achieved, thus heightening stimulation and encouraging continued participation.
3. The gambling world becomes familiar and safe, even in the face of decreasing stimulation (loss of money).
4. Social relationships focused on gambling develop within the social world.
5. Gambling relationships become increasingly important through a process of socialization and differential association.
6. Relationships can be maintained only through continued participation.
7. Gambling participation continues.

Summary

Gamblers typically concentrate on one of the five major gambling games: (1) horse race gambling, (2) sports betting, (3) poker playing, (4) casino gaming, and (5) lottery ticket purchasing. Those who consider themselves regular gamblers feel that gambling is an important part of their everyday lives, whereas occasionals view gambling as a recreational diversion. Most participants attempt to use rational gambling procedures and do not rely on luck or fate. Gambling is conducted in settings that can be considered social worlds. Within these worlds, gambling is the central activity and the main topic of discussion. Gamblers develop continuing relationships with other participants that for regulars often become an important source of social interaction. Such relationships, in most cases, can be maintained only by continuing to gamble.

Notes

1. John Koza conducted several studies of gamblers in which he demonstrated that the various games cannot be easily substituted for one another. Players typically remain loyal to their favorite game. His findings were reported in *Public Gaming Magazine* (March, April, May, and June 1984). Vicki Abt, James F. Smith, and Eugene M. Christiansen, in *The Business of*

Risk (Lawrence: University of Kansas Press, 1985), pp. 2 and 116, concluded that gambling is not monolithic behavior and that individual games attract different participants. In a recent study of the gambling habits of California lottery players, nearly 85 percent of those questioned indicated that they "seldom or never play other games." Roxanne Arnold, "Scratching for Ticket to Big Spin," *Los Angeles Times*, 22 July 1986, p. 1, sec. 1.

2. Alfred R. Lindesmith, Anselm Strauss, and Norman K. Denzin, *Social Psychology*, 4th ed. (Hinsdale, Ill.: Dryden Press, 1975), pp. 439–440.

3. Anselm Strauss, "A Social World Perspective," in *Studies in Symbolic Interaction*, vol. 1, ed. Norman K. Denzin, (Greenwich, Conn.: JAI Press, 1978), p. 121.

4. The Lake Tahoe regulars, like most horse players, lose money from their gambling activities. Igor Kusyszyn, in "How Gambling Saved Me from a Misspent Sabbatical," *Journal of Humanistic Psychology* 17 (Summer 1977): 19–34, estimates that in the long run, 95 percent of horse race gamblers lose.

5. All of the Lake Tahoe regulars had at various times in their lives regularly attended racetracks. For a discussion of the differences between offtrack and on-course gambling, see Marvin Scott, *The Racing Game* (Chicago: Aldine, 1968) pp. 136–146.

6. Some of the following account appeared in my article "Racetrack Buddy Relations: Compartmentalized and Satisfying," *Journal of Social and Personal Relationships* 3 (December 1986): 441–456.

7. A more detailed discussion of sports betting at Lake Tahoe is included in my work "Why Regular Gamblers Don't Quit," *Sociological Perspectives* 29 (July 1986): 357–378.

8. Raymond D'Angelo, "The Social Organization of Sports Gambling" (Paper presented at the Sixth National Conference on Gambling and Risk Taking, Atlantic City, November 1985).

9. See David M. Hayano, "The Professional Gambler: Fame, Fortune and Failure," *Annals of the American Academy of Political and Social Sciences* 474 (July 1984): 157–167.

10. Raymond Gold, "Roles in Sociological Field Observation," *Social Forces* 56(158): 212–223.

11. David M. Hayano, *Poker Faces* (Berkeley: University of California Press, 1982) pp. 123–127.

12. David Oldman, "Compulsive Gamblers," *Sociological Review* 26 (May 1978): 361.

13. Tomatsu Shibutani, "Reference Groups as Perspectives," *American Journal of Sociology* 60 (1955): 566.

14. Oldman, "Compulsive Gamblers," p. 366.

15. For a comprehensive discussion of how casino gamblers develop strategies to explain seemingly random occurrences, see David Oldman, "Chance and Skill: A Study of Roulette," *Sociology* 8 (1974): 407–426.

16. Richard Sasuly, *Bookies and Bettors* (New York: Holt, Rinehart & Winston, 1982), pp. 241–242.

17. Ken Uston, *Two Books on Black Jack*, (Wheaton, Md.: The Uston Institute of BlackJack, 1979).

18. Edward O. Thorp, *Beat the Dealer* (New York: Random House, 1962), and Stanford Woug, *Professional Black Jack* (Atlantic City: Boardwalker Magazine, 1980).

19. Several "experts" are selling their computerized systems for "scientifically" playing the lottery. See Charles Wheeler, "Selling Luck in Long-Shot Lotteries." *Insight*, 15 September 1986, p. 66.

Illegal
Gambling

Gambling is bigger than U.S. Steel.

Meyer Lansky, organized-crime figure and big-time gambler*

A review of the research on illegal gambling in America reveals a welter of inconsistent and conflicting data. Although widespread, illegal gambling is shrouded in misconception, mythology, and misinformation. And the established orthodoxy that exists on the nature and extent of illegal gaming is supported by little empirical or experiential evidence.

A major unresolved research issue is how much of a role organized crime plays in illegal gambling. Some researchers see the Mafia lurking behind every bookie, yet others refute the mob's participation in illegal gambling. The musings of Joseph Valachi, a lowly underworld "soldier," on the role of organized crime in illegal gaming have been accorded credence, when the observations of leading crime bosses on this subject are generally ignored. At the same time that some researchers depict illegal gaming operators as wholesale corruptors of police, others point out that contemporary bookmaking practices and federal involvement in gaming enforcement have made it unnecessary to bribe local officials. A mythology, perpetuated by the media and law enforcement, assumes that bookies routinely employ arm breakers to ensure debt collection. Field work evidence, however, has documented few instances of bookies actually resorting to violence in their business operations.

To understand illegal gambling, other important issues must also be considered. For example, dollar estimates of illegal gaming and the profit margins of illegal operators vary widely. In addition, criminal justice experts continue to argue whether or not gambling laws are enforceable. Paradoxically, although criminologists have long been

* Quoted in "The 1985 Gross Annual Wager, Part II: Revenue," by Eugene M. Christiansen, *Gaming and Wagering Business,* August 1986, p. 27.

skeptical of official reports of criminal activity, these very reports are used almost exclusively in gathering illegal gambling data. Perhaps most perplexing of all is the fact that, despite increasing state legalization, illegal gambling continues to be popular.

To clarify the clouded picture of illegal gambling, our discussion will address six questions:

1. Why does illegal gambling remain popular in a climate of increased state legalization?
2. How much is bet illegally?
3. What are the profit margins of illegal gaming operators?
4. What is the role of organized crime in illegal gambling?
5. What data sources are used in studying illegal gaming?
6. What are the prospects of enforcing antigambling laws?

The Popularity of Illegal Gambling

To the chagrin of many advocates of legalization, illegal gambling continues to flourish and remains an important presence on the American scene. Contrary to expectations, legalization has not sounded the death knell of illegal gambling. The reasons for the vitality of illegal gambling can be found in (1) its price advantages vis-a-vis legal gambling, (2) its superior service and convenience, (3) its control of sports betting, and (4) its growing acceptability.

According to a veteran bookmaker, illegal operators will always have an advantage over legal gambling because they can offer better odds; as he explained it, "the government tends to get stupid with greed and excessive taxation."[1] A classic example of the price advantage offered by illegal bookmakers occurred in New York, where the legislature imposed a 5 percent surcharge on winnings at legal Off-Track Betting offices. Horse players were sensitive to such price differentials, and many of them shifted their offtrack wagers to illegal bookies.[2] In another instance, illegal numbers operators responded to legalized lotteries by increasing their payoffs until their games were a better bet than the state-sponsored games. In addition, the Internal Revenue Service requires legal pari-mutuel operators to withhold a percentage of large winnings as advanced tax payments. Illegal bookies, of course, do not cooperate with IRS guidelines.

In many instances, bookmakers can provide better service and more convenience to their customers than can legal operations. Bookies extend credit, offer a wide variety of wagering opportunities, provide convenient phone betting, and ensure confidentiality. Much of the bookmaker's business is done on credit, a practice forbidden to legal operators. Bookmakers offer a smorgasbord of betting opportunities such as parlays (all the money from a successful wager is applied to another bet), round-robins (a percentage of a winning bet is placed on a future bet), and trains (a series of parlays)—none of which is possible in legal pari-mutuel wagering. Illegal gambling operators conduct most of their business over the phone at the bettor's convenience. Although some pari-mutuel systems operate phone betting lines, the customer must have previously deposited funds to cover the wager (no credit is extended), and phone service is available only during regular business hours. Moreover, illegal bettors can be certain (barring a police raid) that their wagers will not be recorded by government agencies. The new U.S. Justice Department ruling that all those who wager over $10,000 must be identified by gaming operators has driven many high rollers to the illegal gambling market.[3]

Except in Nevada, sports betting in the United States is controlled by illegal operators. At present, no other state has a viable plan to legalize sports betting. Although some have tentatively suggested a pari-mutuel system in which the bettors themselves establish the payoffs,[4] no such scheme is being seriously contemplated. The odds structure currently being offered is insufficient to ensure large profits for state-sponsored operators. This situation has been described by Richard Sasuly in his history of illegal betting:

> Is it possible to imagine football betting turned over, by law, to a nation-wide network of betting parlors? Conceivably. But the problem would come back to the matter of taxation. As pointed out earlier, the bookies $4\frac{1}{2}$ percent vigorish represents very efficient management. It is hard to believe that official betting shops could do better, if as well. Granting of licenses would, also, almost certainly, go along with a tax bite on the handle. Presumably the greater convenience of licensed betting shops might make some small tax tolerable. But how small is tolerable? If state and local taxes came to as much as 3 or 4 percent, the bite on the player's winnings would be painful. And the result would be inevitable. The illegal channels for sports betting are already established. Bettors would return en masse to bookmakers who offered a higher rate of return.[5]

Although legalizing sports betting is unlikely, American sport bettors are going to continue wagering on their favorite teams. For the time being, the market for their wagers is firmly in the hands of illegal operators.

Continuing legalization has fostered the acceptance of all gambling games. This acceptance has stimulated both illegal and legal gambling. As a result, the moral sanctions against illegal gambling have been effectively lifted. Such a trend was predicted by researchers working on the 1976 gambling commission report:

> Benign prohibition of gambling coupled with the continuing trend toward legalization may actually foster the growth of illegal gambling. According

to one Justice Department official, partial legalization makes it more difficult to conduct successful prosecution against illegal gambling. One reason is that partial legalization may have the effect of legitimizing in the public's mind the illegal games as well. . . . With only moderate interference from the law, illegal gambling could one day succeed in exploiting a market of new clients initiated into the world of gambling by their own State or local government.[6]

The Volume of Illegal Gambling

No hard data have been collected concerning the amount of money that is wagered illegally. This lack results from both the clandestine nature of the activity and the bureaucratic nature of data collection. Because of the illegalities involved, bookmakers and their customers are not going to accurately report their wagers (even if they keep accurate records). According to Eugene Christiansen, a leading researcher in this area, "information concerning the nature and dimensions of America's illegal gambling industry remains the exclusive property of impenetrable law enforcement bureaucracies, each with a particular vested interest in maintaining certain public perceptions of bookmaking and illegal numbers, and of illegal gaming and bingo and other games as well, that often appear to bear little relation to the available evidence."[7]

The significance of estimates regarding the amount of illegal gambling is more than academic: these figures are used by law enforcement agencies to justify funding and expansion of gambling enforcement. In addition, revenue estimates influence policy decisions concerning legalization; the argument that large financial resources are being siphoned off by illegal gaming operators and the state should get in on the action is often advanced by advocates of legalization.

Several legislative and administrative commissions, including Kefauver's investigation in the early 1950s, the 1967 Johnson crime commission, and the presidential commission of 1986, have struggled with the question of illegal revenues. Their estimates of annual wagering have ranged from $7 billion to $450 billion. Perhaps the most accurate assessment came from a Kefauver investigator, who stated, "No one has accurate figures regarding illegal gambling."[8] The $450-billion figure was offered by John Scarne, internationally known author of *Scarne's Complete Guide to Gambling*. The methodology he used to arrive at this gigantic figure was never clearly established. Since 1960, however, the $450-billion figure has been so bandied about in the media and before congressional hearings that it has taken on the weight of truth. Gambling estimators have often taken an anecdotal approach; a 1986 *Sports Illustrated* article, for example, quoted a Nevada gambling operator on the volume of sports betting: "In Nevada handle will exceed $1 billion. And there aren't even a million people in Nevada. We're such a tiny part of the whole thing. Figure it out! What do you think they're doing in Philadelphia, L.A., San Francisco? Extrapolate it out! The government says they think it's $40, $50 billion nationally. That's completely ridiculous! I know of a small rural town of thirteen thousand in Wisconsin, and that town alone has three illegal bookmakers. Three!"[9]

Early attempts to pinpoint the volume of illegal wagering used mainly police sources. These estimates were far lower than Scarne's $450-billion figure. In the late 1950s, FBI and Justice Department officials estimated annual illegal gambling at $10 and $11 billion respectively. In 1967, the Commission on Law Enforcement and the Administration of Justice, citing "agreement" among gambling enforcement officials, pegged illegal gambling at $7 to $50 billion per year. This broad range achieved respectability when, in 1969, Donald Cressey included it in his influential book *Theft of a Nation*. Cressey, who had access to the presidential commission's files, confirmed that there was "consensus among law enforcement officials" to justify the $7- to $50-billion estimate. Cressey admitted, however that it was "impossible to determine the calculations on which such estimates are made."[10] In spite of its absurdly wide range and uncertain methodology, the $7- to $50-billion figure remained a frequently cited estimate until the 1970s, when the first independent studies of illegal gambling were conducted.

In 1972, Oliver Quayle surveyed New York City to ascertain the amount of illegal gambling in that area. His survey revealed that illegal gambling was widespread and that a hard core of heavy bettors (those who gambled over $500 per year) accounted for much of the money illegally bet with bookies. Although these heavy bettors represented only 19 percent of the sample, they wagered almost 75 percent of the dollar volume.[11] In 1974, Alfred King of the Justice Department projected figures from Quayle's study of New York City to the nation as a whole, estimating national illegal gambling at between $29 and $39 billion.[12] The accuracy of King's projection was sharply questioned by researchers who doubted that New York City bettors would accurately reflect wagering trends. In 1975, the Survey Research Center (SRC) was commissioned by a federal gambling commission to put an end to the uncertainty over the volume of illegal gambling. The results of the nationwide survey were extremely controversial, however, and raised more doubts as to the amount of illegal wagering.

Using a national probability sample, the SRC researchers estimated the annual illegal handle at $5.1 billion. This extremely low estimate caused consternation among commission members, who refused to endorse the estimate. The commissioners cited political rather than methodological reservations: "If the survey's estimates of a $5 billion illegal handle are taken at face value, and the Justice Department's estimates of $29 billion–$39 billion are refuted, it might be construed that the incidence of illegal gambling in the United States is only one-sixth to one-eighth of what is commonly thought to be, and a significant reduction in enforcement activity would follow. Nothing could be further from the commission's intent."[13]

Researchers who have analyzed the center's findings all agree that gamblers who consistently wager large amounts (heavy bettors) were not included in the survey sample. This glaring oversight led to the inevitable conclusion that the SRC's estimate grossly underestimated the annual amount of illegal wagering.[14] In 1983, the Internal Revenue Service, using the 1976 SRC data, corrected for heavy betting and arrived at its own estimate of annual wagering. Its estimate of $15.79 billion for the year 1979[15]—far lower than prior figures—had some methodological basis and was generally considered credible.

The 1979 IRS figures have been updated and refined by Eugene Christiansen, a consultant to the New York City Off-Track Betting Corporation and one of the authors of *The Business of Risk*. His annual estimates, which appear in the magazine *Gaming and Wagering Business*, are generally considered the best source of illegal-gaming figures. His 1986 estimate fixed illegal gaming during the year at $32.31 billion, which represented 16.00 percent of gross wagering. Christiansen explained how he arrives at his figures: "Estimates of illegal gambling are not hard statistics in the sense that reported legal handles and revenues are hard statistics. They are, rather, the author's best guess, made from an exhaustive examination of the available data including all studies of the subject to date, information generated from law enforcement, and unsystematic polling of illegal operators of the magnitude and consumer cost of illegal gambling."[16]

In arriving at a total for illegal gambling, Christiansen included figures drawn from numbers games, horse books, sports books, and sports cards. While these are the major sources of illegal handle, the exclusion of revenues from illegal casinos seems an oversight. Even though the presence of legal Atlantic City casinos may have put illegal casino gaming out of business on the East Coast, evidence indicates that it continues in other parts of the United States. Personal experience and reliable informants both confirm that illegal casino gambling exists in the Midwest, South, and Southwest. Sociologist William Chambliss has documented the significant presence of illegal casinos in Washington State.[17] Failure to consider illegal casino revenues in an annual estimate may yield total dollar figures far short of actual amounts. Notwithstanding this caveat, Christiansen's figures are far more precise and objective than traditional gambling estimates drawn from "informed police sources" and stand as the best available reference source.

Profit Margins

Just as early estimates regarding the volume of illegal gambling were shrouded in mythology, so were those concerning the profits generated from gaming revenues. The 1967 President's Task Force on Organized Crime heard "evidence" from "knowledgeable" police agencies that illegal gambling operators took in one-third of gross gaming revenues. Although the task force did not "judge the accuracy" of this figure,[18] the figure was subsequently repeated in two influential works. Rufus King and Donald Cressey gave the 33⅓ percentage the academic stamp of approval in their respective books, *Gambling and Organized Crime* and *Theft of a Nation*. The authors also mistakenly assumed that gambling take was synonymous with gambling profit. Those familiar with gaming operations realize that a 33⅓ percent take from bookmaking and sports handle is impossible and that actual take must be reduced by operator expenses—a substantial reduction—to arrive at a final profit figure.

In 1973, Jess Marcum and Henry Rowen took exception to established profit estimates and placed illegal operators' take at approximately 14 percent of revenues.[19] The researchers presented no empirical evidence to substantiate their estimate. In 1979, the FBI estimated profit margins of bookmakers taking sports and horse bets at 15 percent of gross wagering.[20] Though this estimate was more realistic than earlier figures, it was criticized in light of the 4.5 percent retention rate that characterizes legal sports bookmaking in Nevada. The discrepancy between the two figures—specifically, the substantially higher figure for illegal operators—absurdly suggests that bettors using illegal bookmakers are less knowledgeable and lose more than those using legal ones.

Finally, in 1983, the Internal Revenue Service, drawing on a variety of independent sources (not only enforcement officials) developed a credible estimate of illegal take:[21]

Game	% Take
Numbers	49–52
Horses	16.7
Sports	4.5
Sports Cards*	60

Christiansen uses similar percentages to arrive at illegal retention figures in his highly regarded annual estimates of gaming revenue.

In order to understand the profit margins of illegal gaming operators, one must consider the substantial costs of doing business. Peter Reuter

---

* A betting scheme in which the participant must correctly select several winning teams. The payoffs are far lower than the probability of correctly picking the teams.

and Jonathan Rubinstein, after conducting an extensive and comprehensive study of illegal gambling in New York, discussed bookmaker profit margins:

> The estimated return for a bookmaker handling sports bets is usually estimated at 4.4 percent of total wagering. But in fact, the bookmaker's gross profits are much smaller, because he must share some of them with his runners; because of clerical cheating or incompetence, difficulty or delay in collecting runners' or customers' debts; and because baseball betting is less profitable than football or basketball. In addition, bookmakers risk being "middled"—highly informed players can exploit differences in bookmakers' lines on a given day so that the bookmakers are unable to lay off their bets at the original terms. Moreover, a bookmaker also incurs such expenses as labor (clerks are paid $250–400 per week and managing clerks $500), rent ($100 per week), and buying line information. A well-run operation should have a long-run return of 0.5 to 1 percent of total wagers.[22]

Sources familiar with sports bookmaking have pointed out that it is a risky business; in the short run, profit margins can be completely wiped out.[23] Although bookmakers strive to equalize wagers, this is not always possible, and they often must take a financial position, in effect, gambling themselves. It is not uncommon for bookmakers to become financially insolvent after a string of losing weeks. When this occurs, they must shut down their bookmaking business until they locate sufficient capital to resume operation. The exigencies of booking sports bets was clearly demonstrated in the case of the Delaware state lottery. In December 1976, the country's only legal sports betting operation outside of Nevada was Touchdown II, a sports card operation run by the Delaware Lottery Commission. After two weeks, the operation was in a precarious position because large sums of money had been wagered by "professional gamblers." Fearing a possible loss, lottery operators permanently canceled the sports betting and attempted to refund the wagers. Subsequently, the Delaware Supreme Court ruled they must pay off winning bettors. This fiasco stands as a testimonial to the difficulty and risk of running a sports betting operation.

Even though numbers games return a large percentage of the take to the operator, they are also expensive to operate. The cost of maintaining a numbers bank (payment center), paying numbers runners and administrative help, surmounting cheating by employees, and absorbing unexpected player wins is high. This situation is compounded by intensive competition between numbers operators, competition that often results in increased payoffs to participants. Although there are no hard data, Reuter and Rubinstein, after conducting longitudinal and ethnographic studies of bookmaking practices, concluded that, in their sample of numbers banks, the average profit was 6.4 percent.[24] Even though the exact profit margins of illegal gambling operators have not been identified and vary according to the game, operator profits are clearly not as large as was previously thought.

The Mob and Illegal Gambling

The idea that organized crime occupies a central role in illegal gambling has become orthodoxy. Proponents of the idea maintain that organized crime is financed in large part by revenues derived from illegal gambling and that monopolistic control of sub rosa gambling markets is maintained through the discriminate use of violence and bribing of law enforcement officials. The government's definition of organized crime (often used synonymously for the Mafia or La Cosa Nostra) can be found on the first page of the 1967 presidential commission's report:

> Organized crime is a society that seeks to operate outside the control of the American people and their governments. It involves thousands of criminals working with structures as complex as those of any large corporations, subject to laws more rigidly enforced than those of legitimate governments. The actions are not impulsive but rather the result of intricate conspiracies carried on over many years and aimed at gaining control over whole fields of activity to amass large profits.[25]

The report further stated that the high profits generated by organized crime could in large part be directly traced to illegal gambling.

The Kefauver commission in 1950, the McClellan committee in 1962 and the president's commission in 1967 essentially agreed that illegal gambling provided organized crime with its working capital. Using these monies, the mob allegedly diversified its interests into a variety of areas, including legitimate business. Donald Cressey, in 1969, echoed these sentiments when he said, "The members of La Cosa Nostra control all but a tiny part of the illegal gambling in the United States," and, further, that "the profits are hugh enough to make understandable the fact that any given member of La Cosa Nostra is more likely to be a millionaire than not."[26]

President Nixon, in a 1969 statement that was to become a criminal-justice axion, contended that "gambling income is the lifeline of organized crime. If we can cut it or constrict it, we will be striking close to the heart."[27] In 1974, a Justice Department official stated the government's position on illegal gambling: "It is the unanimous conclusion of the President, the Congress, and law enforcement officials that illegal organized gambling is the largest single source of revenue for organized crime. . . . It provides the initial investment for narcotic trafficking, highjacking operations, prostitution rings, and loan-shark schemes."[28]

Since 1974, the orthodox position vis-a-vis illegal gambling and organized crime has remained intact. In 1986 the chairman of the President's Commission on Organized Crime, Irving Kaufman, identified illegal gambling as the "principle source of income" for organized crime. Therefore, Kaufman stated, the goal of the commission "must be to devise ways to prevent the criminals from sharing in the profits from gambling—legal or illegal."[29]

The concept that gambling income is the lifeline of the mob, although deeply ingrained in the orthodox perceptions of government officials, gambling enforcement agents, and a segment of the academic community, has never been accepted by the American betting public. Based on personal experience and discussions with hundreds of illegal bettors, the following comment by a longtime sports bettor appears representative of the public's perception of illegal gambling:

> I've heard all the talk about the Mafia and bookmakers. Well, I don't believe it. I think it's all government propaganda to discourage betting. I've known at least twenty bookies—some of them were my good friends— and only one had any mob connection, and a minor one at that. Bookies are no different from anyone else. Most of them are gamblers who are looking for an edge. They're working stiffs, not guys with ten-dollar cigars and thousand-dollar coats. And all this arm-breaking stuff is pure Hollywood. I've run up a big tab, even walked (welched) on a few bets, but no one ever threatened me. I usually paid up in the end, because if I didn't the word would get out and no bookies would take my action. And that's bad.

Although social scientists generally are unwilling to accept the putative viewpoint, in the case of illegal gambling it may be a fairly accurate one. Researchers who have done independent studies of illegal gambling have also refuted the orthodox view that illegal gambling is inevitably intertwined with organized crime, presenting a view more in line with that of the sports bettor quoted above. Reuter and Rubinstein's portrayal of illegal gambling is typical of those who have conducted field studies of illegal gambling:

> Most bookmakers are just that—bookmakers; perhaps not the worthiest of citizens but certainly not the terrifying monsters of whom we are told. They have few involvements in other criminal activities such as narcotics trafficking or fencing. It is true that they are involved with loan sharks— but as customers themselves, rather than as providers of customers. There is very little use of violence in bookmaking, either for purposes of restricting competition or for disciplining of recalcitrant customers. . . . There is nothing to suggest that bookmakers are part of a coercive cartel, and considerable evidence suggests that they are involved in a risky and highly competitive business. We are certain that there is no territorial control of entry into the business.[30]

In an observational study of two established bookmaking operations, Raymond D'Angelo also found little evidence of mob influence and no instances of bookmakers resorting to violence.[31]

Further evidence of the tenuous link between organized crime and illegal gambling can be found in wire-tapped conversations between leading crime figures. An analysis of recorded conversations between the crime bosses Angelo (Gyp) DeCarlo and Sam (the Plumber) De-Cavalcante and their associates indicated that illegal gambling (mostly numbers banks) was a sideline that generated only modest profits. The crime syndicate heads made no effort to control gambling; they did not restrict entry nor did they establish exclusive territories.[32] After culling through the files of various agencies, Annelies Anderson also concluded that large crime families had only limited control over illegal gambling.[33] Reuter and Rubinstein presented additional evidence to refute the notion that a cartel of operators monopolizes illegal markets, citing the example of an abortive attempt by bookmakers to increase their profits. Prior to the start of the major league season, several large bookmakers reduced their odds on baseball games. The customers reacted by taking their business elsewhere. After suffering a severe drop in baseball wagering for three weeks, the bookmakers cried uncle and returned to the earlier and less profitable odds structure.[34]

Data Sources

Discrepancies in the orthodox view of illegal gambling call into question the data sources used in developing such an orthodoxy. The orthodox view, which assumes that organized crime plays a dominant role in illegal gambling, was developed almost exclusively from reports by gambling enforcement agencies. The various investigation committees and president's commissions provided an influential forum for officials to present their own viewpoints. With few exceptions, public hearings on organized crime in the last twenty-five years have served to validate the opinions of law enforcement officials. Reuter and Rubinstein described the "investigation" practices of the Kefauver Committee, practices that established a precedent for later public hearings on organized crime:

> How did the Committee go about forming these conclusions? What kinds of information did it gather? The answer to these questions raises serious doubts about the validity of its approach and the reliability of its analysis. The Committee recruited a large staff of lawyers and investigators, whose main function was to establish contact with local officials and interested groups, learn their views of local problems and then prepare them to testify for the Committee. The Committee staff initiated no collection of new information, nor did it independently test the assertions of local law enforcement officials. It was assumed that the answers offered by local officials to questions about who "ran" gambling in their towns were correct. No effort was made to analyze the costs of operating these syndicates, the flows of money or the profit margins. It was asserted on all

sides that illegal gambling was a very lucrative monopoly. Since knowledgeable people from all parts of the country seemed to agree, the Committee decided that it must be so.[35]

When public officials testify before legislative and administrative bodies, they rarely present independent evidence to substantiate their statements. Often, to buttress their conclusions, they cite information developed within their own departments. The analytical ability of police departments is open to serious doubt, especially in cases that might shake prevailing doctrine. Moreover, the assumed connection between illegal gambling and organized crime enhances the status and power of those involved with the enforcement of gambling laws, giving them a vested interest in perpetuating belief in that connection.

Traditionally, academics who have studied organized crime have done so by examining the reports of legislative and administrative committees, which in many cases are based exclusively on police reports. Donald Cressey, for example, indicated that his sources consisted of "materials submitted to the Commission" and interviews with "knowledgeable policemen and investigators."[36] Although research into organized crime is fraught with personal and methodological peril, reliance on information from police sources is questionable.

That police reports must be viewed with skepticism and that such reports often tell more about the police than about the criminals, is a sociological axiom that applies to much of the research into organized crime. After analyzing twenty influential criminology books, J. Galiher and J. Cain concluded that "authors of criminology textbooks have purveyed a common belief in the conspiratorial threat by organized crime usually without indicating the limitation of their sources. Since social scientists have largely limited themselves to secondary sources of data, particularly government documents, in their analysis of organized crime, they could not be expected to give an independent challenge to such sources."[37] Chambliss further stated that reliance on "information from police departments, attorney generals' files and grand jury records . . . has distorted our picture of organized crime."[38] More recently, researchers Peter Reuter, Rick Aneskiewicz, John Dombrink, and William Thompson, as well as Jay Albanese have criticized "mainline" organized-crime research for its failure to consider independent and alternative data sources.[39] One important and readily available data source that has been neglected by researchers is participants.

Researchers who generate their own data, rather than relying on official sources, present a far different picture of organized crime than does the government. Joseph Albini, and Francis Ianni and Elizabeth Reuss-Ianni were among the first to conduct empirical studies of organized crime and to challenge the government's view that twelve crime families (La Cosa Nostra) controlled organized crime in the United States.[40] Their pioneering studies of criminal organizations, done in the early 1970s and conducted from an ethnographic perspective, refuted the existence of a national cabal of Mafiosi who dominate organized crime. From a similar perspective, Chambliss, in 1975, called for organized-crime researchers to eschew official reports and instead look for data sources in the field.[41] His own study of Seattle crime activities— one that portrays organized crime differently than traditional research does—is one such example.

Unfortunately only a few researchers have heeded Chambliss's advice. Reuter and Rubinstein used independent sources such as police informants and real-life bookies to challenge the orthodox view of organized crime.[42] Raymond D'Angelo, using no official police contacts, conducted an excellent in-depth study of two ongoing illegal gambling networks.[43] In it, he described bookies and their customers from an insider's perspective, a perspective that had been carefully developed over several years. The picture that emerged from his study of sub rosa gambling groups is one of ordinary people who have made contact with each other through their interest in sports betting. Their betting networks are not linked to organized crime, and mutual interest rather than coercion facilitates the collection of betting debts. Although some with mob connections do participate in bookmaking, these do not dominate the market. Most bettors know several bookies and shop around for the most favorable odds, especially when contemplating a large wager. D'Angelo shows bookmaking to be a financially risky undertaking and not a surefire money-maker and portrays bookies not as cold-blooded automatons with all the odds figured out but as flesh-and-blood gamblers looking for an edge.

D'Angelo's study is unique in that it delineated the social relationships that developed among the various participants. These relationships are neither predatory nor particularly competitive. Bettors and bookies share an abiding interest in sports and develop long-standing associations on that basis. These associations often transcend monetary considerations and help to sustain participation. If a more authentic picture of illegal gambling is to be developed, it will come from first-hand studies like D'Angelo's rather than from information derived exclusively from police sources and their informants. Most illegal gamblers (and, for that matter, bookies) have never been busted, fingerprinted, or indicted, and their story needs to be told.

Enforcing Gambling Laws

Both the public and agents of social control maintain that legal sanctions will not stop gambling, that people will continue to gamble regardless of the legality of such activities, and that enforcement is an ineffective deterrent. Police and prosecutors talk of enforcement as fingers in the dike, while the public maintains that it is impossible to legislate morality. This perspective has led to reduced enforcement, light sentences for those actually charged, and massive violations of gambling laws by the nation's bettors. In 1975, the Boston police commissioner stated in testimony before the federal gambling commission that gambling laws "are unenforceable laws which nobody wants enforced" and that his police department "has been unable to permanently end any bookie operators as of this date."[44] The trend toward decriminalization of gambling laws has continued as the priority given enforcement has dropped. Recently a federal strike force chief stated that authorities "do not prosecute bookmakers unless there is a clear and strong organized-crime presence."[45]

Not all researchers agree that gambling laws are unenforceable. Thomas Mangione and Floyd Fowler, after analyzing 1976 survey data, concluded that the public would support more stringent enforcement of gambling laws. Contending that gambling laws could be effectively enforced if police and prosecutors would coordinate their efforts, they suggested various steps to bring about that coordination.[46] As of yet, their suggestions have not been followed, and gambling enforcement remains on the back burner in most jurisdictions.

An important aspect of gambling enforcement is the issue of police corruption. The Kefauver committee, in 1951, uncovered clear evidence of widespread police corruption with respect to illegal gambling enforcement. Payoffs had become a routine practice that typically involved monthly payments to police groups or pads. Twenty years later, the Knapp commission uncovered similar payoff systems within the New York City Police Department.[47] Developments in the last fifteen years, however, have significantly reduced the prevalence of payoffs for protection from gambling enforcement.

New bookmaking practices, the federal incursion into gambling enforcement, and the emergence of narcotics as a major enforcement concern have reduced the need for bookmakers to bribe local officials. The emergence of telephone betting and the availability of sports results did away with large betting parlors whose obvious visibility required police payoffs. In the 1960s and 1970s, federal authorities, buttressed by enabling legalization, entered gambling enforcement en masse. Strike forces were formed in many major cities. No longer were local police charged with the sole responsibility for gambling enforcement. Local police could therefore no longer guarantee illegal operators protection from prosecution. In many instances, local police departments simply got out of the business of gambling enforcement and let federal and state officials take over. Many indications suggest that the federal effort at gambling enforcement was comparatively short-lived. In recent years, the number of both applications for federal wire taps and gambling convictions have declined significantly. Federal enforcement efforts have instead been directed at prosecuting the heads of crime syndicates that may have peripheral links to illegal gambling.[48]

Narcotics enforcement has become a high priority for federal, state, and local police agencies, whereas gambling enforcement, in large measure, has become a dead issue.[49] In today's climate of decriminalization, bookmakers have no reason to pay off police. In the absence of tempting bribes from "friendly" bookies, police corruption with regard to gambling has been reduced and is no longer a structural part of illegal gambling. The observations of a sixty-five-year-old bookmaker, who has been in the business for over forty years, illustrate the new era in police/bookie relationships:

> I used to pay a police pad regularly. Each month I gave the bag man—a real bruiser cop—five hundred bucks. Some months I couldn't give him the full five hundred. But he usually let it slide, probably was making enough from the other bookies. Then I went tap city and got out of the business for five years. When I started up again I naturally expected to start paying the pad. Well, the other bookies I knew said that was all a thing of the past, the feds were now doing the busts, and you didn't want to bribe them. So I just forgot about paying anyone. Been over fifteen years since I've paid the police for protection. Nowadays I got two cops as customers. Nice guys too. Regular losers, always picking their favorite teams no matter what the spread. You know I got busted only once since I started up again. Paid a thousand-buck fine and did some—what they call community service. That's a lot cheaper than the old days.

Summary

Illegal gambling is a widespread social phenomenon. Illegal operators have retained a loyal betting clientele by offering higher odds, more services, and greater convenience than state-run operations. Early estimates as to the volume of illegal wagering and the profits therefrom (drawn largely from police reports) have been notoriously inaccurate and in many cases grossly exaggerated. Using a variety of information sources, Christiansen estimates that in 1986, $32 billion was wagered illegally. Profits derived from illegal operations remain largely unknown but are clearly not as large as is commonly assumed. For example, an exhaustive study of large sports betting operations in New York City done by Reuter and Rubenstein demonstrated that 1 percent of total wagers was a common profit margin.

Although law enforcement officials have long maintained that organized crime "controls" illegal gambling, there is little empirical evidence to support this contention. On the contrary, actual field studies of bookmakers have not found a pervasive mob influence. Even though organized crime is undoubtedly involved to some extent in illegal gambling, it doesn't dominate the market. Field investigations have revealed bookmakers as small businessmen involved in a risky endeavor and indicate that mutual trust rather than violence ensures the collection of gambling debts. Traditional research efforts have relied on the accounts of law enforcement officials, who often have their own reasons for exaggerating the role of organized crime in illegal gambling. The insider's perspective has typically been overlooked in such studies. When this perspective is considered, a new picture of illegal gambling emerges.

Gambling has been decriminalized as belief in the effectiveness of antigambling laws has waned. The federal government has largely supplanted local agencies in the occasional enforcement of gambling laws. These developments indicate that the widespread bribery of police to overlook illegal gambling has largely become a thing of the past.

Notes

1. Roger Larson, *No Winners* (St. Paul: Ipse Dixit Press, 1978), p. 89.
2. In effect, the 5 percent surcharge has stimulated illegal bookmaking. This finding was reported by Eugene M. Christiansen and Michael D. Shagan, "The New York Off-Track Betting Law: An Exercise in Selective Decriminalization," *Connecticut Law Review* 12 (Summer 1980): 854–869.
3. I. Nelson Rose, "Turning in the High Rollers: The Impact of New Cash Regulations," in *Betting on the Future: Gambling in Nevada and Elsewhere* (Reno: Nevada Public Affairs Review, 1986), pp. 21–26.
4. The most vocal advocate of a pari-mutuel system for sports betting is William R. Eadington, "Sports Betting and Pari-Mutuel Wagering Systems" (Paper presented at the Sixth National Conference on Gambling and Risk Taking, Atlantic City, November 1984).
5. Richard Sasuly, *Bookies and Bettors* (New York: Holt, Rinehart & Winston, 1982), p. 245.
6. Patricia Helsing, "Gambling: The Issues and Policy Decisions Involved in the Trend toward Legalization," in *Gambling in America: Final Report of the Commission on the Review of the National Policy toward Gambling,* app. 1 (Washington, D.C.: U.S. Government Printing Office, 1976), p. 778.
7. Eugene M. Christiansen, "Illegal Gambling," in Vicki Abt, James F. Smith, and Eugene M. Christiansen, *The Business of Risk* (Lawrence: University of Kansas Press, 1985), p. 235.
8. President's Commission on Law Enforcement and the Administration of Justice, *Task Force Report: Organized Crime* (Washington, D.C.: U.S. Government Printing Office, 1967), p. 3.
9. "Gambling: America's National Pastime?" *Sports Illustrated,* 10 March 1986, p. 32.
10. Donald R. Cressey, *Theft of a Nation* (New York: Harper & Row, 1969), p. 74.
11. Oliver Quayle, *A Study of Betting on Sports in New York City: Study #1493* (New York: Oliver Quayle Co., 1972).
12. Christiansen, "Illegal Gambling," pp. 238–239.
13. "Survey of American Gambling Attitudes," in *Gambling in America: Final Report of the Commission on the Review of the National Policy toward*

Gambling, app. 2. (Washington, D.C.: U.S. Government Printing Office, 1976), p. 65.

14. Ibid., pp. 1–15.
15. U.S. Treasury Department, Internal Revenue Service, *Income Tax Compliance Research* (Washington, D.C.: U.S. Government Printing Office, 1983), pp. 198–211.
16. Eugene M. Christiansen, "The 1985 Gross Annual Wager, Part I: Handle," *Gaming and Wagering Business,* July 1986, p. 30.
17. William Chambliss, *On the Take* (Bloomington: University of Indiana Press, 1978).
18. President's commission, *Task Force Report: Organized Crime,* p. 3.
19. Jess Marcum and Henry Rowen, "How Many Games in Town? The Pros and Cons of Legalized Gambling," *The Public Interest* 36 (Summer 1974): 25–52.
20. Peter Reuter, *Disorganized Crime.* (Cambridge, Mass.: MIT Press, 1983), p. 198.
21. Christiansen, in "Illegal Gambling," pp. 246–247, considers the 1983 IRS report to be methodologically sound.
22. Peter Reuter and Jonathan Rubinstein, *Illegal Gambling in New York: A Case Study in the Operation, Structure and Regulation of an Illegal Market* (Washington, D.C.: U.S. Government Printing Office, 1982), p. xvii.
23. See, for example, Sasuly, *Bookies and Bettors,* and Larson, *No Winners.*
24. Reuter and Rubenstein, *Illegal Gambling in New York,* p. 100.
25. President's commission, *Task Force Report: Organized Crime,* p. 1.
26. Cressey, *Theft of a Nation,* p. 65.
27. Quoted in Peter Reuter and Jonathan Rubenstein, "Fact, Fancy and Organized Crime," *The Public Interest* 53 (Fall 1978): p. 47.
28. Ibid., p. 47.
29. John Dombrink and William N. Thompson, "The Report of the 1986 Commission on Organized Crime and Its Implications for Commercial Gaming in America," in *Betting on the Future: Gambling in Nevada and Elsewhere* (Reno: Nevada Public Affairs Review, 1986), p. 70. It should be noted that the full commission took a different position than its chairman by concluding that narcotics had supplanted gambling as the principle source of income for organized crime.
30. Reuter and Rubenstein, "Fact, Fancy and Organized Crime," p. 49.
31. Raymond D'Angelo, "The Social Organization of Sports Gambling: A Study in Conventionality and Deviance" (Ph.D. diss., Bryn Mawr University, 1983).
32. Reuter and Rubenstein, in *Illegal Gambling in New York,* pp. 6–7, report that although these valuable tapes are available to a variety of researchers, they have never been adequately investigated.
33. Annelise Anderson, *The Business of Organized Crime* (Stanford, Calif.: Hoover Institute Press, 1979).
34. Reuter and Rubenstein, *Illegal Gambling in New York,* pp. xviii–xix.
35. Ibid., p. 2.
36. Donald R. Cressey, "Methodological Problems in the Study of Organized Crime as a Social Problem," *Annals of the American Academy of Political and Social Sciences* 374 (November 1967): 104.
37. J. Galiher and J. Cain, "Citation Support for the Mafia Myth in Criminology Textbooks," *American Sociologist* 8 (May 1974): 74.
38. Chambliss, *On the Take,* p. 3.
39. Peter Reuter, "Methodological and Institutional Problems in Organized Crime Research," and Rick Aneskiewicz, "Corruption and Organized

Crime: Historical Trends and Contemporary Issues" (Papers presented at the Annual Meeting of the American Society of Criminology, Atlanta, October 1986). See also Dombrink and Thompson, "Report of the 1986 Commission on Organized Crime," p. 71, and Jay Albanese, *Organized Crime in America* (Cincinnati: Anderson Publishing, 1985).

40. Joseph L. Albini, *The American Mafia: Genesis of a Legend* (New York: Appleton-Century-Crofts, 1971), and Francis Ianni and Elizabeth Reuss-Ianni, *A Family Business* (New York: Sage, 1972).

41. William Chambliss, "On the Paucity of Original Research on Organized Crime: A Footnote to Galiher and Cain," *American Sociologist* 10 (February 1975): 36–39.

42. Reuter and Rubenstein's ethnographic study of New York bookmakers, *Illegal Gambling in New York*, is probably the most comprehensive "non-traditional" study of the relationship between organized crime and gambling yet published.

43. D'Angelo, in "The Social Organization of Sports Gambling," used participant observations to enhance the authenticity of his research.

44. Peter Reuter, "Enforceability of Gambling Laws," in *Gambling in America: Final Report of the Commission on the Review of the National Policy toward Gambling*, app. 1 (Washington, D.C.: U.S. Government Printing Office, 1976) p. 561.

45. Jane A. Morrison, "Illegal Bookmaking Helps Fill Coffers of Organized Crime," *Reno Gazette Journal*, 21 July 1986.

46. Thomas W. Mangione and Floyd J. Fowler, "Citizens' Views of Gambling Enforcement," in *Gambling in America: Final Report of the Commission on the Review of the National Policy toward Gambling*, app. 1 (Washington, D.C.: U.S. Government Printing Office, 1976), pp. 240–300.

47. For an excellent discussion of the Knapp commission's investigation of the New York Police Department, see Alan Kornblum, *The Moral Hazards*, (Lexington, Mass.: D.C. Heath, 1976).

48. Reuter and Rubenstein, *Illegal Gambling in New York*, pp. xii–xiii.

49. The 1986 Report of the President's Commission on Organized Crime (Washington, D.C.: U.S. Government Printing Office, 1986), p. 637, clearly indicates that the government has lost interest in gambling enforcement.

Compulsive Gambling

In a way it is worse than the plague or the quake, for it destroys the soul within. A person without the soul is a burden upon the earth. No doubt war against gambling is not so simple as war against plague or earthquake distress. In the latter there is more or less cooperation from the sufferers. In the former the sufferers invite and hug their sufferings. To wean the gambler from his vice is like weaning the drunkard from the drink habit. This war against gambling is therefore an uphill task.

Mohandas Gandhi*

When friends, colleagues, and acquaintances learn that I am doing research on gambling, they invariably want to know about compulsive gamblers. How many did I know? How much did they lose? Why can't they quit? And finally, they want to know if I am a compulsive gambler. While admitting they have never known a flesh-and-blood compulsive gambler, they are sure that compulsive gambling is a serious social problem. To the disbelief of my questioners, I am unable to satisfy their curiosity: I don't know many compulsive gamblers. To be sure, I know many hard-core gamblers who have experienced a variety of problems related to gambling, but they don't consider themselves compulsive, and I don't either. When pressed, I will acknowledge that Gamblers Anonymous members firmly believe that they are compulsives, but I am not sure that many of them should be so labeled. In these instances, I understand the comment of David Oldman, professor and part-time croupier, who, when questioned about compulsive gamblers, said that he found them as "scarce as the yeti."[1] In this chapter, I hope to clarify this issue by (1) describing how compulsive gambling came to be defined as an illness, (2) depicting the current model of compulsive gambling and questioning its efficacy, and (3) presenting a new model of problem gambling.

* Quoted in *To Gamble or Not to Gamble*, by Walter Wagner (New York: World Publishing, 1972), p. i.

106

Compulsive Gambling as an Illness

The commonly held view that compulsive gambling is a social problem also assumes that it should be treated as an illness, thus affirming the concept that the medical model can best explain problematic gambling. Excessive gambling losses are increasingly being considered manifestations of illness. Troubled gamblers are seen as being driven by an uncontrollable compulsion to gamble and as needing therapeutic intervention to correct their condition.

The process whereby inappropriate behavior becomes defined as a disease is termed the *medicalization of deviance* by sociologists, who suggest that this process should be considered in terms of its historical development. Peter Conrad and Joseph Schneider, leaders in this field, advanced a five-stage sequential model to illustrate the medicalization process:

1. definition of behavior as deviant;
2. prospecting: medical discovery;
3. claims-making: medical and nonmedical interests;
4. legitimacy: securing medical turf;
5. institutionalization of a medical deviance designation.[2]

This model can be applied to demonstrate how compulsive gambling came to be defined as an illness.

Definition of Behavior as Deviant

In the United States, gamblers whose losses have led to serious financial and psychological difficulties have been routinely labeled deviant. Until recently, such behavior has been judged on moral and legal grounds. Those who continually sought financial reward through gambling were seen as flaunting the puritan values of hard work and thrift. Conventional wisdom held that losing gamblers would eventually turn to criminal means to secure additional gambling funds. In colonial America, Cotton Mather warned that excessive gambling was "unquestionably immoral and, as such, displeasing to God,"[3] while a Tennessee Superior Court judge, in 1830, ruled that gambling to excess was "a general evil leading to vicious inclinations, destruction of morals, abandonment of industry and honest employment, a loss of self control and respect. Frauds, forgeries, thefts make up the black catalogue of crime, the closing scene of which ends up in highway robberies or murder."[4]

For much of the twentieth century, the prevailing view of excessive gambling continued to define such behavior as morally and legally reprehensible. The social observer Clyde Davis commented that "gambling is without a doubt the most potent vice cherished by the human race."[5] Attorney General Robert Kennedy warned of the insidiousness of gambling in American life,[6] and an influential sociology textbook advanced the conclusion that gambling was closely linked to organized crime.[7] In the case of excessive gambling, there is ample evidence that this behavior pattern was considered socially deviant before medical science labeled it an illness. The disease label simply validated the folk definition of excessive gambling as deviant, as can be seen in the comments of Robert Lindner, an early proponent of a medical model for deviant gambling: "The fact that the passion to risk possession could assume a pathological form characterized by symptoms related to the various addictions, could marshal behind it compulsions which were beyond reason, could overbear judgment to the very last degree, seems always to have been common knowledge among common folk everywhere."[8]

Prospecting: Medical Discovery

As noted in chapter 4, psychoanalysts were the first to attempt to explain excessive gambling in other than moral or legal terms. In the 1920s, Simmel and Freud concluded that irrational gambling was a substitute for masturbation—provoked by primal, oedipal guilt. Other psychoanalytic researchers contended that this explanation could be extended to most problem gamblers. However, these seminal explanations for excessive gambling were generally unknown outside the psychoanalytical community. The research of Edmund Bergler marked the successful "staking" of a medical claim.[9] After analyzing several patients with gambling problems, he concluded that a distinct type of neurotic gambler could be identified. He labeled this type "compulsive gamblers" and contended that they were driven by an unconscious wish to lose that made them unable to control their gambling. Bergler further stated that compulsive gamblers were in the grips of an illness and, rather than being condemned, should be treated by medical intervention. Although a critical corps of psychoanalysts supported Bergler's conception of gambling, it was a claims-making group that brought his work to the attention of the general public.

Claims Making: Medical and Nonmedical Interests

In 1957, the same year Edmund Bergler's book, *The Psychology of Gambling*, was published, two ex-gamblers founded Gamblers Anonymous in Los Angeles. From this beginning the movement grew steadily. Currently there are approximately 8,500 members in over five hundred chapters throughout the United States and Canada.[10] Gamblers Anonymous is organized for the explicit purpose of aiding its members in their efforts to discontinue gambling. Members believe that helping

other gamblers achieve abstinence helps them maintain their own resolve. The following statement from a Gamblers Anonymous pamphlet
demonstrates their proselytizing mission: "Throughout history untold
suffering and humiliation has been the lot of countless thousands of
men and women due to their addiction for playing games of chance for
money. Today, with the formation of a fellowship called Gamblers
Anonymous, a bright new page has been unfolded in man's struggle
against this insidious problem."[11]

Gamblers Anonymous, modeled after Alcoholics Anonymous, uses
only abstinent gamblers as counselors. Their methods are typical of
those used in conventional group therapy: acceptance of personal responsibility, confession of misdeeds, acknowledgment of guilt, and
penance. Meetings of Gamblers Anonymous typically begin with the
reading of the official credo and the twelve steps to a cure. Each member reports on his or her current behavior and situation (weather reports). A prayer is then followed by refreshments and a general social-
izing session. Members often socialize between meetings and are
available to each other on a twenty-four-hour basis if they feel the urge
to gamble. Spouses are encouraged to join an auxiliary organization
called Gam Anon. Gamblers Anonymous is one of the few groups that
provides an ongoing treatment program for gamblers. Most troubled
gamblers are unaware of other treatment approaches and assume Gamblers Anonymous is the only source of help available to them.

Gamblers Anonymous wholeheartedly supports Bergler's contention
that gamblers who lose repeatedly are victims of compulsion and have
lost the ability to control their behavior. The following excerpt from
their credo illustrates the group's acceptance of this definition:

> We learned we had to concede fully to our innermost selves that we are
> compulsive gamblers. This is the first step in our recovery. With reference
> to gambling, the delusion that we are like other people, or presently may
> be, has to be smashed. We have lost the ability to control our gambling.
> We know that no real compulsive gambler ever regains control. All of us
> felt at times we were gaining control, but such intervals—usually brief—
> were inevitably followed by still less control, which led in time to pitiful
> and incomprehensible demoralization. We are convinced to a man that
> gamblers of our type are in the grip of a progressive illness. Over any
> considerable period of time we get worse, never better.[12]

Troubled gamblers accept the compulsion model to resolve a crisis
that has become unmanageable. The model is a means to both explain
past behavior and gain control over future behavior. Often, the compulsion theory is used to rationalize what otherwise would be considered
socially reprehensible behavior. Debt-ridden gamblers who spend their
time gambling and don't support their families are often unwilling or
unable to verbalize their motivations for such behavior. It is easier for
them to accept the idea that they are driven by compulsive urges than

to admit that self-gratification through gambling has become their rai-
son d'être. In American society, the sick generally are not held morally
responsible for their illness. When troubled gamblers accept a disease
label (compulsion), they are thus able to absolve themselves partially of
guilt for misdeeds.

To admit that one is compulsive is also to reconceptualize the self as
an object to be controlled and treated. This in turn opens the possibility
that the self can change or the crisis be resolved. Acknowledging that
the problem is beyond one's control opens the way for others to inter-
vene and alter the maladaptive behavior. Thus admitting one's compulsion sets the stage for a therapeutic regimen that eventually may control
the compulsion.

In the 1960s, both the public and the medical community were beginning to accept the disease model of alcoholism advanced by E. M.
Jellinek.[13] At the same time, Gamblers Anonymous and proponents of
the compulsion model attempted to link gambling with alcoholism. Dr.
Harry Perlowitz, a psychoanalyst, was quoted in a popular health magazine as saying, "I feel that there are just as many compulsive gamblers
in the United States as alcoholics." The author of the article commented on the success of Gamblers Anonymous in treating this illness
and asserted that compulsive gambling was "America's largest unrec-
ognized health menace."[14]

Legitimacy: Securing Medical Turf

In 1969, members of Gamblers Anonymous approached the psychiatric staff of the Veterans Administration Hospital at Brecksville, Ohio,
for help in dealing with gamblers who were undergoing severe psychological problems. In response, Robert Custer assembled a clinical team
that worked closely with Gamblers Anonymous to establish a therapy
program. The program was later expanded, and the first in-patient treatment facility for compulsive gamblers was opened in 1972.[15] The
Brecksville treatment approach stressed counseling and group therapy
rather than individual psychotherapy. Custer was convinced that regular contact with Gamblers Anonymous was necessary to achieve and
maintain a treatment goal of abstinence from gambling. Because of his
work with problem gamblers, Custer became acknowledged as an authority in the field of compulsive gambling.

In 1972, a group of Gamblers Anonymous members, clergymen, law-
yers, and medical professionals formed the National Council on Compulsive Gambling for the purpose of "educating the public about the
disease of compulsive gambling."[16] The council serves as a lobby for
the medical model by sponsoring research and funding projects that
advance the illness concept. It also publishes a newsletter and journal
to keep its members informed of developments in the field of compul-

sive gambling. Council members actively petition legal and judicial bodies to acknowledge the compulsive and/or pathological nature of excessive gambling.

During the 1970s, the psychiatric model of compulsive gambling changed. Most proponents of the medical model rejected Bergler's unconscious-wish-to-lose theory while retaining the concept that troubled gamblers lose control over their behavior.[17] Other research suggested that the term *compulsion*—an impulse that is felt to be alien and that is therefore dreaded and resisted—was psychiatrically inaccurate and should be replaced with the term *pathological*. This distinction has been largely ignored, however, and the terms *pathological* and *compulsive* remain virtually synonymous and interchangeable.[18] Although rejecting the idea that gamblers unconsciously wanted to lose, subsequent researchers generally supported the basic tenets of the original psychiatric model espoused by Bergler. Custer's comments concerning the nature of compulsive gambling reflect this perspective: "It is a progressive behavior disorder in which an individual becomes dependent upon gambling to the exclusion of everything else in life. Eventually, the compulsive gambler loses all ability to control the gambling impulse and is literally unable to function without gambling. This definition does not include the social or professional gambler, or even a person who gambles heavily every day. Compulsive gamblers are a separate group whose betting behavior is obsessive and uncontrollable."[19]

One explanation for the consensus among clinical researchers on adoption of a medical model is that the source of their data—severely troubled gamblers—is similar. The current prevailing model evolved from the self-reporting of troubled gamblers and psychiatric interpretations of those reports. Later studies of compulsive gambling used similar sources of information—"patients seeking treatment or members of Gamblers Anonymous."[20] The 1976 national survey of gambling behavior estimated that compulsive gamblers represented slightly less than 1 percent of the gambling population.[21] The almost total reliance on information drawn from a small minority of the gambling population has led to a common, but highly selective, view of the problem.

Institutionalization of a Medical Designation

In 1978, the Maryland assembly passed a bill that funded a pilot project for the treatment of compulsive gamblers. Although a treatment center was subsequently opened in Johns Hopkins Hospital in Baltimore, perhaps the most significant implication of this act was its official recognition of compulsive gambling as a social problem that should be "treated." A passage from the Maryland bill is worthy of note:

THE LEGISLATURE FINDS AND DECLARES:

1. That compulsive gambling is a serious social problem and there is evidence that availability of gambling increases the risk of becoming a compulsive gambler; and
2. That Maryland with its extensive legalized gambling has an obligation to provide a program of treatment for those persons who become addicted to gambling to the extent that it seriously disrupts lives and families.[22]

In 1980, the American Psychiatric Association formally recognized pathological gambling as a disorder of impulse control in its *Diagnostic and Statistical Manual III* (DSM III). According to the *Manual*, maladaptive gambling behavior is indicated by at least four of the following:

1. Frequent preoccupation with gambling or obtaining money to gamble.
2. Often gambles larger amounts of money or over a longer period than intended.
3. Need to increase the size or frequency of bets to achieve the desired excitement.
4. Restlessness or irritability if unable to gamble.
5. Repeatedly loses money gambling and returns another day to win back losses ("chasing").
6. Repeated efforts to cut down or stop gambling.
7. Often gambles when expected to fulfill social, educational or occupational obligations.
8. Has given up some important social, occupational or recreational activity in order to gamble.
9. Continues to gamble despite inability to pay mounting debts or other significant social, occupational, or legal problems that the individual knows to be exacerbated by gambling.[23]

The legislative bill and the American Psychiatric Association diagnostic category provided both an instrumental and a symbolic acceptance of deviant gambling as a medical syndrome. A testimonial to this acceptance occurred in 1985, when one of Atlantic City's largest casinos was forced by court order to close its casino operation for one day as a penalty for allowing a known compulsive gambler to lose millions (in stolen funds) at the tables. On the day it was closed, the casino was required to sponsor seminars by treatment counselors on the identification of compulsive gambling.

Proponents of the illness model have succeeded in opening treatment centers in New York, Pennsylvania, New Jersey, and Connecticut that use a basic approach patterned after traditional alcoholism treatment principles. The treatment programs, staffed by professional and medical personnel, have established abstinence from gambling as the only treatment goal and invariably use contact with Gamblers Anonymous as part of the therapy regimen.[24] A chart of compulsive gambling and recovery used in gambling treatment programs (see Figure 7-1) is virtually identical to one used by Alcoholics Anonymous. Despite some criticism within the medical community that the medical label has created a new class of "patients" and public concern over the loss of individual responsibility inherent in a disease designation,[25] advocates of the medical model have gained virtual control over the treatment of problem gambling in the United States. The medical model has been institutionalized.

The Prevailing Compulsive Gambling Model

Treatment advocates, believing that troubled gamblers are incapable of extricating themselves from their problematic situations, have developed an operational model of compulsive gambling. The following composite, drawn from leading researchers in the field, represents the prevailing model of compulsive gambling.[26]

1. There is a single phenomenon that can be labeled compulsive gambling.
2. Compulsives are qualitatively different from other gamblers. Of the three types of gamblers—professional, social, and compulsive—the first two do not exhibit the characteristics of the compulsive.
3. Compulsives gradually manifest a loss of control whereby they are unable to stop gambling.
4. Compulsive gambling is a progressive condition that develops inexorably through a series of distinct phases:
   a. Initial success, augmented by a "big score," leads to unrealistic expectations that increased gambling can yield even larger winnings.
   b. As gambling increases, success slowly diminishes and the gambler's financial resources shrink. The gambler rationalizes that only more gambling will improve his or her situation.
   c. The need to continue gambling, that is, to remain "in action," fueled by irrational optimism, becomes an all-consuming compulsion.
   d. Money becomes a means rather than an end.
   e. The gambler suffers psychological pressure—unresolved guilt feelings leave the gambler unable to stop when winning.
   f. The next stage can be called "chasing." The gambler will go to any length to garner gambling money, including borrowing, stealing, committing fraud, and embezzling.
   g. Self-castigation and frequent attempts to abstain are followed

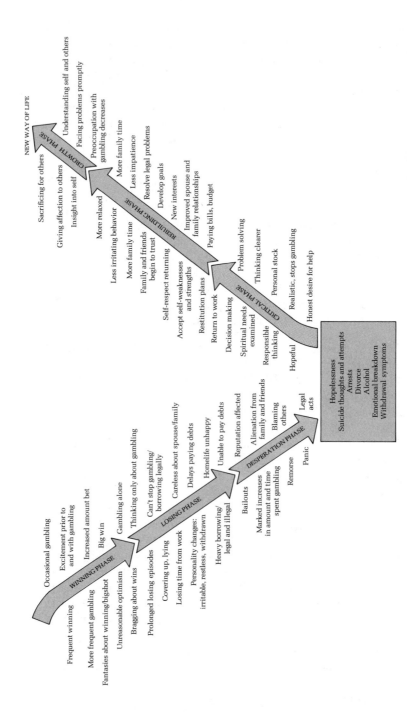

Figure 7-1 A chart of compulsive gambling and recovery. (*Robert L. Custer, M.D., National Council on Compulsive Gambling, Inc., 142 East 29th St., New York, NY 10016*)

by rationalization, culminating in more betting. Gambling is no longer pleasurable, but continues in a frantic ritualistic manner.

    h. The gambler hits rock bottom! He or she has exhausted all funds and rationalization is no longer possible. The individual with sufficient insight acknowledges that any further gambling will be ruinous.

5. Compulsive gambling is a permanent and irreversible condition. The only cure is total abstinence. If the subject resumes gambling, he or she will inevitably manifest symptoms that lead to self-destruction.

A leading spokesperson for a medical explanation of problem gambling is the sociologist Henry Lesieur. Although at first skeptical of the deterministic aspects of the medical model, his study of problem gamblers led him to embrace it, while adding an element of choice to the compulsive gambling model. Lesieur views pathological gamblers as being caught in a spiral of escalating commitment to gambling.[27] As losses mount, the "sick" gambler resorts to *chasing*, or frantic searching for funds for further gambling. When gamblers chase over a long period, they can be considered compulsive or pathological. In his classic work *The Chase*, Lesieur chronicled the lives of persons whose dysfunction led to the concept of compulsive gambling. Compulsive gamblers, he said, suffer

> a high degree of psychosomatic complaints such as ulcers, etc. Gamblers who stop gambling, for example, experience withdrawal symptoms. The rate of suicide attempts is high; there is a high rate of assaults on the gambler by the spouse (a reaction to heavy debts, ruining family finances, etc.); and some of the things this book documents—exploitation of family and work setting and crime to support the habit—are also evident. These are clearly pathological behaviors.
>
>   Whatever all of the above facts indicate, they demonstrate that more than just a crisis point is involved here. There is a complex of problems produced by the defective relationship. While I would contend that the gambler *voluntarily* enters the gambling situation and thoroughly enjoys it, he/she makes side-bets which commit her/him to a career of gambling. The committed gambler engages in pathological behaviors which are never envisioned in advance and which are regretted after having been done. In a real sense, many feel "compelled" to continue because things have gotten out of control. Consequently, the model depicted herein implies a limited voluntarism (or soft determinism if you prefer). People feel compelled yet still have choices which are limited by socio-economic position, options available and options they are aware of.[28]

While Lesieur's arguments are well documented, they derive from a study of severely troubled gamblers who have sought treatment either from professional counselors or from Gamblers Anonymous. Reliance on this type of population base—the hallmark of researchers who espouse a compulsion model—casts doubts upon the effectiveness of the medical approach to problem gambling.

Challenging the Compulsion Model

The general acceptance accorded the compulsion/medical model is more of a social accomplishment than a scientific achievement. Virtually all investigators who have observed gambling groups in natural settings find little empirical evidence of either compulsive or pathological behavior. Ethnographic researchers, studying such diverse groups as racetrack participants, professional poker players, and casino gamblers, have rejected compulsion as an adequate explanation for problem gambling.[29] After conducting empirical investigations of several gambling groups, I too have concluded that the compulsion model is not supported by ethnographic data. The clinical perspective used in developing this model of problem gambling focused on a small minority of persons who were attempting to discontinue their gambling activities. The problems and coping mechanisms of the vast majority of gamblers, who are still in action, have not been fully considered, even though in most cases losing gamblers are able to alter their circumstances and avoid a pattern of progressively larger losses.

The single goal of abstinence presently advanced by treatment programs has limitations and in some cases may be counterproductive to the treatment of problem gambling. For most gamblers, the goal of abstinence is unrealistic. Although therapeutic intervention may result in a temporary remission, a return to gambling activity is common.[30] Often such a return stimulates self-defeating gambling binges, wherein the gambler engages in "the voluptuousness of giving oneself up for lost."[31] Since no alternative treatment methods exist, the problem gambler may be placed in a program that doesn't suit his or her individual needs. Currently, most, if not all, treatment programs require clients to stay in regular contact with Gamblers Anonymous. If the gambler is unable to develop rapport with this group, the success of the treatment is seriously jeopardized. Most counseling researchers stress that, to be successful, a therapist must carefully match individual cases with specific treatment goals. When only one goal (abstinence) is considered legitimate, this is clearly impossible. Although abstinence in some cases is desirable and perhaps necessary, it should not be the only legitimate treatment goal.

A New Model

Invariably when an established concept is challenged, the challenger is asked to propose a better one. With that in mind, I will redefine compulsive gambling and propose an alternative treatment model. These new concepts were drawn from personal studies of ongoing gambling groups and from the findings of other research into natural (as opposed to clinical or experimental) gambling environments. These sources reveal that virtually all regular participants have experienced personal difficulties directly related to gambling losses. Although the severity of these difficulties varied considerably throughout a gambler's career, every participant, to some degree, was at risk. Fortunately, the vast majority were able to deal with their problems in a socially acceptable manner. After analyzing the spectrum of research into compulsive gambling, psychologist Mark Dickerson came to essentially the same conclusion:

> The assumptions that gamblers who seek help are mentally disordered or have a personality that predisposes them to gamble heavily have not been substantiated. Such conclusions have been drawn too readily on the basis of the comparison of the characteristics of those who seek help with those of hypothetical social gamblers who bet infrequently. It seems that so-called "compulsive" gamblers are not uniquely different from many other habitual gamblers who may neither want nor seek help to reduce or control their gambling.[32]

Although the term *compulsive* (or its scientific counterpart, *pathological*) is widely used and accepted in reference to gambling, it does not describe adequately the behavior pattern it seeks to define. *Compulsive* and *pathological* connote psychological aberrations that are not found in the majority of troubled gamblers. *Problem gambling* is a more accurate term, and is defined as the losing of excessive amounts of money through gambling. (The individual gambler's financial situation, of course, determines how much is "excessive.") This definition eliminates psychiatric overtones and focuses on the area of greatest concern to gamblers and their families—excessive monetary loss. Although DSM III does list losing money as one of the criteria of pathological gambling, it emphasizes loss of control as the prime determinant. The following is an attempt to accurately place problem gambling within a conceptual model.

1. Although problem gambling includes a variety of behavior patterns, common to all these patterns is the losing of a relatively excessive amount of money.
2. An individual's gambling can be considered as lying on a continuum, ranging from nonproblematic to severely problematic.
3. Any individual who gambles can develop syndromes of problem gambling.
4. The development of problem gambling does not proceed inexorably but follows a variable pattern.
5. Overcoming or controlling a problem-gambling syndrome does not necessarily require abstinence.

6. Emphasis should be placed on dealing with problem gambling in the environment in which it occurs.
7. The population of problem gamblers is diverse, and treatment programs should be varied to meet individual needs.

Such a model dictates varied and flexible methods of treatment directed toward a wide range of goals. However, during the treatment process, two key variables must be reconciled: (1) commitment to gambling, which can be measured by level of participation, and (2) gambling strategy, encompassing both technique and money management. Virtually all problem gamblers have high levels of commitment, as indicated by their sustained participation. Although their gambling strategies are diverse, it can be assumed that such strategies have, in some measure, proved unsatisfactory; by definition, all problem gamblers have incurred some degree of financial difficulty.

Current treatment efforts deal with only one of these variables—commitment. Patients are urged to stop gambling and find new interests, a difficult process that can involve a drastic change in life-style, ego restructuring, or both. In contrast, an individual's gambling strategy is somewhat more amenable to change, because such change usually does not require life-affecting alterations. If, as implied here, ineffective gambling strategies do contribute to the development of problem gambling, then improving an individual's gambling strategy should reduce the incidence of problem gambling. Although this does not mean financial success for the gambler, it is a means of keeping losses within manageable parameters.

The problem-gambling model supports a controlled-gambling program. Such an approach, rather than demanding total abstinence, aims at helping the gambler cope with the problems of gambling. Oldman delineates the basic premise of the controlled-gambling therapeutic technique: "Perhaps the most important message for those who gamble, or wish to control gambling, or wish to help those in trouble through gambling, is that this particular mechanism whereby one reaches a crisis point is a consequence not of personality defect but of a defective relationship between strategy of play on the one hand and a way of managing one's finances on the other."[33]

Although finding an acceptable gambling strategy can be difficult, it is not impossible. The principles of controlled gambling already have been applied in two cases by British researchers Mark Dickerson, David Weeks, and Howard Rankin.[34] In both cases, the subjects initially exhibited the "classic" syndromes of problem gambling—extensive losses, large gambling debts, decreased work efficiency, and troubled marriages. The patients were allowed to gamble up to a certain limit, with their spouses controlling the outlay of money. Though the subjects participated in individualized therapy, they did not attend Gamblers Anonymous meetings. After one year, both were gambling at an acceptable, somewhat lower level. Their marital, financial, and employment situations showed marked improvement. The results of these two studies, while hardly conclusive, do suggest that a controlled-gambling program is feasible.

Further evidence that a controlled approach is worth serious consideration can be found in a related field of inquiry. In the area of alcohol studies, the question of "controlled drinking" is a controversial one. Several studies, however, have clearly demonstrated that controlled drinking is a viable goal in treating alcoholism.[35] Moreover, leading alcohol therapists are now rigorously questioning the traditional model of alcoholism and its obligatory abstinence.

The new model challenges two basic assumptions of the prevailing compulsion model, namely, that problem gambling, at some stage, proceeds inexorably and that only abstinent gamblers should serve as peer counselors. Available evidence demonstrates that problem gamblers don't progress through inexorably worsening stages but instead are usually able to mitigate their gambling losses using personal coping strategies. Such strategies typically involve changes in gambling technique and money management that allow the participants to continue gambling while keeping losses within acceptable parameters. Recent research of my own indicates that other gamblers can and do aid in this process. These points will be discussed thoroughly in the next chapter.

Summary

Excessive gambling has come to be defined as both an illness and a serious social problem. Gamblers whose repeated losses lead to serious financial and psychological difficulties are increasingly being labeled compulsive or pathological. This redefinition process follows a pattern that sociologists Conrad and Schneider have termed the medicalization of deviance.

Although researchers working in natural gambling settings have reported little empirical evidence of compulsive behavior, various clinicians and nonmedical help groups staunchly advocate a medical model. The help groups have gained public support and currently control the operation of therapeutic programs. Since this control is based more on social–political dominance than on scientific achievement, the efficacy of the prevailing model of compulsive gambling and of standard treatment programs can be questioned and a new model of problem gambling proposed—one that is compatible with diverse approaches to treatment. The new model rejects the idea that problem gambling proceeds inexorably and denies that abstinence should be the only treatment goal. It suggests that severely troubled gamblers in many cases suffer from defective gambling strategies rather than from compulsive tendencies.

Notes

1. David Oldman, "Compulsive Gamblers," *Sociological Review* 26 (May 1978): 349.
2. Peter Conrad and Joseph W. Schneider, *Deviance and Medicalization* (St. Louis: C. V. Mosby, 1980), p. 266.
3. Gilbert Geis, *Not the Law's Business* (New York: Schocken, 1979), p. 223.
4. Robert Bremner, *Traps for the Young* (Cambridge, Mass.: Harvard University Press, 1967), pp. 57–58.
5. Clyde B. Davis, *Something for Nothing* (New York: Lippincott, 1956), p. 15.
6. Robert F. Kennedy, "The Baleful Influence of Gambling," in *Gambling*, ed. Robert Herman (New York: Harper & Row, 1967), pp. 169–177.
7. Paul H. Landis, *Sociology* (Boston: Ginn, 1964), p. 279.
8. Robert Lindner, "The Psychodynamics of Gambling," *Annals of the American Academy of Political and Social Sciences* 269 (1950): 95.
9. Edmund Bergler, *The Psychology of Gambling* (New York: Hill & Wang, 1957).
10. Joseph Dunne, "The President's Message," *National Council on Compulsive Gambling Newsletter* 1 (1983): 2.
11. Jay Livingston, *Compulsive Gamblers* (New York: Harper & Row, 1974), p. 148.
12. Gamblers Anonymous pamphlet (Los Angeles: GA Publishing, n.d.).
13. The "father" of the alcoholism disease model, E. M. Jellinek, delineated the medical symptoms of this "sickness" in *The Disease Concept of Alcoholism* (Highland Park, N.J.: Hellhouse Press, 1960).
14. James R. Berry, an advocate of the medical model, describes the progressive stages of the gambling compulsion in "What Makes a Gambling Addict," *Today's Health*, October 1968, pp. 21–23.
15. Robert L. Custer, "An Overview of Compulsive Gambling," in *Addictive Disorders Update: Alcoholism, Drug Abuse and Gambling*, ed. Pasquale Carone, Stanley Yoles, Sherman Kieffer, and Leonard Krinsky (New York: Human Sciences Press, 1982), pp. 107–124.
16. Margaret Hyde, *Addictions* (New York: McGraw-Hill, 1978), pp. 48–49.
17. Henry R. Lesieur and Robert L. Custer, "Pathological Gambling: Roots, Phases and Treatment," *Annals of the American Academy of Political and Social Sciences* 474 (1984): 146–156.
18. Robert L. Custer, "How Problem Gamblers Can Get Help," *U.S. News and World Report* 88 (29 January, 1980): 75.
19. Ibid.
20. This was the population base used by Robert Roston in his influential study, "Some Personality Characteristics of Male Compulsive Gamblers," *America Psychological Association Annual Convention* 73 (1965): 263–264.
21. Maureen Kallick, Daniel Suits, Ted Dielman, and Judith Hybels, *A Survey of American Gambling Attitudes and Behavior* (Ann Arbor: Institute for Social Research, University of Michigan, 1979).
22. Maryland State Legislature, "Compulsive Gambling: Treatment," Bill no. 1311 (1978).

23. American Psychiatric Association, *Diagnostic and Statistical Manual of Mental Disorders*, 3rd ed. (Washington, D.C.: American Psychiatric Association, 1980), p. 291.

24. Custer, "An Overview of Compulsive Gambling"; Harvey Greenberg, "Psychology of Gambling," in *Comprehensive Textbook of Psychiatry*, 3rd ed., ed. Harold Kaplan, Alfred Freeman, and Benjamin J. Sadock (New York: Williams & Wilkins, 1980), pp. 3274–3283; Johnny Greene, "The Gambling Trap," *Psychology Today*, September 1982, pp. 50–55; and Lesieur and Custer, "Pathological Gambling."

25. Dr. Leon Hankoff seriously questions the disease model in "Compulsive Gambling: Discussion," in *Addictive Disorders Update: Alcoholism, Drug Abuse and Gambling*, ed. Pasquale Carone, Stanley Yoles, Sherman Kieffer and Leonard Krinsky (New York: Human Sciences Press, 1982), pp. 142–147.

26. Some of the material included in this composite appeared in my article "The Next Best Thing: A Study of Problem Gambling," *The International Journal of the Addictions* 20 (1985–1986): 1595–1620.

27. Henry R. Lesieur, "The Compulsive Gambler's Spiral of Options and Involvement," *Psychiatry* 42 (February 1979): 79–87.

28. Henry R. Lesieur, *The Chase: Career of the Compulsive Gambler* (Cambridge, Mass.: Schenkman, 1984), p. 246.

29. Marvin Scott, in *The Racing Game* (Chicago: Aldine, 1968); David M. Hayano, in *Poker Faces* (Berkeley: University of California Press, 1982); and Oldman, in "Compulsive Gamblers," found little empirical evidence of compulsion in their field investigations of naturally occurring gambling groups.

30. Nancy Ashton, "Gamblers: Disturbed or Healthy?" in *Gambling Today*, ed. David Lester (Springfield, Ill.: Charles C Thomas, 1979), pp. 53–70, and David Lester, "The Treatment of Compulsive Gambling," *International Journal of the Addictions* 15, no. 2 (1980): 201–206.

31. Jon Halliday and Peter Fuller, eds. *The Psychology of Gambling* (London: Allen Lane, 1974), p. 24.

32. Mark Dickerson, *Compulsive Gamblers* (London: Longman, 1984), p. 132.

33. Oldman, "Compulsive Gamblers," pp. 369–370.

34. Mark Dickerson, David Weeks, and Howard Rankin, "Controlled Gambling as a Therapeutic Technique for Compulsive Gamblers," *Journal of Behavior Therapy and Experimental Psychiatry* 10 (1979): 139–141, and Howard Rankin, "Control Rather than Abstinence as a Goal in the Treatment of Excessive Gambling," *Behavior Research and Therapy* 20 (1982): 185–187.

35. For a full discussion of controlled-drinking research, see E. Mausell Pattison, "A Critique of Alcoholism Treatment Concepts with Special Reference to Abstinence," *Quarterly Journal of Alcohol Studies* 27 (1966): 49–71, and Jim Orford, "A Comparison of Alcoholics Whose Drinking Is Totally Uncontrolled with Those Whose Drinking Is Mainly Controlled," *Behavior Research and Therapy* 11 (1973): 565–576. For an analysis of how abstinence came to be accepted as the only legitimate treatment goal, see Joseph Schneider, "Deviant Drinking as Disease: Alcoholism as a Social Accomplishment," *Social Problems* 25 (1978): 361–372, and Carolyn Weiner, *The Politics of Alcoholism* (New Brunswick, N.J.: Transaction, 1981).

Coping
with Loss

Some days you can't win for losing.

Anonymous gambler's lament

Studies of naturally occurring gambling groups provide insight into ways of identifying and dealing with the serious consequences of problem gambling. Instead of concentrating on patients seeking treatment, naturalistic studies observe gamblers within the real worlds of gambling to reveal more accurately how they cope with financial loss. In accordance with this approach, I will draw on my own research and that of other ethnographic investigations to tell the story of problem gambling from the participants' point of view.

Gambling is inherently risky, with the rewards intermittent and relatively unpredictable. The rate of return at any particular point in time cannot be assured—as one gambler stated, "When you really need the money, you can't count on winning." Even the most sophisticated gambling strategy cannot, in the short run, guarantee a monetary return. Adapting to periods of financial loss is therefore an inevitable part of sustained gambling.[1] Successful adaptation typically involves a variety of coping mechanisms.

In the gambling context, *coping mechanisms* refer to behavior patterns specifically oriented toward dealing with the interactional consequences and psychological pressures stemming from the loss of money while gambling. An analysis of coping mechanisms provides insight into the origins of problem gambling. In many situations it is a breakdown in coping mechanisms that triggers problematic gambling patterns. Material for this chapter is organized into two sections: (1) coping mechanisms and (2) the origins of problem gambling. The first section describes the four types of coping mechanisms, while the second discusses the origins of problem gambling in terms of attribution theory, locus of control, and the bad beat concept (a gambling term signifying a disheartening loss).

Much of my analysis of coping mechanisms and other adaptive strategies for dealing with financial loss was developed during research at racetracks throughout the country and at Lake Tahoe offtrack betting parlors. Although this research was specifically concerned with horse players, the findings also appear to be applicable to other gambling groups that consider rationality integral to their activity. Most regular participants in the five major gambling games do claim rationality (see Chapter 5). Even though further research is needed to clarify whether or not data from horse players can be generalized to other gambling groups, researchers agree that participants who perceive their gambling as requiring skill are much more likely to develop patterns of problem gambling than are those who perceive their gambling results as being determined entirely by chance.

Coping Mechanisms*

The coping mechanisms used by horse players to sustain their participation in gambling fall into four main categories: (1) voluntary external constraints, (2) goal adjustment, (3) aligning actions, and (4) techniques for increasing short-term rewards. Each type is described and analyzed below.

Voluntary External Constraints

External constraints, known in the racing argot as "tricks to avoid going crazy," constitute a common type of coping mechanism. One of the most frequently used ploys is to temporarily distance oneself from the scene: the horse player stops gambling for a period of time in an attempt to gain a fresh perspective. One veteran player explains this process: "I know it sounds stupid, but even a day away from the races can change my outlook. Sometimes I get so involved I can't see anything but the next race. I've lost my sense of proportion, my control." A Lake Tahoe race book regular has been nicknamed "Hiker," after his distancing technique. His method of coping with a losing streak is to hike or ski in the nearby mountains. Hiker said that his alpine adventures refreshed him, preparing him for "another go at the ponies."

Another constraint used by horse players calls for placing a certain percentage of the winnings in an inviolate trust, where the player will not have ready access to them. This way, the player retains at least some of the winnings while avoiding the psychologically shattering loss of all of them. Such a loss can catalyze reckless gambling behavior.

* I would like to thank Human Sciences Press for permission to adapt materials used in this section from my article "Adapting to Failure: The Case of Horse Race Gamblers," *Journal of Gambling Behavior* 2 (Fall/Winter 1986): 81–94.

One regular reported that after a big score he made several advance mortgage payments. Another winning player purchased long-term treasury notes, reasoning that the early withdrawal penalties would dissuade him from using those funds for future gambling.

Players who feel they are no longer able to adequately control their own gambling often seek to reduce losses by relinquishing some or all control of the gambling process. The most common form of relinquishment is to have a significant other (spouse, live-in partner, parent, sibling, close friend) dole out gambling funds on a regular basis; one gambler's wife, for example, gives him $25 every Monday, Wednesday, and Friday.

In rare instances, the losing gambler will seek more rigid constraints by entering a therapy program—most often, at least for horse players, Gamblers Anonymous. Interviews with horse players who had attended meetings of Gamblers Anonymous indicated that most had gone at the urging of relatives. Some commented that the rigidity of the program had "turned them off," and after paying a "a few bills," they stopped attending meetings. Several researchers have noted the high drop-out rate of those who attend Gamblers Anonymous meetings.[2]

Most regular horse players invoke external control mechanisms only during periods of severe financial losses. When their immediate financial crisis is resolved, players usually discontinue the external controls.

Goal Adjustment

This strategy is used by losing gamblers who are willing to change their overall approach to gambling. A common technique is to switch from high-risk, high-reward wagers to less risky ones with corresponding lower rewards. In the horse racing world, this is referred to as "moving from prices to chalk." Conservative betting may include avoiding certain unfavorable races, concentrating on particular kinds of horses, decreasing the amount wagered, establishing a rigid allotment of available gambling funds, or invoking a progressive betting system wherein the amount wagered remains at a fixed, low level, increasing only after the gambler recovers a certain percentage of prior losses. Switching to a more conservative style often allows the gambler to sustain his or her participation.

Gamblers willing to alter their gambling strategy, rather than assume a dogmatic position, adjust to new contingencies by changing methods. Although this may seem self-evident, a gambler's strategy often is so well established that changing it is difficult. For many, the change means a shift in goal orientation; for example, the goal is no longer financial reward but sustained participation. Gamblers who have sustained large losses or who live on relatively fixed incomes are often forced into a conservative betting stance in order to remain active. As one veteran horse player put it: "I used to be a real action bettor, always trying for a big score. After a while, I lost too much and realized if I wanted to keep coming here, I'd have to change. So now I just piddle around, two bucks here, five bucks there. Maybe I'll get lucky. It's tough to build a bankroll this way. But for now it's the best I can do."

The goal of many regular players is to earn their living from gambling by becoming professional handicappers. Great discipline and skill are needed to achieve the status of a professional handicapper; according to racing columnist Bill Barich, one must have "a high tolerance for the drudgery of daily handicapping and record keeping, a cold emotionless eye, a tightly controlled system, an accountant's approach to cash flow, and the cut-throat managerial attitude of a Harvard Business School graduate."[3]

The majority of those who try to sustain a livelihood at the racetrack fail. Some quickly realize they will never succeed and quit trying. Do those who give up seeking professional status—"bailouts," in the racing argot—cease gambling? A small minority do, in fact, stop participating at this point, but my research indicates that most individuals in this category continue gambling. Several such bailouts reported no appreciable change in their overall participation but showed a significant decline in problems related to gambling after they had ceased trying to earn their living from gambling. Goal adjustment led to new and more appropriate gambling and money management techniques. These individuals still attended the track or race book regularly, but gambled smaller sums or used more conservative approaches.

Some horse players who succeed in participating frequently with few problems have retired from work and now attend the races regularly. Although members of this group have a reduced income, they are able to sustain attendance through the use of conservative betting strategies. The primary goal of this group is not financial gain but regular attendance. Members are willing to forego a big score for high-probability, low-reward bets. The gambling careers of the retired are often replete with instances of past gambling problems. However, these gamblers have developed strategies compatible with their present goals.

Aligning Actions

Aligning actions are defined by sociologists Randall Stokes and John Hewitt as "verbal efforts to restore or assure meaningful interaction in the face of problematic situations."[4] These verbal remarks stem from the gambler's desire to preserve his or her gambling-related identity, an identity drawn both from an internal self-image and from the perceived opinions of fellow gamblers. These identities are known and understood by the horse players, and their relations with one another are influenced by such perceptions. When these identities are subject to question, the interaction between the participants can be disrupted. This process has been described by Hewitt and Stokes as follows: "Indeed, the thematic organization of meaning by interactants usually depends upon their ability to interpret each others' actions as manifestations of particular identities. It follows that when events fail to fit themes in interaction, identities may come into focus as problematic: if the acts of another fail to appear sensible in light of his identity in the situation, perhaps he is not who he appears to be."[5]

During the gambling process, the players attempt to negate possible disruptions in their gambling-related identities by using verbal statements that serve to maintain their self-respect and that take the form of disclaimers and rationalizations.[6] Before wagering, inveterate horse race gamblers use disclaimers to reduce their commitment to the outcome of a race. Faced with the possibility, once their bets are placed, that their selections might lose, the bettors try to demonstrate verbally that such a loss will not alter their basic identity as rational horse players. This phenomenon can be considered a kind of side bet, a gambling strategy that works to reduce the gambler's psychological commitment to the outcome of an uncertain event. After the race, the players offer rationalizations to explain why their selection lost. In this retrospective process, the players assure themselves and others that the loss was not the result of personal inadequacy but, in fact, stemmed from an unforeseen contingency.[7] The following examples illustrate this concept.

Disclaimers (prospective)	Rationalizations (retrospective)
It's a shot, only a flyer.	It was a boat race (fixed).
It's only a small bet.	The jockey stiffed him (held the horse back).
I'm trying to beat the chalk.	The trainer was not trying to win.
I don't have any real conviction.	It was bad racing luck; the horse stumbled.
What the hell, somebody has to win.	It was worth a bet anyway.

Virtually all horse race gamblers use aligning actions to some extent, though less successful ones use this coping mechanism more frequently. Gamblers know from experience that overstating the case, bragging about a "sure thing," often leaves overconfident bettors looking foolish when their selection loses. As one inveterate player said, "There's nothing worse than touting all your buddies on a sure thing and then having the piece of shit run up the track. You're afraid to show your face at the track." The use of disclaimers reduces this possibility. Rationalizing a loss by attributing it to an unforeseen but explicable event is a sign of perceived control, and the perception of control, according to psychologist Herbert Lefcourt, greatly ameliorates negative sanctions and anxiety-provoking situations.[8] Thus, if players can explain why their horse lost, they remain in control. Appearing in control in turn helps reinforce the serious horse player's credibility. The coping mechanism of retrospectively manipulating information, popularly termed the "certainty of hindsight,"[9] is no doubt the most familiar of the four types discussed here.

Techniques for Increasing Short-Term Rewards

Ironically, certain coping mechanisms, used in part to sustain participation, in the long run usually result in the player's losing money, rendering continued participation problematic. The following is a description of these less than successful mechanisms.

Many losing gamblers bet on more than one horse in a race or purchase multiple combinations of exotic[10] or daily double tickets, a technique known as "saving." Bettors who regularly use this technique appear to share an intolerance for losing, resorting to saving after a few consecutive losing races to boost their chances of collecting a winning ticket, albeit for less financial gain. These horse players thus cope with the psychological pressures of an infrequent reward pattern by increasing their short-term rewards.

The practice of saving, if used regularly, virtually guarantees long-term financial loss. Most racing experts agree that in the long run, the most financially rewarding method is to place straight wagers, that is, to bet only to win and only on one horse per race.[11] Using this method, the gambler may lose the majority of races but stands to gain enough from an occasional win to offset prior losses.

Behavioral research has empirically demonstrated that individuals tend to find short-term rewards more attractive than long-term rewards.[12] The appeal of saving techniques to horse players is thus to be expected. Like most individuals, horse race gamblers find it difficult to trade the assurance of immediate reinforcement for the possibility of a larger gain in the future. It is extremely difficult to lose race after race and wait patiently for a skewed reward structure to pay off.

Gamblers' attempts to improve the reward structure, even in the short run, often prove unsuccessful. Some bettors, unsettled by losing, take rash risks, letting the need for instant reward preclude all logic. In the words of one impatient gambler: "I slaved for six months, really busted my ass. Built up my bankroll, slowly, carefully, logically, doing just the right thing. Then I lost for four straight days; big deal, why didn't I shrug it off? I couldn't stand the pressure. I had to win. So I bet all the money on one stupid race—the race wasn't even playable! Couldn't wait—no, not me—just had to prove myself—stupid, stupid. Guess I'll eat shit all my life."

A similar behavior pattern can be identified in the practice known as "hitting the tables." Gamblers with access to a casino may, in the midst of a losing streak or after a particularly disheartening loss, try to recoup their losses instantly by playing blackjack or craps. Normally patient and steady race handicappers turn into rash casino gamblers. Horse players who rarely bet over fifty dollars on a race can be observed wagering several hundred dollars on the turn of a card or a throw of the dice. "Hitting the tables" is rarely successful, and the resulting losses can be substantial and traumatic. What happens when a gambler's coping mechanisms prove totally inadequate? An analysis of such situations illuminates the origins of problem gambling, and challenges traditional views of the progression of problem or compulsive gambling.

Origins of Problem Gambling

Proponents of the compulsion model have identified three significant stages in the development of problematic gambling: (1) a winning phase, (2) a losing phase, and (3) a desperation phase.[13] A crucial turning point in this progression occurs when the winning phase ends and the losing begins. The trigger for this reversal is often a big win, which fuels unrealistic expectations of future gain. Unbridled optimism prompts gamblers to increase the size of their wagers. However, the odds of continued winning are low, and the gambler's losses mount predictably until he or she becomes desperate.

Logical as this progression may seem, after analyzing the patterns of regular horse race gamblers at the racetrack and at Lake Tahoe's offtrack betting parlors, I have concluded that although the big win is a significant event in the gambling careers of inveterate horse players, it is not the catalyst for the development of problem gambling. On the contrary, I found that a devastating loss, commonly referred to as a "bad beat," is the trigger for a chain of events that often leads to problem gambling. The bad beat involves a large financial loss that is particularly disheartening because it results from a seemingly inexplicable occurrence, as when, for example, a winning horse is disqualified for minor interference, a horse with an insurmountable lead dies shortly before the finish line, or a selection wins but the race is declared void because of an electrical outage.[14] In such improbable situations, the gambler's coping mechanisms are inadequate.

Bad beats frequently disorient gamblers to such a degree that they drastically alter their established betting strategies and money-management techniques. Typically, these changes prolong the financial loss. The length of time gamblers remain in this disoriented state, referred to as being "on tilt" by Hayano in his study of poker players, varies, but most gamblers eventually "come to their senses" and are able to continue gambling in a relatively acceptable manner. Virtually all serious gamblers face bad beats at some time in their gambling histories. How a gambler regains control after a period of disorientation offers important clues to ways of coping with problem gambling. After observing and chronicling this phenomenon in a naturalistic setting, I am convinced that attribution theory can provide a useful framework for understanding problem gamblers.

Attribution Theory

Attribution refers to the process whereby individuals seek to explain and understand the causes and meanings of behavior. The various theories of attribution share a view of ordinary people as intuitive scientists attempting to understand, explain, and make inferences about themselves, others, and the surrounding environment.[15] One of the pioneers in attribution research, George Kelly, introduced this concept: "Might not the individual man, each in his own personal way, assume more of the stature of a scientist, even seeking to predict and control the course of events with which he is involved? Would he not have his theories, test his hypotheses and weigh his experimental evidence?"[16]

Regular horse players are classic examples of intuitive scientists, weighing evidence and developing theories to explain the results of horse races. Marvin Scott considers it the hallmark of a regular horse player to "perceive a race as a natural event ordered and capable of being determined by analysis." He has further observed that regular horse race gamblers are generally able to explain their losing selections while maintaining a subjective sense of rationality and purposefulness.[17] Regular horse race gamblers are sustained by the assumption that their activity is ordered and that eventually their knowledge and skill at prediction will allow them to win or, as one veteran race-goer put it, "at least not lose too much."

Attribution researchers have also studied people's attempts to gain control over their physical and social world, focusing to a large extent on whether the actor perceives the locus of control as being external or internal to him- or herself. One of the pioneers in this area, Julian Rotter, defined locus of control as follows:

When a reinforcement is perceived by the subject as following some action of his own but not being entirely contingent upon his action, then, in our culture, it is typically perceived as the result of luck, chance, fate, as under the control of powerful others, or as unpredictable because of the great complexity of the forces surrounding him. When the event is interpreted in this way by an individual, we have labeled this a belief in external control. If the person perceives that the event is contingent upon his own behavior or his own relatively permanent characteristics, we have termed this a belief in internal control.[18]

People who attribute the consequences of their actions to internal control typically show vitality as they grapple with life events, while those who credit external control are generally passive or complaining and do not work constructively to change their situation. Lefcourt maintains that an "internal locus of control may be a prerequisite of competent behavior [whereas] an external control orientation seems common to many people who do not function in a completely healthy manner."[19]

Although the internal–external continuum cannot be applied indiscriminately and may in fact be overly simplistic, the concept may still help sensitize researchers to the importance of individual perception.[20] Research has demonstrated that an individual's causal attributions of success or failure can influence subsequent behavior. Internal attributions generally spur the individual to additional effort, whereas external attributions evoke frustration and anger. According to attribution researcher Mark Snyder, causal attribution is often self-fulfilling; thus "an individual's construction of his or her social world can be a fairly good match to the actual state of affairs."[21]

Regular horse race gamblers, like regular participants in other gambling games, generally exhibit an internal locus of control. Regulars are able, in part, to cope with periodic swings in fortune because they believe that rational practices will prevail over chance elements. An understanding of race results, even if erroneous, reinforces the gambler's sense of personal control. However, when a bad beat occurs, the gambler's sense of rationality is temporarily displaced. Although locus of control is a relatively enduring aspect of one's personality, the catastrophic nature of the bad beat causes a shift in the perception of control. Distraught losers no longer believe they have control and tend to attribute the success or failure of future wagers to "cruel fate." The gambler's perceived locus of control thus temporarily shifts to an external one. This reaction may occur regardless of the gambler's prior skill at handicapping, money management, or coping techniques. Attributing an inexplicable occurrence to factors beyond human understanding then undermines the gambler's existing adaptive skills.

The shift in locus reported by racing regulars typically results in a disoriented state in which the gambler attempts to recoup much (or all) of the loss as soon as possible. During such attempts, gamblers passively and fatalistically wager large sums of money hoping for a quick resolution of their situation instead of actively using their known skills to rebuild their gambling funds. These blind appeals to fate, known to gambling regulars as "giving it up," often lead to reckless risk taking, ultimately culminating in a blowout (large loss). Most gamblers eventually regain their equilibrium and take steps to continue gambling participation, having been forced by the desire to remain in action to reappraise their betting behavior. This process eventually allows gamblers to once again seem themselves as being in control of their destiny. Empathetic interaction with other gamblers can facilitate the shift back to believing in internal control. Some gamblers, however, are unable to return to an internal orientation. Their bad beats have been so traumatic that they remain in an external-control mode. This condition can further impair the gamblers' handicapping and result in continuing loss. As long as gamblers perceive themselves as being caught in a spiral of events beyond their control, their gambling usually remains problematic.

Thus, though horse players generally are able to cope with periodic losses and routine vicissitudes, extremely improbable events present a special challenge. A veteran horse player summed up the problem: "Nobody can keep cool when a really bad beat strikes. It's as if the fates are out to screw you personally. You can't help but get a little crazy."

The Bad Beat

Data developed from observation and interviews reveal that coping with bad beats typically follows three distinct stages: (1) manic reaction, (2) realization, and (3) regaining internal control. During the manic phase, the normal locus of control is displaced, and gamblers abandon their rational betting techniques. The realization phase involves the restoration of some control over gambling patterns and the application of more rational betting strategies. In the racing argot this stage is referred to as "coming to your senses." In the third stage, the gambler regains an internal locus of control and returns to prior betting patterns—commonly termed "putting it all behind you." Not all gamblers are able to move smoothly through the stages. Usually the longer one takes to regain control, the greater the likelihood that gambling will become problematic. In order to illustrate the response of gamblers to bad beats, I will present two case studies,[22] reported to me by reliable informants.

Ed had played the horses for fifteen years with moderate success when he came across a prime betting opportunity in an outstanding horse that, through a series of unfortunate mishaps, had never been able to demonstrate its true potential. Ed followed this hard-luck horse for over three months, and when it was entered in a race with rather mediocre animals, he felt certain it would win. He decided to go "all in" by betting $10,000 from his accumulated bankroll. Ed bet $5,000 at the racetrack and (in order not to reduce the odds) had acquaintances bet $5,000 spread among three race books in Nevada.

Since the trainer had entered two horses in the race, Ed's horse went to the post as part of an entry. The betting public didn't realize the horse's capability, and the odds were over eight to one when the race started. The horse easily went to the front and maintained a long lead throughout the race. When the horse passed the finish line, Ed felt an incredible sense of exhilaration: the $80,000 winnings, he realized, would change his life. He was confidently walking to the cashier's window when the track announcer intoned, "Hold all tickets; there has been a claim of foul." "So what," Ed mused, "my horse was always in front and hadn't been in anyone's way." However, after viewing the race film, the stewards disqualified Ed's horse and placed it third. The other horse in the entry had interfered with the original third-place finisher, and since the horses were considered a team, the winner was penalized for its entry mate's action.

The turn of events left Ed in a state of frenzy. He kept repeating, "But my horse didn't do anything wrong," while pacing up and down the grandstand. Almost as an afterthought, he bet the remainder of his funds ($5,000) on a long shot in the next race. He was not surprised when the horse finished out of the money.

During the next three months, Ed continued to gamble, with funds borrowed from his parents. He played nothing but long shots to try to recoup his losses. His strategy was unsuccessful, and he finally decided to quit playing the horses. Ed's resolve lasted for three months, after which he resumed gambling on horse races. After his return, he demonstrated more purposefulness and no longer wagered exclusively on long shots. Using a more conservative betting strategy, Ed has been able to maintain participation for another thirteen years. However, he is subject to frequent bouts of depression and fits of anger, and seems to be an "unhappy horse player." Although a knowledgeable handicapper, Ed loses consistently. He attributes his lack of success to "incredible, unbelievable bad luck" and frequently comments that he probably never will win any real money betting the ponies. When questioned about his persistence, he replied, "After all these years of horse playing what else can I do?"

Bill lived in southern California and had played the horses for ten years. He liked to wager on horses running on the East Coast and frequently traveled to Tijuana, Mexico, to wager legally at Aqua Caliente Race Book. Bill located a horse running at Pimlico Race Track in Maryland that appeared to be a "good thing." He planned to bet $5,000 on the horse. Since he was well known at Caliente, he would have no difficulty placing the wager.

On the day of the race, he left sooner than necessary to ensure an early arrival and drove toward Tijuana. Upon reaching the Mexican border crossing, however, he encountered a gigantic traffic jam caused by immigration crackdown. He was delayed over three hours. Once through the border crossing, he drove frantically through Tijuana and arrived at the track just in time to see his horse's number being placed on the board as a winner that had paid over ten to one. Bill couldn't believe what had happened and said over and over to himself, "I've never been shut out before. I've always gotten my bets down in time." He wagered his $5,000 on the last race of the day and watched his fifteen-to-one shot run third. He drove home, took the rest of his $6,000 bankroll to the night harness races, and lost it all.

Bill stopped going to the races for thirty days before resuming participation. He started slowly and only took $50 each time he went to the track. Bill returned to his former strategy of betting on horses in good form regardless of the odds. He has played the horses regularly for fifteen years since the bad beat and plans to continue "as long as I can walk up to the betting windows." Bill works hard at handicapping and enjoys the mental stimulation of the activity. He attributes losing to poor handicapping rather than to a "conspiracy of the fates." While not amassing sizeable winnings, Bill has been able to manage regular participation without suffering financial problems related to gambling.

Locus of Control

A central element in the process of dealing with a bad beat is the gambler's locus of control. In both cases studies, the gamblers demonstrated similar behavior while in the manic and the realization stages, but in the third stage, they differed in their efforts to regain an internal locus. In the first case, the gambler was never able to regain a sense of internal control, and although he continued to participate, his gambling remained problematic. This corroborates the idea that the likelihood of manifesting problem gambling is related to the length of time it takes to regain internal control. Ed remained in an external locus that was ultimately self-defeating. He fit the pattern of a losing gambler described by Hayano: "Most consistent losing gamblers tend to be Externals who believe essentially that gambling, along with life's other problems, is ultimately beyond their control and that bad luck and bad games are the major causes of loss. Losing players do not expect to win, and they find a culpable external reason when they do not. Even when they do win the reason is likely to be external to themselves and traced to good luck or good timing."[23]

In the second case, the gambler was able to restore his internal locus in a fairly short time and quickly regained the positive, optimistic outlook that is characteristic of an internal locus. This confident attitude was reflected in his betting tactics and helped him maintain regular participation without suffering financial difficulties. A similar sequence was reported by a horse-player-turned-author, who after experiencing a "dramatic disaster" that knocked him "completely off stride," concluded, "My mental state determined my fortunes at the track. I lost because of mental excuses. I won when I maintained an air of calm self-confidence."[24]

Bad beats can be placed on a continuum ranging from disturbing to traumatic. The two case studies presented showed responses to traumatic situations or "super bad beats." Adaptation to less distressing but nonetheless improbable events follows a similar process of resolution. The specific reasons some gamblers are able to bounce back from a bad beat and regain their internal locus and others are unable to do so are difficult to pinpoint. A variety of financial, situational, and psychological factors affect the losing gambler's perception of control. One important (and frequently overlooked) factor is the gambler's access to peer support. Ed was unable to draw on the support of other horse players. On several occasions, he spurned the observations of track acquaintances, saying, "These guys can't tell me anything I don't already know about horses. Why should I pay any attention to people who know less about gambling than I do?" This attitude eventually severed his access to peer support. One horse player who had known Ed for many years remarked, "We've given up on him. There's no point in trying to reason with him—he knows it all. He'll just have to work out his problems by himself."

On the other hand, Bill was willing to consider the opinions of other players. When Bill found himself mired in a losing streak, he was receptive to the views of other gamblers and sometimes sought their help. In one instance, I observed Bill approach a group of horse players and say, "I'm salty as hell—can't seem to cash a ticket. Anybody got any ideas what I'm doing wrong?" Although Bill remained an independent handicapper, he also subscribed to the gambling adage "There's no player so smart that he can't learn from his friends." In the case of Bill and Ed, their differing receptivity to peer support was an important factor in their respective ability to regain an internal locus.

Regular horse players frequently attempt to aid troubled gamblers by providing empathetic understanding. Those particularly adept at this are called "race book shrinks." Regulars often serve as devil's advocates or sounding boards in order to help another objectively assess a prospective bet. In so doing, they provide a touchstone of reality that can bring disoriented gamblers to their senses.

Virtually all regular horse players have experienced bad beats of varying degrees of seriousness and can empathize with other gamblers who are attempting to cope with one. Players often initiate communication by assuring the losing gambler that his or her experience is not unique and that someone else understands. The following verbal exchange is representative:

> "Did you see what happened to me? My horse jumped the rail. I can't believe it!"
>
> "Man, that's a tough beat."
>
> "I'll never cash a bet. Guess I'll chuck in my wad on the next race and then take off."
>
> "Same thing happened to me a couple of months ago. Best thing to do is to stay calm. Don't change your betting style. Don't get crazy."
>
> "There's no point in doping out these stupid nags. Something bad always happens to me."
>
> "That's bullshit. You know better than that."
>
> "Every time I get something good it fucks up somehow."
>
> "Just last week you got that three-horse round-robin; that was good picking, and things worked out OK. Don't get rattled."
>
> "Yeah, but . . ."

The reactions of individuals to highly unlikely events is an underresearched area; according to Lefcourt, a leading attribution theorist, "no one has constructed devices which ascertain control beliefs about events that are extremely improbable."[25] My findings indicate that adaptation to inexplicable occurrences presents unique difficulties. Previously learned coping skills, at least in the short run, are inadequate to overcome the resulting psychological disorientation.

Two findings have particular significance for those trying to comprehend inappropriate gambling behavior: (1) the process of becoming involved in problem gambling is reversible rather than inexorable, and (2) other gamblers can provide help in coping with gambling problems. These findings belie the traditional contentions that one must quit gambling permanently to relieve the symptoms of problem gambling and that abstinent gamblers such as those in Gamblers Anonymous are the only acceptable peer counselors. On the basis of the two case studies described here, personal observations, and several ethnographic studies, I believe that although reversing a problem gambling pattern is not easy, it is possible. The causal attributions of gamblers play a significant role in their ability to satisfactorily manage participation. A change in attribution often signals the beginning of troubled gambling. The origins of problem gambling are reflected in the observation of a race book regular: "It's real easy to be cool when you're winning. You can be so logical, so confident. Everything's working for you. But the real crunch comes when you start losing—especially if you get hit with a bad beat or, God forbid, a bunch of them. Suddenly everything looks different. Then let's see how you handle yourself. That's the real test."

Summary

This chapter explores problem gambling from the participants' perspective. All gamblers must deal with an unpredictable reward structure that cannot guarantee financial profit. Regular gamblers therefore inevitably develop coping mechanisms for dealing with periodic losses. These coping mechanisms allow most participants to withstand the losses inherent in sustained participation. Coping mechanisms typically fall into four categories: voluntary external constraints, goal adjustment, aligning actions, and techniques for increasing short-term rewards.

Although coping mechanisms are adequate for most situations, certain inexplicable events, or bad beats, can disorient gamblers. Such disorientation often catalyzes the development of problem gambling. Attribution theory provides a useful framework for understanding the process whereby troubled gamblers regain control of their betting. When dealing with bad beats, most gamblers succeed in regaining an internal locus of control, which in turn aids them in managing their behavior. An analysis of the process of regaining control reveals two important findings: problem gambling can be reversed, and other gamblers can provide valuable assistance in coping with problem gambling. Although most controlled gamblers don't make money from gambling, they are able to keep their losses within manageable proportions.

Notes

1. For an understanding of the difficulty of coping with loss, see Thomas M. Martinez and Robert La Franchi, "Why People Play Poker," *Transaction* 6 (1969): 32–52, and Andrew Beyer, *My $50,000 Year at the Races* (New York: Harcourt Brace Jovanovich, 1978).
2. See, for example, Gordon Moody, "The Facts about Money Factories," *London Churches Council on Gambling* 1 (1972): 64–86; David Lester, "The Treatment of Compulsive Gamblers," *International Journal of the Addictions* 15, no. 2, (1980): 201–206; and Frederick W. Preston and Ronald W. Smith, "Delabeling and Relabeling in Gamblers Anonymous: Problems with Transferring the Alcoholics Anonymous Paradigm," *Journal of Gambling Behavior* 1 (Fall/Winter 1985): 97–105.
3. Bill Barich, "Laughing in the Hills," *The New Yorker*, 12 May 1980, p. 117.
4. Randall Stokes and John P. Hewitt, "Aligning Actions," *American Sociological Review* 41 (October 1976): 838–849.
5. John P. Hewitt and Randall Stokes, "Disclaimers," *American Sociological Review* 33 (February 1968): 46–62.
6. A discussion of disclaimers was included in my book *The Degenerates of Lake Tahoe* (New York: Peter Lang, 1985), pp. 75–85, and in my article "Adapting to Failure: The Case of Horse Race Gamblers," *Journal of Gambling Behavior* 2 (Fall/Winter 1986): 81–94.

7. See Marvin B. Scott, *The Racing Game* (Chicago: Aldine, 1968), p. 92., for a further discussion of the rationalizations employed by horse players.

8. Herbert Lefcourt, "The Functions of the Illusions of Control and Freedom," *American Psychologist* 28 (1973): 417–425.

9. Baruch Fischoff, "The Silly Certainty of Hindsight," *Psychology Today,* April 1975, pp. 71–76.

10. Exotic wagering includes *quinella,* in which the bettor specifies horses to finish first and second in either order; *exacta,* in which the bettor selects horses to finish first and second in exact order; *trifecta,* in which the bettor picks horses to finish first, second, and third in exact order; and *pic six,* in which the bettor chooses the winning horse in each of six consecutive races.

11. See Thomas Ainslie, *Ainslie's Complete Guide to Thoroughbred Racing* (New York: Simon & Schuster, 1979).

12. Howard Rachlin, *Introduction to Modern Behaviorism* (San Francisco: W. H. Freeman, 1970).

13. Henry R. Lesieur and Robert L. Custer, "Pathological Gambling: Roots, Phases and Treatment," *Annals of the American Academy of Political and Social Sciences* 474 (1984): 146–156.

14. These are examples of actual events.

15. Richard E. Nisbett and Lee Ross, *Human Inference: Strategies and Shortcomings of Social Judgment* (Englewood Cliffs, N.J.: Prentice-Hall, 1980).

16. George A. Kelly, *The Psychology of Personal Constructs* (New York: Norton, 1955), pp. 4–5.

17. Scott, *The Racing Game*, p. 40.

18. Julian Rotter, "Generalized Expectancies for Internal versus External Control of Reinforcement," *Psychological Monographs* 80 (1966): 1.

19. Herbert Lefcourt, "Belief in Personal Control: A Goal for Psychotherapy," *Journal of Individual Psychology* 22 (1966): 191.

20. E. Jerry Phares, *Locus of Control in Personality* (Morristown, N.J.: General Learning Press, 1976), p. 23.

21. Mark Synder, "Attribution and Behavior: Social Perception and Social Causation," in *New Directions in Attribution Research,* vol. 1, ed. John Harvey, William Ickes, and Robert Kidd (Hillsdale, N.J.: Erlbaum, 1976), p. 69.

22. These two case studies were cited in my article "Attributions and the Origins of Problem Gambling," *Sociological Quarterly* 27 (Winter 1986): 463–478.

23. David M. Hayano, *Poker Faces* (Berkeley: University of California Press, 1982), p. 110.

24. Beyer, *My $50,000 Year at the Races*, p. 13.

25. Herbert Lefcourt, *Locus of Control: Current Trends in Theory and Research* (Hillsdale, N.J.: Erlbaum, 1976), p. 141.

Gambling on the International Scene

Of the universality of gambling there is no doubt, and it seems to be inherent in human nature.

John Ashton*

Russians, Australians, Yugoslavians, South Koreans, Uruguayans, New Guineans, Norwegians, Zimbabweans, and others of various nationalities share a fascination with form and speed that leads them to take up the search for a winning horse. In my travels throughout the world, I have seen horse racing on ice-covered surfaces in Quebec, on tropical beaches in the Caribbean, over green grasses in New Zealand, and in dust bowls in California. Although the geography and climates of these far-flung places varied, the racing patrons were surprisingly similar. I observed the same behavior in the offtrack betting parlors of Christchurch, New Zealand, that I had seen in the casinos of Lake Tahoe, Nevada. The railbirds at El Comandante Race Track in Puerto Rico were like their counterparts at Fort Erie, Canada; Aqueduct, New York; or Agua Caliente, Mexico. Like horse racing, other betting games share a cross-cultural appeal, for gambling is truly a universal endeavor. Figure 9-1 (on pp. 140–141) is testimony to gambling's ubiquity.

Gambling activities in England, Europe, and Australia have directly affected the American gambling scene. For example, gambling games such as baccarat and roulette were imported to the United States from European casinos. The widely used totalizator systems, developed to rapidly display pari-mutuel odds, originated in Australia. The English regulatory system for gambling has been advanced as a model for regulatory agencies in this country. However, cross-national influences have not been unidirectional; popular American games such as craps and poker have been exported to England, Europe, and Australia. The particularly American glitz and ambiance associated with Las Vegas

* From *The History of Gambling*, by John Ashton (1899; reprint, New York: Burt Franklin, 1968, p. 2.)

and Atlantic City have been emulated by casinos in other countries. American gambling is further linked with Anglo-European developments by the increasing multinational, corporate ownership of gambling operations and by competition among the various countries. English companies have entered the Atlantic City market, and Harrah's (controlled by the publicly traded Holiday Corporation) has proposed building the world's largest casino in Sydney, Australia.

The material for this chapter is organized into four sections: (1) gambling in England, (2) European gambling (France, Germany, Holland and Spain), (3) Australian gambling, and (4) a comparison of practices in England, Europe, and Australia with those in the United States.

Gambling in England

England, with a long history of gambling, has earned its reputation as a "nation of gamblers." According to social commentator Ordericus Vitalis, gambling was prevalent in eleventh-century England.[1] Geoffrey Chaucer observed in the fourteenth century:

> Gaming is the mother of all lies,
> And of deceit and cursed villainies,
> Manslaughter, blasphemy and wasteful sore
> Of cattle and time. And furthermore,
> 'Tis shameful and repugnant to honour
> To be regarded as a hazarder.[2]

In the seventeenth century, the poet Charles Cotton wrote the classic *The Compleat Gamester*, in which he chronicled the influence of gaming upon England's citizenry.[3] Gambling participation in the twentieth century continued to be an important part of English life, and in 1966 politician Roy Jenkins declared, "This country has become a gamblers' paradise more wide open in this respect than any comparable country."[4]

England has also had considerable experience with the regulation of gaming. In 1190, Richard I prohibited gambling among common soldiers while restricting knights and clergymen to stakes of no more than one hundred shillings in any one gambling session. In 1541, an act was passed controlling gambling at amusement parks and fairs. During the reign of Queen Anne in the eighteenth century, a series of laws was passed specifying the maximum allowable wagers at various gambling games. In 1845, the omnibus Gaming Act rendered gambling debts unenforceable by law, restricted gambling to cash, and made most tavern gaming illegal. The 1845 law was not a suppression of gambling per se but a pragmatic attempt to control its pervasiveness. The acceptance of gambling itself is evident in the preamble to this act: "At present,

AFRICA

	Bingo	Cock fighting	Casinos	Football pools	Greyhounds	Horse racing	Jai-alai	Lottery	Off-track betting	Slot machines	Misc.
Algeria			●			●					
Angola						●					
Benin			□			●					
Bophuthatswana			●							●	
Botswana	●		●			●				●	
Burkina Faso								●			
Cameroon								●			
Cape Verde								●			
Central Af. Republic									□		
Ciskel			●							●	
Dahomey								●			
Egypt			●			●		●		●	●
Ethiopia								●			
Gabon			●					●		●	
Gambia, The			●								
Ghana			●			●		●		●	
Guinea-Buissan					●						
Ivory Coast			●					●		●	
Kenya			●	●		●				●	
Lesotho	●		●							●	
Liberia			●	●				●			
Madagascar			●								
Mali								●			
Morocco			●	●	●	●		●			
Mozambique			●					●			
Niger								●			
Nigeria								●			
Senegal			●			●		●		●	
Sierra Leone								●			
South Africa						●					
Swaziland			●	●				●		●	
Tanzania								●			
Togo			●					●		●	
Transkei			●							●	
Tunisia					●	●		●	●		
Uganda								□			
Venda			●							●	
Zambia			●		▲			●	●	●	
Zimbabwe	●		●	●		●		●	●	●	●

ASIA, AUSTRALIA

	Bingo	Cock fighting	Casinos	Football pools	Greyhounds	Horse racing	Jai-alai	Lottery	Off-track betting	Slot machines	Misc.
Afghanistan								●			
Australia	●	✔	●	●		●		●	●	●	
Bangladesh								●			
Bhutan								●			
Burma								●			
China (Taiwan)								□			
Fiji								●			
Guam	●		●			●		●			
Hong Kong						●			●	●	
India						●		●			
Indonesia	□		□	□				□		□	
Iran	□		□								
Iraq								●			
Israel						●		●			
Japan						●		●	●	●	
South Korea			●			●		▲		●	
Macau			●			●	●	★	●	●	
Malaysia			●			●		●			
Mauritius			●	●		●		●	●	●	
Nepal			●							●	
New Caledonia			●								
New Zealand	●		●			●	●	●	●		
Papua New Guinea						●		●	●		
Philippines	●	●	●			●	●	●	●	●	●
Samoa								●			
Seychelles			●							●	●
Singapore						●		●	●		
Sri Lanka	●		●			●		●	●	●	
Syria			●								
Thailand						●		●			
Turkey			●	●		●		●			
USSR						●		●			
United Arab Emirates	□										
Viet Nam								●			

EUROPE

	Bingo	Cock fighting	Casinos	Football pools	Greyhounds	Horse racing	Jai-alai	Lottery	Off-track betting	Slot machines	Misc.
Austria			●	●		●		●	●	●	
Belgium			●	●		●	●		●	●	

Figure 9-1 Gambling throughout the world. (*Reprinted with the permission of Gaming and Wagering Business, August 1986, Vol. 7(8), pp. 20–21.*)

wagers are chiefly confined to sporting events, but the practice of wagering is still deeply rooted . . . and the practical imposition of pecuniary penalties for wagers would be so repugnant to the general feelings of the people, that such penalties would scarcely be enforced, or, if enforced, would be looked upon as an arbitrary interference with the freedom of private life."[5]

Over the next one hundred years, a variety of laws were passed to control and tax gambling. After World War I, Winston Churchill, while serving as chancellor of the exchequer, introduced a betting tax. In 1929, the tax was repealed and Churchill admitted, "In practice it has

	Bingo	Cock fighting	Casinos	Football pools	Greyhounds	Horse racing	Jai-alai	Lottery	Off-track betting	Slot machines	Misc.
Bulgaria			•			•		•		•	
Cyprus						•		•			
Czechoslovakia						•		•			
Denmark		•	•		•	•		•	•	•	•
Finland	•					•		•	•	•	•
France			•	•		•		•		•	
Germany, East			•			•		•			
Germany, West			•	•		•		•		•	•
Gibraltar			•					•			
Great Britain	•		•	•	•	•		•	•	•	
Greece			•	•		•		•	•		
Hungary			•	•	•	•		•		•	
Iceland								•			
Ireland (Eire)	•				•	•		•	•	•	
Ireland, Northern (U.K.)	•			•	•	•			•	•	
Italy			•	•	•	•		•	•		
Luxembourg			•					•		•	
Madeira			•							•	
Malta	•		•			•		•		•	
Monaco			•								
Netherlands	•	✔	•			•		•	•	•	★
Norway				•		•		•	•		
Poland						•		•			
Portugal	•		•	•	▲	•					
Rumania		□	•			•				•	
Spain	•		•	•	•	•	•	•	•	•	
Sweden	•			•	•	•		•		•	□
Switzerland			•	•		•			•		
Yugoslavia			•	•		•		•		•	
NORTH AMERICA, CENTRAL AMERICA, THE CARIBBEAN											
Antigua	•		•			•		•		•	
Aruba	•		•					•		•	
Bahamas			✔							✔	
Barbados						•		•			
Bonaire			•								
Canada	•		•	□		•		•	•		
Costa Rica								•			
Curacao	•		•	□				•		•	
Dominican Republic		•	•			•		•	•		
Guadeloupe			•	•		•					
Guatemala	•		•			•		•		•	
Haiti		•	•	□				•			
Honduras			•								
Jamaica	•					•		□			
Martinique			•	•		•			•		•
Mexico					•	•	•	•			
Nicaragua	•										
Panama		•	•			•		•	•	•	
Puerto Rico	•	✔				•		•	•	•	✔
St. Kitts	•		•							•	
St. Lucia	•										
St. Maarten (Dutch)		✔						•		✔	
Trinidad and Tobago	•		□			•		•	•		
United States	•	•	•	•	•	•	•	•	•	•	
U.S. Virgin Islands	•							•			
SOUTH AMERICA											
Argentina	•		•	•		•	•	•	•	▲	
Bolivia	•	•	•					•			
Brazil	•			•		•		•			
Chile			•	•		•		•	•	•	
Colombia	•	•	•	•		•		•	•	•	
Ecuador	•	•	•	•		•		•		•	
Paraguay			•	•		•		•		•	•
Peru	•		•			•		•			
Surinam			•					•			•
Uruguay			•			•		•	•	•	
Venezuela	•					▲	•	•	•		

Explanation of symbols:

• legal and operative
★ legalized and implemented since August 1985
✔ additional new operation(s) since August 1985
▲ authorized but not yet implemented
□ previously operative, currently inactive

failed. The volatile and elusive character of the betting population, the precarious condition in which they disport themselves, have proved incapable of bearing the weight of even the repeatedly reduced burdens we have tried to place upon them."[6] By the end of World War II, legal gambling had been effectively confined to football pools, horse racing, and dog racing. At the same time, however, illegal casinos, unregulated lotteries, and unlicensed bookmakers flourished. A Royal Commission on Betting, Lotteries, and Gaming concluded that "a social habit as deeply ingrained as gambling could not efficiently be prevented by restrictive legislation; that by toleration of flagrantly illegal practices, progressive disrespect would be shown to the law and that, as a result of random enforcement and arbitrary interpretation due to ambiguity, the law officers, and in particular the police, could be exposed to charges of overt favouritism and active participation in corruption."[7]

The commission's report convinced Parliament that massive change was needed, and subsequently the Betting and Gaming Act of 1960 was enacted. The effect of this act was to legalize gambling games such as chemin de fer, blackjack, bingo, lotteries, and offtrack horse and dog race betting. An unintentional consequence was the proliferation of unregulated casinos. Capitalizing on various loopholes in the bill, over one thousand quasi-legal casinos opened between 1960 and 1968. By 1967, it was evident that additional legislation was needed, and after considerable debate and lobbying, the sweeping and comprehensive Gaming Act of 1968 became law. This act has been widely acclaimed as an apt and effective regulatory response to gambling. The act's purpose was twofold: to minimize the social and economic impact of gambling and to quash illegal gaming. In order to achieve these goals, a powerful Gaming Board with broad licensing authority was created. The Gaming Board was an independent body charged with the tight regulation of gaming. Toward this end, the board became involved in virtually all aspects of gaming, from specifying the number of tables in a casino to setting the hours for offtrack betting shops.

The most important provision of the 1968 act was the strict licensing of casinos and offtrack betting shops. The Gaming Board invoked its licensing authority, and three years after its formation, the number of casinos in England had declined almost tenfold, from 1,100 to 120.[8] The number of offtrack betting shops remained fairly constant, but their operations were carefully monitored by agents of the Gaming Board. The guiding philosophy of the board is to prohibit stimulation of demand for gaming. Gambling is permissible only where there is an inherent demand for it. Gambling operators are therefore not allowed to advertise, promote junkets, offer entertainment, or sell liquor. Casinos must enforce the club system, under which only members or their guests are allowed to gamble. To discourage impulse betting, casinos require a forty-eight-hour waiting period for the processing of club membership applications. The granting of credit by casinos or offtrack betting shops is strictly prohibited. However, casinos are able to cash checks provided they are processed within two banking days; thus gambling debts are now legally enforceable.

The 1968 act also attempts to protect the betting consumer, or punter, by limiting the operators' edge. Unlike their American counterparts, English casinos are prohibited from increasing their advantage by using a double zero in roulette or offering sucker bets like the Big 8 or Big 6 in craps. Operators must clearly post gaming rules and suggested playing strategies to aid gamblers in making rational betting decisions. Lottery managers must specify the approximate odds of collecting a winning ticket. Betting shops are required to give their patrons a wagering receipt and to promptly pay off winning tickets.

An important test of the Gaming Board's licensing authority occurred in the late 1970s, when the licenses of several large casinos came up for renewal. Gaming investigators charged that certain London casinos, competing fiercely for Middle Eastern high rollers, had circumvented provisions of the 1968 act. The offending casinos had allegedly engaged in player recruitment, junket operations, illegal advertising, and extension of credit. Subsequently the Gaming Board found the casinos in violation of the act and took decisive action by revoking the licenses of several casinos, including the well-established Playboy, Coral Leisure, and Ladbroke clubs. Despite vigorous appeals, the board's action was upheld, and the casinos were forced to close. Its success at imposing its rules on powerful international gaming corporations strengthened the Gaming Board's position, as gambling operators realized that they must follow the board's edicts or be put out of business. The Gaming Board thus emerged as the czar of English gambling. Its authority to control gaming operations is virtually unquestioned.

Legal gambling opportunities in England, while tightly controlled, are abundant, and the English punter is offered a host of betting opportunities. Casino games, bingo, and lotteries are all readily available. In addition, betting shops abound in English neighborhoods. In 1984, there were approximately ten thousand betting shops in England.[9] A manager of over one hundred English betting shops described their operation:

> One of the major features within the betting shops is a display board showing the programme for the day's racing events, and showing fluctuations in betting and results. Around the shops are fixed seats or stools and there is also a shelf around the shops upon which customers can write their bets on their betting slips. Shops can be situated practically anywhere providing planning permission and a license have been obtained, but are usually found in main shopping streets, beside public houses and bars, or on housing estates. Different bookmakers operate different systems and take bets very often on different things. For example, although we do approximately 80 percent of our business on horse racing, we also take bets on greyhound racing, on English soccer, on cricket, golf, boxing, rugby, boat races, athletics, general and presidential elections and so on. We pride ourselves on offering the customer the opportunity of betting on practically anything.[10]

There is general consensus that England's gambling industry is relatively crime-free and that bettors, although offered numerous opportunities, are not enticed to participate.[11] English gaming has gained the reputation of being an honest operation where the bettor is given a fair shake. Much of the credit for this image must be given to the provisions of the 1968 act and to its implementation by the Gaming Board.

European Gambling

As in England, gambling in European countries has established historical roots. Horse racing and dice games were popular in the time of Charlemagne. The sailors aboard the Niña, Pinta, and Santa Maria were avid card players. National lotteries were conducted in eighteenth-century Europe, and large-scale casinos appeared in the early part of the nineteenth century. Europeans also have struggled with the regulation of gambling and with illegal activities. In seventeenth-century France, *hoca* (roulette) parlors were banned, and in 1838, the country closed down all its gambling houses. Similarly, Bismarck banned all German casinos in 1872, an action rescinded by Hitler in the 1930s.[12] In the 1960s, many European countries liberalized their gambling laws in an effort to either discourage or regulate popular but illegal forms of gaming. These new laws, in many cases, led to an increase in the number of legal casinos.

There are interesting national variations within European gambling. In order to present a comprehensive picture, I will briefly describe contemporary gambling in (1) France, (2) Germany, (3) Holland, and (4) Spain.

France

Horse racing is a popular sport in France. Race meetings at Deauville and Longchamp are internationally famous for both their horses and their jet-set patrons. Both on-course and offtrack horse betting are well established, and trying to pick the *tierce* (similar to the American trifecta, in which the first, second, and third place finishers must be specified in exact order) is a national pastime. Playing the national lottery and weekly lotto games are French prerogatives. The casino industry in France comprises approximately 150 casinos, many of which offer only low-stakes wagering on *boule* (a variation of roulette). Major casinos are in resort areas often called spas. The French Riviera, for instance, is home to several large gaming clubs, as is the Atlantic coastal region. Slot machines are prohibited; casino games are roulette, chemin de fer (a form of baccarat), blackjack, and trente et quarante, or 30/40.[13]

Gambling is rigidly controlled by a national gambling commission, supervised by the minister of the interior. An important rationale for the legalization of gambling is to raise governmental revenues, and consequently, gaming operators are heavily taxed. Cooperation is emphasized; government inspectors work closely with gaming operators and, so doing, lend legitimacy to gambling. French regulation of casino gaming is representative of other European countries.

The casinos are encouraged to increase their profits (thus increasing tax payments) by exploiting tourists. Casinos charge entrance fees, bar local inhabitants from gambling, and cash only foreign checks. Identification and passports are inspected at casino entrances to ensure that the participants are not nearby residents. Locals are thus protected from losing money at the tables. Casinos enforce dress requirements (typically, men must wear jackets and ties, and women may not wear pants) to further ensure a well-heeled clientele. Casino workers are paid largely in tips, which are a routine part of gambling participation; winners are expected to contribute a portion of their winnings to the *pourboires,* or tip pool.

Not all French gambling is so tightly regulated. Although illegal, slot machine gaming is a popular activity. Unauthorized French bookmakers, like their American counterparts, offer credit and convenience unavailable from legal operators. The French underworld, including the infamous Union Corse, is allegedly involved in large-scale illegal casino operations.

Germany

The German view of gambling is an interesting mix of paternalism, optimism, elitism, and tourism. Paternalism is manifest in the innumerable legal restrictions created to protect German workers from gambling away too many of their hard-earned pfennings. Optimism is present in the expectation that gambling operations will actually contribute to the cultural and social well-being of the community. Elitism lies behind the oft-invoked provision that gamblers must show proof of fiscal solvency before being allowed to gamble. Tourism is the basis for the German casino industry.

The German gambling industry is so tightly controlled by the ministries of finance and the interior that a de jure partnership exists between government and gaming operators. Football pools, horse race betting, and lotteries are officially licensed and their operations closely supervised by government agents. Nowhere is the relationship between government and gaming operators more apparent than in the casino business. The state governments are allowed to collect an 80 percent tax on gross gaming revenues. Government inspectors maintain a constant presence on the premises and oversee every casino operation.[14] Government inspectors are present when money is counted, labor assignments are made, new equipment is installed, and hours of operation are established. Casino facilities are generally leased from government agencies rather than owned outright. Each casino has been franchised by the government and has a monopoly in its geographical region. Casinos are allowed to advertise their existence; this, however, is usually done in conjunction with civic functions (concerts, plays, symphonies) that are sponsored jointly with local agencies.

The German government takes a pragmatic position on gambling. On the one hand, they acknowledge its inevitability; on the other, they seek to minimize its adverse effects on the German wage earner. Gaming operators are charged with seeing to it that German gamblers don't lose excessively. Government agents enforce regulations that require gamblers to show that they have sufficient funds to withstand gambling losses before being allowed to participate. To ensure that this regulation is followed, gambling debts are not legally collectable. Credit is rarely, if ever, given to participants. Casino gaming (thought to be particularly conducive to excessive gambling) is prohibited for most local residents. Residents of Baden-Baden, for example, are forbidden to gamble at their town's world-famous casino. This prohibition is occasionally waived for individual gamblers in possession of written permission from the mayor. Casinos are allowed only in areas frequented by tourists.

The substantial taxes obtained from gaming significantly reduce the tax burden placed on wage earners. By licensing all gaming operators, German officials hope to control the amount of gambling in any one region and keep it relatively unobtrusive. Because of the traditional German respect for authority and a wide range of legal betting opportunities, the illegal gaming market is small. Although casino development has increased somewhat during the last ten years, gambling remains a significant but limited activity in German society.

Holland

The Dutch have traditionally championed personal freedom and have been reluctant to interfere with individual behavior as long as it does not directly harm others. This attitude has fostered the decriminalization of "victimless" crimes such as prostitution and drug use— with the understanding that such activities be confined to certain neighborhoods.[15] This tolerance extends to gambling, and there is an established Dutch gaming tradition; for example, Holland boasts the oldest government lottery in the world, and its tulip speculation in the seventeenth century was perhaps the most frenzied gambling scheme in the Western world. Recently, the Dutch have struggled with extensive illegal gaming. Their answer to this problem has been to increase the scope of legal games.

In the years following World War II, large-scale illegal gambling operations became a fact of life in Holland. By the late 1950s, illegal lotteries, sports pools, offtrack horse betting, and casinos were well established. In 1960 the Netherlands government legalized most sports pools and attempted to tax and regulate them. In addition, in an effort to attract the guilders that had been going to illegal operators, legal lotteries were expanded to include lotto games. In 1975, after much discussion about the prevalence of illegal casinos and their unregulated revenues, the national government legalized casinos. Under the casino bill, no advertising is permitted, a dress code is enforced, taxes are set at approximately 40 percent of gross revenues (win), and a national casino board was created to oversee operations. Four casinos have since opened, and three more are scheduled to begin operation by 1990. Legal offtrack horse race betting facilities were significantly expanded in the 1980s in an attempt to wean the horse player away from illegal bookies.

To establish legal casinos and expand their offtrack betting operations, the Dutch turned to foreign companies. Casinos Austria, the group that runs all of Austria's casinos, was given a large contract to start up casino operations. The Austrian group provided management and labor to staff the first casinos. Subsequently, they helped train local Dutch casino workers. Legal offtrack betting had been languishing when Ladbroke, England's largest betting shop operator, was given franchising privileges. Ladbroke immediately expanded the number of outlets and provided more efficient service. There are now more than one thousand betting shops throughout Holland, most run by Ladbroke.[16]

Holland's attempt to put illegal gambling out of business by legalizing its own games has not succeeded. Illegal gaming operators there, like their American counterparts, have proved adaptable. Illegal casinos continue to offer roulette, blackjack, and baccarat, allowed by police bribery and judicial leniency to remain in business. On occasion, their operations are interrupted by well-announced police raids, which often occur during the slow season.[17] A new type of illegal game— Golden Ten—has sprung up throughout Holland. Golden Ten, also called observation roulette, allows participants to bet after a ball has begun its downward spiral through a series of funnels until it comes to rest on numbered squares. Operators of Golden Tens have convinced Dutch courts that it is a game of skill and therefore cannot be considered gambling. This legal maneuver has allowed Golden Tens to operate openly. They now advertise extensively and offer their customers food, drink, entertainment, and twenty-four-hour service—amenities not offered by legal casinos. Illegal lottery operators and bookmakers have seen their business decline somewhat since Golden Tens received quasi-judicial approval.[18] By offering their familiar combination of credit and superior service, however, they have been able to maintain a loyal patronage. Illegal gambling in Holland remains widespread.

Spain

The contemporary Spanish experience with gambling is particularly interesting because of a tremendous increase in participation after certain games were legalized. Before 1977, the Spanish gaming industry was dominated by four games: the weekly national lottery, the daily local lottery, soccer pools, and illegal numbers.[19] Horse race betting and illegal casino gambling were relatively insignificant activities. Gaming participation, as measured by national surveys, was on the whole relatively stable.[20]

In 1977, the central government legalized casinos and bingo and, in 1981, slot machines. Legalization of these games ushered in a period of phenomenal growth in gambling participation. From 1977 to 1985, gross gaming revenues increased from approximately 150 billion pesetas to a staggering 2.45 trillion pesetas.[21] The new games, which appealed to a different segment of the Spanish population, changed conventional views of gambling. A Spanish social scientist described the revolution in Spanish gambling:

> The result is a massive eruption of new gaming consumers, new gamblers, drawn by the overwhelming availability of gambling (women moving from home card games into bingo parlors, youngsters alternating between amusement and slot machines, young couples sharing the weekend at a casino) and the insinuation of a "new morality" or attitude towards gambling, alteration of personal and family habits, different values, problem or pathological gambling, new forms—legal and illegal—of gambling and, on the whole, a profound redistribution of the leisure and entertainment money.[22]

The traditional games (lotteries, illegal numbers, and soccer) have continued stable but unspectacular growth, while horse race betting remains moderate. Since 1977, 20 casinos have opened, 1,100 bingo sites have been authorized, and approximately 500,000 slot machines have been installed. These developments suggest that in Spain the various games are not interchangeable; each has its own particular market niche. The most popular new games, bingo and slot machines, are characterized by short intervals between wagering and collection and by fast action based largely on chance rather than on skill. The phenomenal increase in Spanish gaming may indicate that a vast untapped reservoir of participants exists for such low-skilled games.

The sudden growth of gaming has revealed a host of regulatory problems. Illegal operators have begun to offer slot machines and casino gaming to the Spanish consumer.[23] Lax governmental control has allowed fly-by-night operators to capitalize on the gambling boom. The tax dollars obtained from gambling are becoming substantial, and some skimming scandals have already emerged.[24] Political infighting between various factions has hampered gambling regulation. In addition to these problems, some unscrupulous operators have been boosting the house edge to unconscionable levels. It will be interesting to observe how Spanish officials cope with the embarrassment of gaming riches that have resulted from legalization.

Australian Gambling

Gambling is an integral part of Australia's self-image. An Australian historian, Russell Ward, echoing the sentiments of social commentators since 1790, observed that the "typical Australian gambles heavily and often."[25] There's little doubt that gambling is a pervasive influence in Australian society. The general acceptance accorded the national image of Australians as heavy gamblers has given gambling a legitimacy rare in other countries. While Australian history is replete with abortive reform and prohibition movements, Australians' view of themselves as gamblers was sufficient to deflect these efforts. A cartoon in the *Sydney Truth* in 1906 clearly showed the relative importance of gambling to Australians in the first decade of the twentieth century. The importance

(*From Sydney* Truth, *June 24, 1906*)

of gambling eventually resulted in state support of some gambling games. Since the nineteenth century, state governments in Australia have assumed responsibility for administering the most popular forms of legal gambling: horse race betting and lotteries.

Organized horse race betting began in Sydney Town in 1810 (only twenty-two years after the first Europeans set foot in Australia). Subsequently, hundreds of private clubs were given government approval to conduct horse race meetings. At present, almost five hundred separate race clubs are officially registered as thoroughbred racing operators.[26] Lotteries were given a quasi-legal standing when nineteenth-century Australian courts ruled that sweepstakes betting based on the outcome of horse races was not illegal. Shortly thereafter, several state governments established commissions to conduct lottery games. Illegal gambling—often with the tacit approval of legal authorities—has also been an Australian tradition. Illicit casinos, offtrack bookmakers, and social clubs that sponsored card playing and illegal slot machine gaming were commonplace in early twentieth-century Australia.

The 1960s saw important changes in Australian gambling as new games were legalized and the demand for existing ones was stimulated through advertising. These changes led to significantly increased participation and ultimately opened a Pandora's box of regulatory problems. In 1960, Australia legalized offtrack betting by establishing a Totalizator Agency Board (TAB). Under this system, horse players place their bets at retail outlets throughout the states, and the bets are pooled through computerized networks. The TAB was an instant success, and today its outlets are in almost every neighborhood; Australians wishing to place a horse bet have no difficulty in doing so. In 1956, the Victoria State government legalized slot machines, commonly referred to as pokies, and by 1962, most other state governments had also approved their use. This led to support for the legalization of casinos. After considerable debate, the first state-approved casino opened in 1973. Legalizing casino games introduced a new breed of Australians to gaming. Relatively unsophisticated gamblers soon discovered the fascination of poker machines, and today this form of gambling ranks number one in terms of dollar expenditure.[27] A contemporary Australian sociologist, Jan McMillen, analyzed the recent changes in Australian gambling:

> Three important changes are worthy of note. First, the introduction of TAB (Totalizator Agency Board) off-course betting systems in the 1960s marked a major turning point in Australian gambling policies at a time of increased social affluence and leisure time. Previous policies had been based on conservative moral principles which, for over a century, had restricted commercial stimulation of gambling. With the establishment of TAB agencies throughout the community, governments began to move from a cautious limitation and regulation of gambling to the explicit promotion and legalization in some forms for the revenues that could be produced. Second, there has been a shift away from the dominant emphasis upon state-owned and operated gambling monopolies (lotteries, TAB) toward active government support for large commercial gambling corpora-

tions (Lotto, Pools, casinos). The encouragement of market competition between a diverse range of commercial gambling industries has facilitated the introduction of new types of gambling for which there previously had been no public demand. A third catalyst for change associated with the growth of the tourist industry has been the recent proliferation throughout Australia of casinos. There are eight in operation in 1986, and the ninth is planned for Sydney in 1987 or 1988. Commercial casino gaming, historically prohibited in Australia, is now being enthusiastically supported for its stimulation of international tourism and its anticipated 'trickle down' benefits to local economies.[28]

As Australian gambling has diversified and expanded, its regulatory structure has not kept pace. There is growing criticism within Australia that regulation of gambling is both haphazard and undemocratic.[29] In some cases, the responsibilities of various regulatory agencies overlap, since federal and state governments have not coordinated their gambling policies; consequently, there is no way of knowing precisely who is responsible for gaming regulation. In other cases, gambling policies are the result of pressure from local government and regional interest groups. Particularly disturbing to some observers is a growing tendency to remove gambling policy decisions from public scrutiny. The customary hearings on gaming have been circumvented by gaming boards, who issue edicts and make wide-ranging decisions without being subject to political review. Recently, casinos were opened in Queensland and the Northern Territory by government decree without public debate or input. At present, fragmentary and unresponsive regulation of gaming is a fact of life in Australia.[30]

Comparisons

There are striking parallels and similarities between the United States and Anglo-European countries with respect to the spread of gambling and attempts to regulate it. Most countries had an active but stable gambling population (both legal and illegal) until governments legalized new games or greatly expanded existing ones. Wholesale entry of the government into gaming (typically begun in the early 1960s) drastically changed patterns of participation. Legalization and government participation gave gambling new legitimacy as well as new markets. While participation in established games like horse racing, lotteries, and card games showed moderate growth, newly legalized games such as casino gaming, slot machines, lottos, and instant lotteries attracted large numbers of players who together wagered large sums of money. The new games appealed to a different segment of the population, consisting of relatively unsophisticated gamblers who were drawn by quick action and uncomplicated rules; slot machines and instant lotteries didn't require players to learn subtle nuances or complicated strategies. In most countries the new games have not yet reached their saturation point; thus their ultimate market potential remains uncertain.

The riches gained by legalization have in many cases been a mixed blessing. While increased gaming participation has swelled tax coffers, social and regulatory problems have multiplied. New gaming operations invariably affect the community in unforseen ways. Many of the new gambling participants lack the acquired skill and informal coping mechanisms of traditional gambling groups. This has led to increased problem gambling, calling for the development of community agencies staffed by professionals. Although gaming legalization does generate visible economic benefits in the form of new investment and jobs, such benefits often prove illusory. Gaming expansion tends to concentrate economic gains in one industry, often to the detriment of others;[31] the public's gaming expenditures, for example, reduce the pool of spendable dollars that, if not for gambling, might have been used to purchase other commodities or to fuel growth in nongaming areas.

All countries have claimed that an important goal of legalization has been to reduce or eliminate illegal gambling. This, of course, assumes that illegal operators would be put out of business by state-sponsored gambling. In most instances, this goal has not been reached, and in some cases, legalization has proved counterproductive. Germany and England have been most successful in limiting illegal gaming, but this may be due more to traditional attitudes of respect for authority in those countries than to legalization itself. In Holland, the United States, and Spain, however, illegal operators have adapted to legalization, and because of the general legitimacy accorded gambling, their business has actually increased. In Australia and France, illegal gaming, though not increasing significantly, has certainly not been eradicated.

Not all gaming developments follow similar historical patterns. The regulatory efforts of various countries have tended to follow two different approaches. The United States and Australia allow individual state governments to regulate gaming within their geographic borders while keeping the federal government's role at a minimum. Other countries generally have opted for a more active federal presence and have appointed administrative boards, with varying degrees of power, to oversee gaming throughout their countries. Both of these approaches have drawn criticism. Individual state governments are accused of being parochial and incapable of regulating the multinational gaming corporations that operate within their jurisdictions.[32] Federal gaming boards have been criticized for their authoritarian handling of licensing and their paternalistic control of routine operations.[33] In any case, the all-powerful British Gaming Board is generally considered the world's most effective regulatory body, and is being considered by other countries as a model for their own efforts. Whether or not other countries will be able or willing to follow England's example of granting a single board full authority over gaming remains to be seen.

Countries also differ in their approach to advertising. On the one hand, England and European countries (with the exception of Spain) have opposed advertising, believing it would overstimulate participation. On the other hand, the United States (with the exception of Puerto Rico) and Australia sanction gaming advertisement. In fact, state governments in both countries advertise their games extensively. Radio announcements, TV spots, and newspaper columns carry continuous advertising for state lotteries in the United States, and Australians are similarly bombarded with reminders about the merits of state-sponsored TAB betting.

Casino development has continued briskly throughout the world (with the possible exception of England), but it has done so in different ways. The United States has pioneered a Las Vegas–Atlantic City model wherein several casinos are allowed to compete openly in a relatively small geographical area. Consequently, casinos tend to dominate a community, as they do on the Las Vegas Strip and the Atlantic City Boardwalk. In the European model, a single casino operates (often in resort areas) without extensive advertisement or undue fanfare. The result is a relatively unobtrusive gaming environment that doesn't dominate local communities. Australia has borrowed from both models by granting single-casino monopolies within specified geographical areas; at the same time it has sanctioned wholesale advertising and allowed casinos to offer a Las Vegas ambiance.

Newly legalized games have attracted hordes of participants and publicity, and horse racing is making a comeback of sorts. Offtrack betting, computerized pooling of money, large-scale televising, betting gimmicks, advertising, and promotions have revived interest in horse racing, and its future as an international industry looks promising.

Summary

Gambling is a universal phenomenon with worldwide participation. International gaming activities, especially in England, Europe, and Australia, directly influence developments in the United States. England has a long history of gambling participation and state regulation. In 1960, it legalized virtually every form of gambling and, in 1968, tightened regulations by creating an all-powerful national Gaming Board. The power and authority of the board was solidified in the 1970s, when it succeeded in permanently closing several large casinos.

European countries also have a long history of gambling. In the 1960s, many European countries liberalized their gambling laws, and participation, especially in casino gaming and slot machines, increased significantly. French and German gaming are tightly controlled by powerful federal boards that have succeeded, for the most part, in maintaining a low profile for gaming. Holland is experiencing considerable difficulty with illegal gambling operators, who have successfully circumvented legal restrictions and openly operate officially unsanctioned Golden Ten parlors. Spanish gambling has seen phenomenal increases in slot machine and bingo participation as new participants are attracted to these low-skill games.

Australians have a national image of themselves as heavy gamblers and actively support state-sponsored gambling. They have updated off-track horse race betting by initiating a sophisticated computerized system (TAB). The regulation of newly opened casinos has proved difficult for government agencies.

There are many parallels in gaming throughout the world, including ongoing regulatory problems, significant increases in wagering on low-skilled games like slot machines and lotteries, and inexorable legitimation buttressed by continuing state legalization. At present, there is considerable debate over whether or not a powerful gaming board like that in England would be an appropriate model for other countries to emulate. A question that concerns many countries is the extent to which gambling should dominate local communities. Most countries reject high-visibility gaming environments similar to those found in Las Vegas and Atlantic City and instead favor less obtrusive gambling situations.

Notes

1. Cited in John Ashton, *The History of Gambling*, (1899; reprint, New York: Burt Franklin, 1968), p. 13.
2. Quoted in Otto Newman, *Gambling: Hazard and Reward* (London: University of London Athlone Press, 1972), p. 2.
3. Charles Cotton, *The Compleat Gamester* (1674; reprint, London: Kennikat Press, 1930).
4. *London Times*, "A Nation of Gamblers," 13 September 1966, p. 21.
5. D. M. Downes, B. P. Davies, M. E. David, and P. Stone, *Gambling, Work and Leisure: A Study across Three Areas* (London: Routledge & Kegan Paul, 1976), p. 31.
6. Newman, *Gambling: Hazard and Reward*, p. 2.
7. Ibid., p. 24.
8. Joseph Kelly and William R. Eadington, "The Regulation of Casino Gambling in Europe: A Comparative Analysis," in *Betting on the Future: Gambling in Nevada and Elsewhere* (Reno: Nevada Public Affairs Review, 1986), p. 58.
9. Leonard Steinberg, "Running a Betting Shop Group and a Casino Group in the United Kingdom" (Paper presented at the Sixth National Conference on Gambling and Risk Taking, Atlantic City, November 1984), p. 21.

10. Ibid., pp. 18–19.
11. Vicki Abt, James F. Smith, and Eugene M. Christiansen, *The Business of Risk* (Lawrence: University of Kansas Press, 1985), p. 162.
12. Kelly and Eadington, "The Regulation of Casino Gambling in Europe," p. 59.
13. Trente et quarante, prominently featured at Monte Carlo, is also called rouge et noir (red and black). For a full explanation, see Arnold Abrams, *Gaming around the World* (Hollywood: Gambling Times, 1982), p. 25.
14. Kelly and Eadington, "The Regulation of Casino Gambling in Europe," p. 60.
15. The Dutch generally don't bother drug dealers or prostitutes in the central canal area of Amsterdam. See William Thompson, "The Dutch Gamble" (Working paper, University of Nevada at Las Vegas, November 1986).
16. Teri La Fleur, "Ladbroke Brings a Bit of Britain to Detroit," *Gaming and Wagering Business*, January 1986, p. 18.
17. Thompson, "The Dutch Gamble," p. 20.
18. Ibid., pp. 21–24.
19. José L. Guirao, "Gambling in Spain: The Unplanned Revolution" (Paper presented at the Sixth National Conference on Gambling and Risk Taking, Atlantic City, November 1984).
20. National surveys, compiled to measure gambling expenditures, were begun in 1970 and have continued on a yearly basis. The findings were reported by Guirao (see above).
21. "Lo que nos Jugamos," *Cambio 16*, 28 October 1985, p. 41.
22. Guirao, "Gambling in Spain," p. 7.
23. "Lo que nos Jugamos," p. 39.
24. Guirao, "Gambling in Spain," p. 8.
25. Russell Ward, *The Australian Legend* (Sydney: Oxford University Press, 1966), p. 2.
26. John O'Hara, "The Australian Gambling Tradition," in *Sport: Money, Morality and the Media*, ed. R. Cashman and M. McKernan (Sydney: New South Wales University Press, 1981), p. 69.
27. Reported by Arthur Nielson in "Gambling Policy and Experience in Australia" (Paper presented at the Sixth Annual Conference on Gambling and Risk Taking, Atlantic City, November 1984).
28. Jan McMillen, "The Other Revolution: The Legalization of Commercial Gambling in Australia," in *Betting on the Future: Gambling in Nevada and Elsewhere* (Reno: Nevada Public Affairs Review, 1986), p. 60.
29. *Report of the Committee Appointed to Inquire into and Report on Gaming in Western Australia* (Perth: West Australian Government Printing, 1984), and *Report of the Committee of Inquiry into Gaming in New South Wales* (Sydney: New South Wales Government Printer, 1985).
30. McMillen, "The Other Revolution," pp. 68–69.
31. William R. Eadington, *Trends in the Legalization of Gambling in America in the 1980s and the Implications of Australia*, Bureau of Business and Economic Research Paper 86–2 (Reno: College of Business Administration, University of Nevada at Reno, 1985), pp. 1–22.
32. Jan McMillen, "The Other Revolution," and Jerome Skolnik and John Dombrink, "The Limits of Gaming Control," *Connecticut Law Review* 12 (Summer 1980): 762–784 both describe the limited ability of state governments to adequately control gambling in Australia and the United States, respectively.
33. For a full discussion of the English gaming board's authority, see David Miers, "The Mismanagement of Casino Gaming," *British Journal of Criminology* 21 (January 1981): 79–86.

The Future
of Gambling

*If I could buy options on the future of gambling, I wouldn't take a
short position.*

A commodity speculator

In order to make informed personal and political decisions regarding
gambling participation, one must understand the consequences of gambling's increasingly pervasive influence. In this final chapter, I will
pinpoint future trends in gambling and analyze their significance. Such
projection, though necessarily speculative, is based on the evidence
presented in the first nine chapters. This discussion of future trends
may aid individuals and groups in developing strategies for coping
with emerging gambling developments.

The legitimation of gambling is likely to continue until gambling
becomes taken for granted. Although the extent and form of legal gambling will remain controversial, its continued existence will thus no
longer be an issue. Reform movements, which in the past have limited
gambling's acceptance, are unlikely in the future. With no support for
the elimination of gambling, future debate will center on how to regulate and tax it. While some citizens may continue to question the ethics
of state-sanctioned gaming, most will have to face the reality of a growing gambling presence in their community.

For the majority of Americans, gambling is not a moral issue and
participation is no longer considered an "evil." Instead, gambling is
perceived as an enjoyable activity. Americans are becoming more pragmatic about gambling and no longer view it from an ethical perspective.
Separating gambling from moral condemnation has allowed it to be
defined as a legitimate social activity, and such legitimation has allowed, for the first time, a mass of middle-class gamblers to regularly
and openly participate. The significant broadening of the base of acceptable participation has further changed American perceptions of
gambling, and it is no longer accurate to state, as Abt, Smith, and

Christiansen did in 1985, that gambling retains an "ambiguous cultural status."[1] The overwhelming evidence indicates that Americans have resolved their ambivalence toward gambling by opting for participation. In the future, increasing legitimation will most likely lead to more legalization, which in turn will stimulate even greater participation. These developments will dramatically affect American society. In the remainder of this chapter, I discuss the economic, social, and political impact that emerging gambling trends are likely to have on American society.

Economic Impact

The American gaming industry of the 1990s can be expected to be intensely competitive. As more gambling games are legalized or decriminalized, the number of gaming operators vying for consumer dollars will also increase. Although at present the demand for gaming remains high, it is not infinite. In some areas, such as the Northeast corridor and Nevada, gambling participation has reached or will soon reach the saturation level. It is thus doubtful that gaming will continue to experience unlimited growth. Gambling consumers of the future can afford to be more discerning. They will not have to participate in a game in which they are not comfortable, simply because it is the "only game in town."

Increased competition will bring about significant changes in gaming operations. The evolution of casino gaming in Atlantic City illustrates this phenomenon. When gambling was first introduced to Atlantic City in 1978, Resorts International was the only operating casino. Demand for participation was phenomenal, and hordes of eager patrons waited hours for the privilege of playing. The only marketing problems for Resorts were security, crowd control, and cleanup.[2] Within a year, two more casinos, Caesars and Bally's, opened to packed houses. The success of these three operations encouraged operators to open eight more casinos. In a relatively short period, Atlantic City had more than enough casinos to satisfy local demand. Increased competition spurred casino operators to actively recruit customers and led to a massive bussing operation that currently transports over 12.5 million visitors to Atlantic City.[3] To lure additional patrons, casinos undertook massive promotional campaigns that ranged from distributing passes to lounge shows featuring big-name entertainers to handing out coupons for free nickels. As the operators struggled for a market share, a new type of operation emerged—the premium-grind casino, which simultaneously catered to high rollers playing games like craps, baccarat, and blackjack and to quarter slot players.[4]

The active recruitment of customers, while initially successful, eventually reached its limit. Noting that bus patronage increased only 2 percent between 1984 and 1985, a casino executive observed that if people in the New York and Philadelphia areas "haven't been to a casino by now, they're either dead or they just don't care."[5] The leveling off has led casino operators to suggest that for growth to continue, they must attract a broader national and international clientele. In order to attract such customers, casino executives are urging the development of massive convention facilities that, at present, are unavailable in Atlantic City.

Increased competition has proved costly, and opening a casino in Atlantic City is no longer an El Dorado. The Atlantis Casino, for example, is currently being reorganized after declaring bankruptcy, while the Claridge Casino has yet to show a profit after seven years of operation.[6] In addition to competing with one another, the Atlantic City casinos are also in competition with racetracks, OTB operations, state lotteries, and large-scale illegal sports betting.

Racetrack operators have adopted year-round racing, undertaken the refurbishing of track facilities, begun offering races with higher-caliber horses, and initiated new betting gimmicks to lure more horse players. OTB operators in New York and Connecticut have made their operations more attractive by improving and expanding the televising of races, offering more hospitable surroundings, and providing a greater number of betting opportunities (additional tracks and new gimmick bets). State lotteries in the Atlantic City area have responded to the competitive market by developing instant lotteries, lotto games, and daily drawings. In addition, lottery operators plan to offer super jackpots with top prizes as high as $30 million. Illegal bookies offer the public not only wagering on football, baseball, and basketball, but also easy access to credit. The gambling consumer in the Northeast corridor has a multitude of games in which to participate.

Atlantic City is not the only casino area to be hit by competition from other games. Gambling in northern Nevada (Reno, Lake Tahoe, and Sparks) has lost revenues to the new California lottery. With tourism in this area remaining flat as well, several casinos have filed for bankruptcy. Older, less physically attractive casinos are especially threatened by shrinking patronage and the financial difficulty that accompanies it. Nevada casinos have responded to competition from the California lottery by offering giant slot machine jackpots ("megabucks") that can run into the millions. They have also started in-house lotto games that are heavily advertised as offering "much better odds than the California lottery."[7] Nevada legislators, also fearing loss of revenue to the California lottery, have introduced a bill to sanction a Nevada state lottery. In addition, the financially solid casinos are refurbishing their facilities while undertaking aggressive advertising campaigns in national markets, especially in southern California.

The examples of Atlantic City and northern Nevada provide valuable clues to future developments. They demonstrate that gambling participation does have a saturation point, that unlimited gaming growth is not possible, and that market conditions will mature. Gaming operators in most situations respond to added competition by attempting to make their product more attractive to the consumer. In this respect, gaming operations have emulated well-established economic principles, such as creative marketing, careful attention to the life cycle of the product, and frequent innovation. Gaming operations, whether privately owned, state-run, or illegally operated, are subject to the same "revenue imperatives" (the need to continue to expand sales and profits) that drive most private-sector companies. The gaming industry of the future will probably be easily understood by MBAs, and running a modern gambling operation will resemble managing a conventional business. Robert Trump, the epitomy of an enlightened entrepreneur, is currently attempting to translate his business acumen to management of Atlantic City casinos. As gambling operations come to be controlled by corporate business executives, they will no doubt lose some of their unique, colorful character and become more routine and bureaucratic.[8]

The trend toward corporate ownership of legal gaming establishments (see chapter 3) is sure to continue, leaving the small corner operator unable to compete with the large gaming companies, but lending further credibility and legitimation to the gambling industry. The American gaming market will remain a target for international interests. Indications of a growing foreign presence include the following: (1) Ladbroke, England's leading offtrack operator, has purchased the Detroit Race Course; (2) Japanese interests have invested heavily in American gaming; and (3) English casino interests have penetrated the Atlantic City market.[9] At the same time, American gaming interests have attempted to expand overseas. Although Harrah's was temporarily thwarted in its bid to build a casino in Sydney, such efforts will undoubtedly continue.

Even though saturation may lead to mature market conditions in some areas, in most parts of the United States gambling will continue to grow. New legalization and continuing legitimation will stimulate a demand whose potential is yet unknown. Low-skill games like lotteries and slot machines will be the leading revenue producers. In 1986, these two games accounted for over 40 percent of national gross gaming revenues, a significant increase from the 1985 percentage.[10] The market for this type of gambling obviously has not been fully tapped. Lotteries have room for significant expansion as interstate cooperatives like the ten-state America's Game offer larger prizes and as additional lotto games become fully implemented. More aggressive advertising by state lottery commissions will also stimulate participation. The public is willing to accept lotteries; ballot initiatives authorizing them have rarely been defeated. It appears safe to predict that the "lotterizing of America" will continue.[11]

As casinos have become accessible to a larger segment of the population, slot machine play has increased dramatically. This trend can be shown by comparing revenue-generated games in Nevada. William Eadington reported, "In 1971 the mix in casino win between table games and slot machines statewide was 67.4 percent to 31.4 percent, and by 1984, the percentages had shifted to 44.4 percent and 51.8 percent respectively."[12] Considering that slot machine gaming is legal in only two states, its national growth rate has been substantial—up 57 percent in gross gaming revenues since 1982.[13] Slot machine gaming may soon undergo de facto legalization in the form of state-approved Video Lottery Terminals (VLTs). These terminals are similar in principle to slot machine games. Several states (for example, Illinois, Nebraska, and California) are considering implementing VLTs. The demand for this type of gaming is expected to be significant, and if legal VLTs become a reality, phenomenal increases in participation can be anticipated. When slot machines were legalized on a national level in Spain, revenues from them far outstripped even the most optimistic estimates.

The growth of more established games, such as horse racing, poker, and casino games other than slot machines, has been moderate recently and will continue to be so. This doesn't mean that such games will die out, merely that their market potential seems more predictable than that of low-skilled games. As Americans become more familiar with gaming, however, they are likely to shift gradually to more complicated games. Slot machines and lotteries will lose some of their appeal as Americans become more sophisticated at gaming. The logic and skillful application of learned techniques that characterize poker and horse and sports betting will attract the more savvy American gambler. While many will be introduced to gambling through lotteries and slot playing, some will eventually gravitate to games where they can exert more rational control over their wagers. The shift to more skilled games, although gradual, will affect overall gambling participation. Already slight increases in horse race betting and poker playing and even more noticeable increases in sports betting have occurred.[14] I believe in the future these trends will expand as more Americans discover the intellectual challenge and camaraderie offered by horse race gambling, sports betting, and poker playing.

The projected increases in all forms of gambling participation mean economic gains in the form of new jobs, tax revenues, and civic improvements. These gains will be visible and highly concentrated in those areas where gambling is conducted. Many of the economic benefits to gaming jurisdictions are siphoned from surrounding areas. Thus, the actual economic gain may be overestimated by legislators seeking an infusion of seemingly painless tax revenues. Eadington has argued that this was true in Atlantic City:

> In this context, it could be argued that the legalization of casinos in Atlantic City has resulted in a situation not unlike the levying of a tax on various merchants and residents of the rest of New Jersey, Pennsylvania and New York, so that jobs and profitable opportunities could be created in the deteriorated seaboard community of Atlantic City. Much of the economic activity that is apparent around the casino industry has only been shifted from other regions that compete generally for consumer expenditures with casino gaming, but because those reductions are so dispersed, they are virtually invisible and, for the most part, go unnoticed.[15]

Although the overall economic gains may be overestimated, there is no question that increased gambling participation will have significant social consequences.

Social Implications

The social costs of gambling can include an increase in crime, prostitution, and alcohol and drug use in the immediate gaming area. Some researchers have reported a noted increase in these kinds of activities in Atlantic City since casinos were approved. Other researchers have commented on the social malaise that results from gambling.[16] In the 1990s, however, the major social concern will be the issue of problem gambling, putatively termed compulsive gambling. I have shown that all serious gamblers have at times lost more money than was comfortable; in so doing, they have experienced varying degrees of problem gambling. Thus, an increase in the number of American gamblers will inevitably result in more instances of problem gambling. This situation will also be exacerbated, as least temporarily, by the participation of groups relatively unfamiliar with gambling contingencies. Many of the new gambling participants will be drawn from the ranks of the middle class.

Historically, gambling has been an accepted activity of the working and upper classes. In contrast, serious and sustained gambling has not been practiced by the middle class. Until recently, then, middle-class individuals had relatively limited personal or secondhand experience with gambling and its possible consequences. Lacking such experience, many middle-class gamblers are unprepared for the psychological pressures of losing and winning. On the one hand, they lack a repertoire of techniques for dealing with the periodic losses that are an integral part of sustained gambling. On the other hand, a large win or "big score" early in the gambling career of a middle-class participant can lead to unrealistic and unfulfilled expectations of continued winnings. The middle-class gambler often has access to lines of credit and other sources of funds that are unavailable to working-class gamblers. Such resources allow gambling to continue to the point where large debts may threaten the gambler's financial and social status.

Middle-class players, seeking relief from their gambling-related problems, will increasingly label themselves compulsive. The potential for incurring large losses, combined with the ready acceptance of medical explanations, makes middle-class "bust-outs" (heavy losers) prime candidates for an illness label. This follows the prediction of sociologists Peter Conrad and Joseph Schneider: "As a particular kind of deviance becomes a middle-class rather than solely a lower-class problem, the probability of medicalization increases."[17] If they are correct, the medical monopoly on the definition and treatment of this form of deviance will be strengthened as middle-class gambling is declared a major social problem by the mass media and by advocates of disease designations such as Gamblers Anonymous. The following exchange between a problem gambler and Ann Landers reflects a situation that is likely to become commonplace.

> Dear Ann Landers: I need some kind of help desperately. Please come to my rescue. I can't sign my name so I am praying that you will print this letter and your advice.
>
> I am a 35-year-old married man with three kids. I gamble every day and am in great financial trouble. My family doesn't know I gamble the way I do. I lie to everyone to cover up the losses. The bill collectors keep calling and all we do is fight. The bookies are demanding their money, too. After every loss I promise myself I will never gamble again but in a few days I am back placing bets, shooting craps and playing poker. Please help me before I kill myself.—Hurting in Chicago
>
> **Dear Hurting: Gambling, like alcoholism and drug addiction, is an illness. In the case of all three, the best approach is a self-help group. Nothing is as effective as the emotional support of people who share the problem. I strongly recommend Gamblers Anonymous. Write to Box ——. This splendid group has saved many a life.**[18]

A growing public concern with problem gambling will affect American gaming operators, who traditionally have ignored the consequences of excessive losses by patrons. Regulatory agencies, court decisions, and public opinion are presently forcing operators to seriously consider the issue of problem gambling. In the future, it will no longer be considered good business to milk customers of their last dollar. Casino operations are especially open to criticism, as their policies of providing "comps" (complimentary rooms, meals, and transportation) and extending credit to high rollers can be seen as unfair temptations. Two recent events have demonstrated casinos' vulnerability to charges of unethical conduct when they allow gamblers to lose excessively. In

1985, Caesars Boardwalk in Atlantic City was forced to close its doors for one day because it had allowed a "compulsive gambler" to lose millions of embezzled funds.[19] In 1987, the Florida Supreme Court refused to enforce New Jersey's gaming laws in Florida, wiping out a $100,000 gambling debt owed by a Florida resident to an Atlantic City casino.[20]

Without minimizing the seriousness of problem gambling, I believe that most American gamblers will satisfactorily come to terms with its risks. Few Americans will become regular gamblers, but the vast majority will restrict their participation to an occasional wager. These occasional participants will view gambling as a legitimate recreational activity and not as an integral part of their lives. They will consider gambling losses to be the price of participation and will not allow them to seriously affect their lives. Some will have a brief fling with gambling, decide it's not for them, and avoid further participation. Most of those who decide to participate regularly will eventually develop coping mechanisms to satisfactorily manage participation. Neophyte gamblers will develop the informal skills that have allowed more experienced players to remain "in action." New participants will learn strategies that allow them to gamble regularly without incurring disastrous losses. While new gambling groups are learning these skills, they will be especially vulnerable to problem gambling. In time, however, they too will learn how to gamble reasonably, in turn influencing others in their group to use restraint.

Those who decide to become regular gamblers will also discover the social rewards of gambling social worlds. These rewards include companionship, empathy, and social interaction. As gamblers become socialized into a gaming mileu, their contacts with nongamblers often become less meaningful, and they find that other settings lack the social rewards offered by the gambling world. In order to remain part of that social world, individuals must continue their gambling. Excessive financial losses seriously jeopardize participation and eventually restrict access to the gambling world. The potential loss of membership in that world will force many participants to change their gambling strategies, for in order to remain part of it, they must have available funds. This means cutting down on losses. Thus, the threat of losing contact with the gambling social world will force many participants to wager more responsibly.

In summary, I am optimistic that inappropriate gambling will not become a major social problem. Even though there always will be a few troubled players who are unable to cope, most Americans will learn to gamble responsibly. The majority will gamble occasionally as a recreational outlet, and regular players will develop skills that will allow them to participate without losing excessively. Informed political activity will also help minimize the social costs of gambling.

Political Impact

The legitimation of gambling has been enhanced significantly by various political actions. The voting public has approved legalization, and regulatory bodies have given an official stamp of approval to gaming operators. As Jerome Skolnick has noted, "Sociologically speaking, licensing in the gaming business constitutes a formal affirmation of non-deviance. One cannot participate in it without being investigated, reviewed, and found acceptable."[21] Gambling in the United States will continue to be a highly regulated and politicized activity. Gaming will be conducted under the watchful eye of state and federal regulators, the licensing of gaming operators will remain controversial, and further legalization will be subject to the political process.

Until recently the federal government played only a minor role in gambling regulation. States were allowed to establish their own regulatory policies relatively free from federal scrutiny. The federal government may be about to end its hands-off policy, however. The Treasury Department has redefined casinos as "financial institutions." As such, they fall subject to regulations of the Bank Secrecy Act; thus casinos must now report to the IRS the names, addresses, and social security numbers of high rollers—gamblers who bet over $10,000 in cash or $2,500 in credit over a twenty-four-hour period.[22] In addition, the IRS is seriously considering a plan to force casinos to withhold taxes from the winnings of foreign gamblers. A casino executive commented that a strict interpretation of the proposed regulation would "require you to stop the game before every roll of the dice and withhold on whatever someone won, and it wouldn't matter if, on a subsequent roll, the man lost everything he owned."[23] A number of court decisions have indicated that the Supreme Court may be forced to consider the constitutionality of state gaming regulations. Legal scholar Blaine Rose has said that states like Nevada "may not long be able to get away with its protestation of constitutional exemption" and, further, "that the spread of gambling legalization will result in an increasing awareness of the courts concerning the questions of gambling in general and the procedures applied to its regulation in particular."[24]

Although the federal government's interest in gambling may be considered an unnecessary intrusion by some, it could introduce an important source of balance into systems that traditionally have favored gaming operators at the expense of regulatory goals. In the past, states typically have initiated regulatory constraints in response to real concerns, such as the possible infiltration of organized crime into gaming. However, as states become more dependent on gaming revenues, they often become more concerned with the expansion of gaming than with a strict interpretation of the original regulations. Thus regulations are frequently relaxed in order to allow gaming operators to prosper, incidentally increasing the state's take. Although both Nevada and Atlantic City adopted stringent restrictions to keep illegal operators from being licensed, regulations were relaxed when it appeared that former bookies and illicit casino managers were the only ones capable of running a profitable gaming operation.

Jerome Skolnick and John Dombrink commented that a classic example of economic expediency occurred when the Atlantic City Casino Control Commission licensed Resorts International to operate a casino, in spite of a negative recommendation from the enforcement division (based on allegations that Resorts officials had engaged in unethical practices in their Bahamian gaming operation and that "unsavory characters" were part of casino management). The licensing of Resorts was granted despite New Jersey regulations that stipulated, "Since casino operations are especially sensitive and in need of periodic control and supervision the regulatory and investigation powers and duties shall be exercised to the fullest."[25] Thus, according to Skolnick and Dombrink, "Although the logic of licensing said 'deny,' the logic of economic pressure dictated, 'affirm.' Economic logic won out."[26] Eadington observed similar tendencies in Nevada's approach to regulation:

> To the extent that discretionary decisions are allowed for the regulators, there is the potential for abuse or, at minimum, the regulatory body becoming overly influenced by those it is supposed to be regulating. The tendency within the regulatory structure, when confronting a trade-off between the profitability of the gaming industry or expansion of the regulated gaming and a constraining regulation that had initially been established for some socially desirable purpose, is to allow the regulation to be relaxed.[27]

As gambling becomes more national in scope, the federal government will be pressed to form partnerships with states to set standards that can be applied to all gaming operations. Already there have been efforts to establish federal guidelines with regard to drug use in horse racing. Proposed legislation would require that individual tracks establish a comprehensive drug testing program that would allow Drug Enforcement Agency operatives to administer the tests.[28] There has been considerable discussion about the federal government establishing policies for Indian gaming. An Arizona senator has proposed federal control, citing concern among Indian tribes, "about their ability to continue to regulate gaming free from the influence of organized crime, racketeers, professional gamblers, and those who would defraud or otherwise attempt to exert corrupt influence upon them."[29] Congress has also debated the feasibility of instituting a federal lottery. Advocates suggest that lottery revenues could be used to significantly reduce the national debt.

There is little doubt that in the 1990s the federal government will play an important role in gaming. Furthermore, if state regulatory agencies prove unable to adequately control gaming, and widely publicized instances of fraud, skimming, or unethical conduct by gaming operators occur, support for the establishment of a powerful national gaming board could develop. Undoubtedly, such a board would be given full authority to control gaming. If this should occur the success of England's all-powerful Gaming Board in keeping gambling relatively free of crime and scandal would serve as a model.

Although some games, like VLTs and offtrack horse wagering, can be authorized by state legislatures, the American electorate will decide whether new jurisdictions will offer casino gaming. Recent ballot initiatives to sanction casinos (those, for example, in Florida, Colorado, Massachusetts, Minnesota, Arkansas, and Texas) have been soundly defeated. This has occurred in spite of a changing casino image. The public no longer sees casinos as being controlled exclusively by the mob but instead sees them as corporate entities. Regulation, regardless of its effectiveness, has lent an aura of respectability to casinos. However, voters remain unwilling to approve new casinos. The negative examples of Nevada and Atlantic City have been powerful.

Communities fear being overrun by wide-open casino development, believing that approving casinos is an irreversible process—once established, the casinos will not go away. Politicians, for the most part, have been unwilling to support casino legalization, afraid of voter backlash if something went wrong. Nonetheless, I expect that additional casinos will be approved, but with a different format from that currently existing in Nevada or Atlantic City. The new casinos will operate on a more limited basis. Franchises will be granted for the operation of a single casino in a specified geographical area. Single casinos will be far less intrusive on local communities than the casino complexes found in Nevada or Atlantic City. The franchising of casinos could follow European and Australian practices. I predict that future American casinos will take two forms. One will showcase the casinos within a tourist complex, with the casino an important part of a larger recreational area such as a fairground, a theme park, a mountain resort, or an urban redevelopment project. The other form will be relatively unobtrusive and more mundane than those currently in operation. This type of casino will be fairly commonplace and will offer low-stakes wagering. North Dakota already has this second type of operation. There, two-dollar table stakes are played in settings that have been described as "ordinary."[30] The small-stakes legal poker games currently being played in Gardena, California,[31] are a further example of scaled-down gambling.

There is nothing to suggest that the public will decide to enforce existing gambling laws. State support of certain forms of gambling reduces public pressure to crack down on illegal operations. Even though the array of laws against gambling will probably remain on the books, enforcement will be downplayed and even disregarded. Police agencies at all levels will overlook illegal gambling, effectively decriminalizing it. Federal enforcement agencies will continue their campaign against organized crime figures. This will weaken the already tenuous organized-crime presence in gambling[32] and allow more independent operators to enter the market. I envision a significant increase in the number of small-time illegal bookmakers who cater to a local clientele. As long as sports betting is not legalized, bookmakers are assured a steady patronage.

Summary

The future of American gaming appears healthy. Additional legalization and continuing legitimation ensure that participation will increase significantly. Since states have come to depend on gaming revenues, any serious reform efforts to restrict gambling will be short-lived. Increased gambling participation will affect economic, social, and political issues.

Increased competition in areas like the Northeast and Nevada will lead to an economic situation wherein supply (available games) has caught up with demand (the desire to gamble). When this occurs, gambling participation will be near or at the saturation point, and continued gaming growth cannot be expected. However, the economic potential of gaming in other areas will remain high. Even though the demand for low-skill games like lotteries and slot machines will continue, participants will no doubt gradually shift to more skilled games such as poker and sports and horse betting. As Americans become more accustomed to wagering, they will seek games in which rational skills and learned strategies increase the likelihood of winning. Although gaming produces concentrated economic gains for certain geographical areas, such gains may be overestimated. In reality, they may represent redistribution of consumer expenditure rather than an overall gain.

The major social concern stemming from increased participation will be the incidence of problem gambling. Middle-class participants who are new to gambling will be especially vulnerable to excessive losses. Inappropriate gambling will increasingly be defined as compulsive behavior. Proponents of the disease model will remain in charge of treatment programs that invariably require abstinence. However, as gambling becomes more prevalent and its contingencies better understood, gamblers will develop their own coping skills to avoid excessive losses. In time, the vast majority of American gamblers will learn to gamble responsibly.

The political issues of gaming will center on regulation, licensing, and new legalization. The federal government will markedly increase its involvement with gaming regulation and licensing. This could be a positive force, as state gaming regulators, representing regional concerns, have often opted for relaxed regulation to protect the state's economic gains from gambling. The decision to legalize casinos will remain in the hands of an electorate whose reluctance will force casino advocates to propose a new model. Wide-open casino operations, like those existing in Nevada and Atlantic City, will be rejected in favor of single operation monopolies, often of an unobtrusive character. The American casino of the future is likely to resemble its subdued European cousin more than the familiar Las Vegas glitter palace.

Notes

1. Vicki Abt, James F. Smith, and Eugene M. Christiansen, *The Business of Risk* (Lawrence: University of Kansas Press, 1985), pp. 206–207.
2. James F. Smith, "Las Vegas East: Atlantic City Ten Years after the Referendum," in *Betting on the Future: Gambling in Nevada and Elsewhere* (Reno: Nevada Public Affairs Review, 1986), p. 54.
3. Ibid., p. 53.
4. An excellent review of this type of casino can be found in James F. Smith, "The Premium-Grind: Atlantic City Hybrid," *Nevada Review of Business and Economics*, 6, no. 1 (1982): 5–12.
5. J. Lloyd, "Wooing the Low-Roller with Freebies and Showroom Strategy," *Philadelphia Inquirer*, 1 April 1986, sec. E, p. 1.
6. Smith, "Las Vegas East," p. 53.
7. This advertisement ran on TV and radio in the Reno–Lake Tahoe area for several months in 1986 and 1987.
8. James Frey believes that the "old style, sneak-joint gamblers will be replaced by business school graduates employed by conglomerate owners." See his article "Labor Issues in the Gaming Industry," in *Betting on the Future: Gambling in Nevada and Elsewhere* (Reno: Nevada Public Affairs Review, 1986), pp. 32–38.
9. "Foreign Interests Scramble for a Piece of the Action," *Gaming and Wagering Business*, March 1986, pp. 10–11, and Teri La Fleur, "Ladbroke Brings a Bit of Britain to Detroit," *Gaming and Wagering Business*, January 1986, pp. 18–19.
10. Eugene M. Christiansen, "The 1986 Gross Annual Wager, Part II: Revenue," *Gaming and Wagering Business* 8 (August 1987): 7–14.
11. Abt et al., *The Business of Risk*, pp. 55–67.
12. William R. Eadington, *Trends in the Legalization of Gambling in America in the 1980s and the Implications for Australia*, Bureau of Business and Economic Research Paper 86-2 (Reno: College of Business Administration, University of Nevada at Reno, 1985), p. 16.
13. Christiansen, "The 1986 Gross Annual Wager," p. 8.
14. Ibid., p. 28.
15. Eadington, *Trends in the Legalization of Gambling*, p. 7.
16. David Lester reported that in the months following the opening of casinos, street crime increased 27 percent. "The Impact of Casino Gambling on a

Small Town," in *Gambling Today*, ed. David Lester (Springfield, Ill.: Charles C Thomas, 1979), pp. 3–11. Similar findings were reported by New York State in *Report of the Attorney General in Opposition to Legalized Gambling in New York State* (Albany: Department of Law, 1981). It should be noted that Jay Albanese, in "The Effect of Casino Gambling on Crime," *Federal Probation Quarterly* 49 (June 1985): 39–44, disputed these findings, blaming the increasing crime rate in Atlantic City on factors other than casino gaming. The following researchers have explored the generally negative effect of gambling on communities that have sanctioned widespread gambling: George Sternleib and James Hughes, *The Atlantic City Gamble: A Twentieth-Century Fund Report* (Cambridge, Mass: Harvard University Press, 1983), and James W. Hulse, *Forty Years in the Wilderness: Impressions of Nevada 1940–1980* (Reno: University of Nevada Press, 1986).

17. Peter Conrad and Joseph W. Schneider, *Deviance and Medicalization* (St. Louis: Mosby), p. 275.
18. "Ann Landers," *Tahoe Daily Tribune*, 2 February 1987, sec. 1, p. 10.
19. Smith, "Las Vegas East," p. 52.
20. "Florida Supreme Court Refuses to Enforce Gambling Debt," *Reno Gazette Journal*, 5 February 1987, sec. A, p. 3.
21. Jerome Skolnick, *House of Cards* (Boston: Little, Brown, 1978), pp. 174–175.
22. I. Nelson Rose, "Turning in the High Rollers: The Impact of the New Cash Regulations," in *Betting on the Future: Gambling in Nevada and Elsewhere* (Reno: Nevada Public Affairs Review, 1986), p. 51.
23. Ken Miller, "IRS Plan Will Scare off High-Rolling Foreigners," *Reno Gazette Journal*, 10 January 1987, sec. C, p. 3.
24. Blaine S. Rose, "Constitutional Questions of Nevada Gaming Licensure: A Rights-Based Analysis," in *Betting on the Future: Gambling in Nevada and Elsewhere* (Reno: Nevada Public Affairs Review, 1986), p. 20.
25. Jerome Skolnick and John Dombrink, "The Limits of Gaming Control," *Connecticut Law Review* 12 (Summer 1980): 778–784.
26. Ibid., p. 784.
27. Eadington, *Trends in the Legalization of Gambling*, p. 12.
28. John Dombrink and William N. Thompson, "The Report of 1986 Commission on Organized Crime and Its Implications for Commercial Gaming in America," in *Betting on the Future: Gambling in Nevada and Elsewhere* (Reno: Nevada Public Affairs Review, 1986), pp. 70–75.
29. Ibid., p. 74.
30. Charles Hillinger, in "Gambling the Gackle Way in North Dakota," *Los Angeles Times*, 14 April 1985, describes low-profile gaming in North Dakota, where gaming revenues are earmarked for charities.
31. See David M. Hayano, *Poker Faces* (Berkeley: University of California Press, 1982).
32. See Peter Reuter, *Disorganized Crime* (Cambridge, Mass.: MIT Press, 1983).

Index